A DICTIONARY OF LACE

PAT EARNSHAW

SHIRE PUBLICATIONS LTD

Preface

My grateful thanks are due to the museums, private individuals and firms who have kindly allowed the use of photographs from their collections. These are acknowledged on page 239. My most grateful thanks go also to Ronald Brown, who has, once more, coped so admirably with the patience-straining arrangements, lighting and close-ups of lace for the other pictures. I am much indebted to Pat Squires and to Alastair Thompson for translations from the antique and modern French; to Anne Kraatz, Fulvia Lewis and Jane Merritt for their stimulating discussions; to Giorgio Calligaris and to Mme Risselin-Steenebrugen for their comments; and to Ann Woodward and Eva Cummings for their advice on lacemaking.

In the extremely few cases where information given in this book differs from that in *The Identification of Lace*, it is where facts or opinions which have come to light since publication of that book have made some slightly different point of view seem more plausible.

The cover shows a portion of the flounce of Queen Victoria's wedding dress, a Honiton lace appliqué on bobbinet. The flounce measures 675 millimetres (26½ inches) at its deepest point and is 3,590 millimetres (141 inches) in circumference. It is reproduced by gracious permission of Her Majesty Queen Elizabeth II.

Copyright © 1982 by Pat Earnshaw. First published 1982. ISBN 0 85263 602 4.
All rights reserved. No part of this publication may be reproduced or transmitted in any form or by any means, electronic or mechanical, including photocopy, recording, or any information storage and retrieval system, without permission in writing from the publishers, Shire Publications Ltd, Cromwell House, Church Street, Princes Risborough, Aylesbury, Bucks, HP17 9AJ, UK.

Set in 10 on 11 point English Times by Permanent Typesetting & Printing Co Ltd, Hong Kong, and printed in Great Britain by C.I. Thomas & Sons (Haverfordwest) Ltd, Press Buildings, Merlins Bridge, Haverfordwest.

A dictionary of lace

Abruzzi, Aquila. A silk or linen bobbin lace of vermiculate design, not unlike East European forms, was produced in this area of central Italy, east of the Apennines, in the eighteenth century. Lace is still made in the mountain village of Offida. (Fig. 25d.)

Aemilia Ars. A society founded in Bologna in 1898 for the revival of the decorative arts. Designs for reticella and punto a fogliami (see *Pagano* and *Venetian lace*) from the Bolognese Passarotti's *Libra di Lavorieri* (1591) were copied by skilled needlewomen, and their productions were illustrated in a large book published in 1929. They included representations of the heraldic arms of noble families such as the Orsinis and Malvezzis. Though the society as a whole was disbanded in 1903, the lacemaking continued, and gold medals were awarded at various exhibitions, for example at Liège (1905), Milan (1906) and Paris (1925). Original designs were also made. (Fig. 48a.)

Aficot. A small polishing instrument used to give a smoothness and shine to the solid parts of a lace, especially in needlepoints, e.g. Alençon. It was made of a lobster's claw, a wolf's tooth or, more recently, of steel.

Aglet, eyelet lace. See *Trou trou.*

Ajours (French, adorned with openwork). See *Fillings.*

Alb flounce. An 8–12 inch (203–305 mm) flounce of lace attached to the skirt of a priest's alb, or long-sleeved linen robe. A short form of alb, called a cotta, is decorated in a similar way, with matching cuffs.

Alençon. A town in Normandy famous in the sixteenth century for its cutworks, reticellas and punto in arias. It was chosen as one of the main centres for the development of the Points de France in 1665. The type of lace now referred to as Alençon became distinctive about 1717 as a meshed lace of classical design with architecturally arranged flowers and swags neatly and precisely suspended in the Alençon ground. Progressive simplification followed until, by the time of Louis XVI, with the fashion for froths of lace so closely frilled that no design was visible, there was little left but spots.

    At its best Alençon had a sharp, clear, firm texture, achieved by the hard rim of cordonnet supporting every smallest piece of the design and often extended into picots made over horsehair (qv). The numerous fillings were like traceries studded with tiny jewels. See *Stitches.* Four types of reseau are distinguished:

(a) Reseau ordinaire (ordinary reseau), made of twisted buttonhole stitches worked from left to right, with the thread carried back from right to left. It has a light and delicate appearance and is the only one used in the earlier forms. (Fig. 14(6).)

(b) Brides tortillées (twisted reseau): this is (a) with the meshes twisted around with thread to make it look like Argentan.

(c) Reseau mouché (fly reseau). The clear ground is spattered with spots like flies clinging to a window pane. A variation is the semé de larmes (sown with tears), where the spots are shaped like falling tears.

(d) The petit reseau (little reseau) is not used as a ground but as a filling. It is (a) on a smaller scale.

In making the lace the thread is knotted to the needle, and the entire work is made in buttonhole stitch. In all it involves ten distinct procedures and, in the past, each was completed by a different group of workers. The final process was the lissage, or 'cold ironing' with the aficot, to give a smooth waxy finish.

The production of Alençon lace ceased with the Revolution (1789) but was revived in the early nineteenth century by Napoleon I, who wore a collarette and cravat of Alençon at his coronation by the Pope, in Paris, in 1804. A garniture du lit, begun for the Empress Josephine, was completed for Napoleon's second wife, Marie-Louise, in 1810. In all it totalled 20 yards (18 metres) square and cost 40,000 francs. Within a border of the lilies of France, the reseau ordinaire of the canopy and coverlet swarmed with bees, symbolic of Bonaparte – an idea borrowed perhaps from Bernini.

After Napoleon's defeat and banishment in 1815, Alençon languished until 1830, when the disestablishment of the Spanish convents (see *Lacemakers* (a) and *Spanish lace*) brought a lot of Alençon lace, made there by French nuns, on to the market, reviving the interest. The Lefebure manufactories, established at Bayeux in the previous year, produced in the 1860s some very expensive pieces, including a dress and flounces bought by Napoleon III for the Empress Eugenie (see *Hours of work* (iv)). The Russian aristocracy was especially fond of Alençon, and one order for a bridal dress, handkerchief, fan and parasol, and for a layette, totalled £6,000. The fall of the Second Empire in 1870 closed the royal market. More ordinary pieces continued to be made – in Belgium and Burano, as well as at Bayeux. From the 1880s there was machine competition.

Lacemaking is still taught at the workshops in Alençon, by nuns, and small commercial items are produced.

All-overs. Machine lace produced as yardages rather than as shaped pieces such as collars and cuffs.

Aloe. A group of sub-tropical plants, some of the lily family, others of the Amaryllidaceae (daffodil family). The latter includes the century plant, *Agave americana*. In all of them there is a huge basal cluster of fleshy leaves, and from these the aloe fibres used in lacemaking are obtained.

In Paraguay a kind of sun lace similar to nanduti (see *South American Lace*: Paraguay) was made until the early twentieth century; from the 1840s openwork stockings and shawls of extremely fine knitting were made in the Azores; and in the Philippines (qv) simple rosette designs were made by plaiting and tatting. Small amounts of aloe were also used in Spain, Portugal and parts of Italy.

The fibres from the liliaceous plants become gummy on contact with water and so are completely unpractical, except for tourist souvenirs. The fibres from the century plant – sometimes known as pita fibres, hence pita lace – can be washed in soap and water provided they are not, while wet, exposed to a hot sun.

American lace. Lace was taken from Europe to North America by the Pilgrim Fathers, formerly known as the Old Comers or Forefathers, who settled in Massachusetts in 1620. They had at first no specialist manufactories, and the greater part of their energy was expended in survival. However, other Protestant refugees and immigrants were far from impoverished and arrived not only with their stitching samplers, needles and thread, but with quantities of lace. Only one example of an imported pillow and bobbins is known: the equipment was much too bulky to be easily carried. In the second half of the seventeenth century, inventories and wills, as well as accounts of robberies, show that the new Americans were well supplied.

There are rare records of lace, possibly drawnwork on muslin, being made on Long Island in the eighteenth century, and of both bobbin and machine laces at Ipswich, Massachusetts, in the nineteenth century. In the first half of the nineteenth century, tambour and needlerun embroidered nets, hand netting and fringing for bed and table covers, and crochet work were all popular. In the 1870s and 1880s, though there was little lacemaking that could be called commercial, there was a strong craft revival, and cutworks, Battenburg Renaissance laces, and knotted Modano laces all flourished. The Needle and Bobbin Club was established in 1916, the International Old Lacers in 1953. Somewhat similar institutions in England are the Embroiderers' Guild, established in 1906, and the Lace Guild, in 1976.

Anti-Gallican Society (anti-Catholic). This was founded in 1750, when the War of the Austrian Succession and the Seven Years War had placed Protestant England on unfriendly terms with Catholic France. Its main object was to promote English workmanship and so reduce importations. The Dublin Society and the Society of Edinburgh, founded at about the same time, had similar aims for Ireland and Scotland.

Antwerp. A city and important seaport of Flanders, almost on the border with Holland. Its lace is of a continuous bobbin type, with a cinq trous or point de Paris ground, a silky cordonnet and a straight heading. It most closely resembles Mechlin but is a great deal heavier and more sturdy. The design often incorporates vases of flowers, and then it is known as potten kant, or pot lace. In the eighteenth and nineteenth centuries, it was made extensively in the béguinages, not only in Antwerp itself, but as far afield as Ghent, and used mainly for trimming the caps of the peasant women. Antwerp was also a centre for fine, and expensive, flax thread. See also *Trolly lace.*

Appliqué. The stitching or gluing of design motifs to a continuous background began in the late eighteenth century, with the bobbin-made ground, droschel. With the invention of widths of bobbinet in 1809, the droschel became replaced by the far cheaper machine product (15d instead of £15 for an 18 inch or 457 mm square, i.e. 240 times less).
(a) Bobbin appliqué, Brussels and Honiton. Only non-continuous laces, adapted to the production of quite separate and distinct motifs, were suitable, since in continuous laces the motif threads would automatically be carried over into the ground. When the motifs were assembled, they would be placed face downwards (i.e. in the position in which they were made), the net stretched over them and stitched on from the reverse side.
(b) Needlepoint appliqué, Brussels. The motifs were made, sometimes rather sketchily, in buttonhole stitch, and applied to the net as above. It was especially popular in the second half of the nineteenth century.
(c) Mixed bobbin and needlepoint appliqué also occurred.
(d) Muslin appliqué. This was a labour-saving, and therefore money-saving, form in which a woven cotton cloth was attached to the net, either by a couched outlining thread (Carrickmacross), or by chain stitch embroidery (Belgium), and the excess material was cut away after the pattern had been completed.
(e) Net-on-net appliqué, mainly Belgium. A two-twist bobbinet was laid over a three-twist net and attached by chain stitching. Then the overlying surplus was cut away. It copied the designs of a good Brussels needlepoint appliqué and could easily be mistaken for it, and also in some cases for a needlerun embroidery.

(f) Machine copies of muslin appliqué were made on the Swiss hand-embroidery and Schiffli machines. Some hand finishing was still needed. (Fig. 35.)

Aquila. See *Abruzzi*.

Argentan (Normandy). This differentiated from the original point de France in the early eighteenth century, and the name is first recorded in 1724. It is distinguishable from Alençon only in the reseau, which appears to the naked eye larger and firmly hexagonal. With adequate magnification, it can be seen that every mesh is closely worked over with buttonhole stitches, as many as ten to each side. Argentan shared the fate of Alençon at the time of the French Revolution, but not its early nineteenth-century revival: being a heavier lace, it did not fit with the gauzy silks of the First Empire. Lefebure produced Argentan at his Bayeux factory in 1874, but for exhibition purposes rather than for use. Today Argentan is made only in the Abbaye Notre Dame of that town. The 300-count thread makes the work extremely slow, and the hours of labour alone would put the price beyond all reach. (Fig. 15b.)

Argentella. A rare eighteenth-century needlepoint lace, usually regarded as a form of Argentan, distinguished by its elaborate ground of reseau rosaceae – a solid hexagon within a skeletal hexagon. Nevill Jackson ascribes it to Burano, Palliser and Lowes to Genoa, but these views are generally regarded as erroneous. (Fig. 16c.)

Armenian lace. A knotted lace of the nineteenth and twentieth centuries made around the shores of the eastern Mediterranean. It was worked in Armenian edging stitch and was said with doubtful truth to resemble the seventeenth-century punto avorio (ivory point). See *Groppo* (vi).

Armure, Fond d' (French, armour ground). A rare type of bobbin reseau found in some Mechlin laces of the first quarter of the eighteenth century. It is thought to be named from its resemblance to chain mail.

Artificial fibres. These are of two main types:
(a) Derivatives of naturally occurring staples. The cellulose of cotton waste or wood pulp is treated by either a viscose or an acetate process to produce an artificial silk. Though both processes were patented in the 1890s, the fibres were not used commercially until 1905. In 1927 'artificial silk' was changed to 'rayon'.
(b) Completely synthetic fibres formed by the polymerisation of non-fibrous materials obtained from oil or coal, such as polyamides, poly-

esters and acrylics. Long molecules are created which can be used as textile filaments. Synthetic fibres can be used on Levers machines but are especially suited to the Warp Frame, or Raschel, laces. The first to be used was nylon (1938), followed by the acrylic orlon (1951), and a little later courtelle. Polyesters were marketed as dacron (1953) and as terylene (1955). Elasticated polyurethane fibres were first used for underwear in 1962. See also *Fibres*, and Fig. 23e.

Austria. See *Vienna*.

Aurillac, in the Auvergne, not far from Le Puy. In the seventeenth century it was a noted centre for gold and silver guipures, i.e. laces built up from thin strips of precious metal wound around a silk core.

Avorio, Punto (Italian, ivory stitch). (a) A buttonhole stitch knotted tightly just below the loop it has passed through. (b) A form of lace made with this stitch, e.g. puncetto. (c) A sculptured Venetian lace where the pale colour and waxy lustre are reminiscent of the smooth patina of carved ivory. See also *Groppo, Gros point* and *Ragusa* (d).

Ayrshire work. A white embroidery associated with Ayrshire, a county in South-west Scotland. The material first used was a sheer muslin imported from India and decorated with tambour work. In the early nineteenth century Scottish weavers were able to make a very adequate muslin themselves, and the influence of both Dresden drawnwork and French pierced embroidery enriched the decoration until it developed a distinctive characteristic of its own. Mrs Jamieson, who lived in Ayr c 1814, started a cottage industry which expanded to include thousands of both Scottish and Irish workers by the 1850s. They were paid a shilling a day. The large variety of patterns were stamped, rolled or lithographically printed on to the material. All were of flowers, and the work was therefore sometimes called flowerin, and the workers flowerers. The minute flower centres were either perforated with drawnwork (Fig. 38c) or actually cut out and then filled with plain net, with embroidered net or with delicate buttonhole stitching.

   The American Civil War of the 1860s cut off the supply of raw cotton. Bolder laces, too, were coming into fashion. Also Swiss machines were achieving a marvellous proficiency. They could turn out not only broderie anglaise but intricate white embroideries with openwork fillings, so like handwork that only the printed outline of the pattern in the latter distinguished it. Even this distinction was easily eliminated by the simple device of inking in faint marks around the finished machine product. The machine embroideries were of course cheaper, and also their somewhat heavier style was better suited to the gaudy ostentatious clothes then coming into fashion. See also *Whitework*.

Azores. See *Knitted lace, Aloe*.

Baby caps, vests and robes. For centuries swaddling bands were applied like bandages to the new-born infant to hold it together. The shirt or vest, over which they were bound, was at first of plain linen, but by the end of the seventeenth century it was being decorated along the shoulder seam, often with a narrow insertion of hollie point, while the soft bobbin laces of Mechlin or Binche were applied, quite straight, around the neck and cuffs so that their well considered designs were clearly visible. Several linen caps, or biggins, were worn, one on top of the other, the topmost alone being decorated, with hollie point medallions to match the shirt. For special occasions additional sleeves, mittens and a long bib were added. During the eighteenth century, christening gowns of ivory satin were worn. Their sack-back, or open robe, effects, modelled on adult fashions, were trimmed with tasselled braids rather than lace. The familiar long gown of white lawn appears not to have developed before the end of the eighteenth century. One of its earliest decorations was a form of white embroidery known as Ayrshire work. Matching caps were made to accompany the gowns, decorated all over with pierced eyelet holes, or cut into a hundred tiny windows filled with needlepoint panes, every single stitch made by hand.

From the 1840s gowns overlaid with Honiton or Brussels appliqué began to replace the Ayrshire. They became little by little more elaborate, with first broderie anglaise, then a mass of tucks, frills and lace of all kinds. Throughout the nineteenth century necks were square, sleeves short, bodices shallow or V-shaped, and skirts very long. In the twentieth century sleeves became longer, necks rounder and gowns shorter.

Baby lace. Very narrow (¼ inch, or 6 mm, wide) lace edgings used for the multiple frills around baby's caps in the mid nineteenth century. They were made in the East Midlands, of flax thread, in a miniature torchon fan design, or of a plain net ground sprinkled with tiny point d'esprit. (Fig. 4d.) See *Tulle* (v).

Band. See *Ruff*.

Barbe. See *Lappets*.

Barleycorn. A term used in Bedfordshire Maltese for a long square-ended wheatear.

Barmen. See *Machine lace* (g).

Baroque. See *Design*.

Bars, brides, legs, ties, straps, bridges, plaits. A term used in bobbin, needlepoint and some embroidered laces. See *Brides*.

Bath Brussels. A rare bobbin lace made in the Somerset and Devon area of England in the eighteenth century. The general appearance resembles Brabant laces: the edges of the flowers and the veins of the leaves show raised and rolled work, and the ground is droschel. But the design is more diffuse, lacking the competent self-assurance of Brussels urbanity, having indeed a 'lost' look; while the droschel, instead of being arranged in neat narrow strips side by side along the length of the lace, meanders in a disorderly way around the convolutions of the design.

Battenburg. A form of renaissance lace, giving the appearance of a floppy edging made up of big loops of tape caught together by 'spiders' or by tenuously twisted brides. It was used for the borders of afternoon teacloths around 1900 and was a favourite pastime in the USA.

Bavaro (plural bavari). An embroidered or jewelled edging used to decorate, and sometimes even to fill, the low-cut square neckline of a woman's bodice in the late fifteenth century. It is referred to in the Sforza inventory as 'Pecto uno d'oro a grupi' (a breast cloth of knotted gold). Some very beautiful designs for needlepoint bavari appeared in the pattern books of Ostaus (1557) and Vecellio (1591). Here they were shaped more like a yoke, with straps over the shoulders, since the Venetian gowns of that period came no higher than the armpits.

Bayeux. See *Blonde, Caen* and *Lefebure*.

Bead edge, beading. A narrow tape-like border of bobbin lace, made in hem stitch, faggot stitch or ribbon hole, to attach the footing of a lace to the fabric it is to decorate, in order to prevent direct strain on the lace itself. It is often machine-made. (Fig. 7c.)

Beam. The large roller which holds the threads which make the warp of bobbinet and Levers laces. The warp threads on these machines are sometimes, for this reason, called beam threads. (Fig. 32a.)

Bebilla, bibila, oya. A needle-knotted lace, using a special knot (Fig. 40a), and made in Turkey, Syria, Armenia and parts of Greece. It often takes the form of a three-dimensional decoration of brightly coloured silks, like a garland of flowers, said originally to have embellished the yashmaks of the harem women. It was revived in the second half of the nineteenth century as dentate borders to head scarves and handker-chieves, sometimes using cotton instead of silk. In the 1920s it was copied in crochet. Some good pieces were shown at the Colonial Exhibition of 1886. (Fig. 40f.) See also *Knotted lace.*

Bedfordshire. This county name (often abbreviated to 'Beds') was first used for a type of lace in the 1850s; it was then strongly disapproved of as encouraging bad workmanship since mistakes could so much more easily be concealed than in the parental Buckinghamshire. It was a deliberately imitative lace, copying popular continental forms. Bedfordshire Maltese is associated with the name of Thomas Lester, who transformed the lace designs from a mere imitation to a work of art. His raised wheatears, first used in 1856, sit on top of the closely textured whole stitch like clustered cherries on the icing of a cake, reminiscent of similar raised effects in the late seventeenth-century North Italian bobbin laces. In Beds Maltese the wheatears are finer and more slender than in the original form from Malta, and there is a nine-pin border; Beds Cluny has a divided trail; and in Beds Le Puy the wheatears are in pinnate rows. (Fig. 3.) See also *East Midlands.*

Bedfordshire trailers. Large trolly bobbins used to hold the outlining, or gimp, thread.

Beds. See *Bedfordshire.*

Beer (Devon). The home of Jane Bidney, who was put in charge of the making of Queen Victoria's wedding lace in 1839. Also the site of the famous lace shop, formerly run by Ida Allen, a descendant of Jane Bidney.

Béguinage. A sort of upper-class workhouse for pious single ladies of the Catholic faith. Some of the finest laces of the Low Countries were made in their sheltered and dedicated atmosphere. See also *Lacemakers.*

Belgian lace. Most laces named by their nationality are easy to place within geographical limits of latitude and longitude. Belgium, however, because of frequent wars and fluctuating boundaries, is not; and the rela-tionship between the groups of laces known respectively as Belgian,

Brussels, Flemish and Dutch is difficult to define with precision.

These laces come from the Low Countries, which from the early six-teenth century were part of the Holy Roman Empire, whose Catholic rulers persecuted the Protestant inhabitants without mercy. Holland became independent in 1648, but Belgium was not a distinct kingdom until 1831. In spite of the vacillation of boundaries during almost cease-less wars, with border towns being tossed back and forth in various con-quests, 'Belgium' nevertheless approximates to the old geographical limits of Flanders.

The sixteenth to eighteenth century lacemaking centres of Antwerp, Mechlin, Binche and Valenciennes are regarded as 'Flemish'. They made bobbin laces of the continuous kind.

'Brussels' laces were non-continuous, and they are recorded in the seventeenth, eighteenth and nineteenth centuries. Brussels lies in the province of Brabant, and Brabant lace is similar, technically, to Brussels. So-called 'Dutch' lace may have been made in Holland, formerly known as the United Provinces.

'Belgian lace' refers to products from the same, and other, towns after 1831, though Valenciennes had long been part of France and in the nine-teenth century was producing a typically French lace. The monopoly of its manufacture was later acquired by Belgium.

During the French Revolution (1789) 'Flemish' lace foundered. In the early nineteenth century Brussels, revivified by Napoleon I, produced some exquisite veils; but the spark was extinguished again with the Emperor's defeat at Waterloo in 1815. In the second half of the nine-teenth century Belgian lace flowered again in duchesse, point de gaze and Bruges. In the 1880s, competing with their beautiful and expensive pieces, came the Swiss chemical laces. The 45,000 workers of 1914 had diminished to 30,000 by 1922; and the quality of the thread, detail of work and originality of design had deteriorated. By the late 1950s the situation was much the same as in England: lace schools and workshops had closed down, and there was only a handful of makers to be found from one end of the country to the other. The late twentieth-century revival in England and America extended to Belgium, and a Kantcen-trum (Lace Centre) was founded in Bruges in 1972 for the teaching of bobbin lacemaking.

The following is a list of the laces of the Low Countries from the six-teenth to the twentieth centuries. Further details of most of them are given under their separate heads. (Figs. 5, 6, 7, 10c, 11, 19a, 35c.)

(a) Embroidered laces: cutworks, sixteenth to seventeenth centuries.

(b) Needlepoints: (i) Netherlands/Dutch, seventeenth century; (ii) Brussels, eighteenth century; (iii) Brussels point de gaze, nineteenth to twentieth century; (iv) point de Venise, twentieth century (see *Venetian*

Lace (h)).

(c) Bobbin: (i) sixteenth-century (see *Flemish lace* (b)); (ii) seventeenth-century Dutch; (iii) seventeenth-century Flemish: collar lace, vermiculate, and peasant; (iv) Flemish continuous, seventeenth to early nineteenth century: Binche, Valenciennes, Antwerp, Mechlin; (v) Belgian continuous: mid nineteenth and twentieth centuries: point de fée, also Cluny, torchon, Valenciennes, blonde, point de Paris, Lille, Chantilly; (vi) eighteenth-century Flemish non-continuous; (vii) Brussels non-continuous, eighteenth century: Brabant, point d'Angleterre; (viii) Brussels non-continuous, mid nineteenth to twentieth century: point d'Angleterre (mixed), duchesse (mixed), Old Flanders (mixed), rosaline; (ix) Bruges, late nineteenth to twentieth century: flower lace, Russian.

(d) Renaissance: Belgian, late nineteenth to twentieth centuries: (i) point de Milan; (ii) princess.

(e) Decorated nets, mostly referred to as Brussels. (i) Appliqué: (1) on droschel – motifs may be bobbin, needlepoint or mixed, late eighteenth to early nineteenth century. (2) On three-twist bobbinet – motifs may be bobbin, needlepoint, mixed, muslin or net, c 1840 to twentieth century. (ii) Tambour embroidery: Lierre, Ghent.

Bemberg. A special matt finish to rayon machine laces.

Bérain. See *Design* and *Points de France* (a).

Bertha, berthe. A long (3–4 foot, 0.9–1.2 metre) collar worn around the shoulders leaving the neck and upper chest bare. The berthe came into fashion for women with the Restoration (1660), as the era of the falling collar ended. In the seventeenth century it was worn straight, to display to the best advantage the quality and design of those memorable laces: Venetian gros point, point de France and Binche. The nineteenth-century berthe, on the other hand, was shaped like a circle with a wide centre so that, placed around the decolletage it fell naturally into gentle folds. Burano, point de gaze, Limerick, Buckingham, Brussels and Honiton appliqué were all used, as well as chemical laces of varied designs.

Beveren. A town a few miles west of Antwerp. Lille bobbin lace, as well as Belgian laces, was made there in the nineteenth century.

Bidney, Miss Jane. She was appointed 'Honiton Brussels Point Lace Manufacturer' to Queen Victoria on 14th August 1837. She is said to have organised the making of the Queen's wedding lace. Payments to her in 1839 amounted to £34 and in 1840 to £250.

Binche. A Belgian town 20 miles east of Valenciennes. In the late seventeenth century the continuous bobbin laces of the two towns were alike in design, texture and technique, distinguishable only by their ground: oeil de perdrix in Binche, cinq trous in Valenciennes. Both towns were annexed to France in 1678, but Binche was returned to Flanders twenty years later, while Valenciennes was not. Binche therefore remained Flemish in character, so fine and smooth that it looked like a weightless cambric with the filmy design caught in a web of partridge eye ground, and separated from it by a thin picket of tiny pores or pinholes. (Figs. 7c, 17b.)

In the first half of the eighteenth century, Binche was much sought after by the fashionable Parisiennes, but its importation was severely restricted, and the dog within a dogskin packed with lace and sent bounding across the frontier did not often escape the sharp eye of the French customs men.

Since 1972 the Kantcentrum at Bruges has revived the making of Binche, by advanced students, in a form known as point de fée. The modern form is seven times less fine than the old: only a 180-count flax thread is available instead of a 1200. Even so, it takes two hours to complete one square centimetre. (Fig. 7d.)

A hand-made commercial 'Binche', produced in the 1920s or 1930s, is more like a very simple Antwerp, with either an imitation point de Paris or cinq trous ground. It even has an outlining gimp, which is never present in Binche. Machine copies of this 'Antwerp Binche' were made on the Barmen, one width at a time, or on the Levers, fifty widths at a time.

Bisette. A lace mentioned several times in the sixteenth century, made apparently of gold, silver, coloured silk or black thread, and used sometimes laid flat like a braid. It also sometimes referred to an ecru silk lace or a peasant lace. See *Saxony* (a).

Black lace. The natural colour of all the natural fibres is a slightly creamy white. This colour shows to advantage the intricate lace techniques and designs, allowing a soft shading of the minutely three-dimensional threads, so that it is relatively seldom that it is obscured by dyeing. Black lace has occurred as a fashion need, as a sign of mourning or of matronliness, or as a concealment for hasty workmanship, from the sixteenth century, and it is shown in portraits of, for example, Mary Queen of Scots, Mme de Maintenon (Louis XIV's second wife) and Queen Charlotte (wife of George III). That almost none has survived from these 250 years is probably an effect of the dye: it contained iron salts which oxidised to form corrosive compounds, which rotted the silk until it disintegrated. Silk thread was most commonly used: black is notoriously difficult to work with, and tiring for the eyes, because of the lack of contrast and lack of shadow as the threads cross, and the gloss of silk provided faint highlights to aid the maker. (Figs. 2, 11.)

The lack of contrast was no problem to machines, and tons of black lace poured off the nineteenth-century looms in silk, cotton and rayon – indeed there is a common belief that no black lace is 'real'. It also tended to fade (to a dingy brown colour), go mouldy and rot. The mould gave it a musty smell, and the recommended method of cleaning the lace with vinegar did not improve its aroma. Recipes for preserving black lace included mixing bullock's gall with hand-hot water, perfuming the gall with musk, squeezing the lace in it, rinsing, and tingeing the cold water with blue, then 'make stiffening by pouring water on a small piece of glue, squeeze it out, stretch and clamp it'. Another recommended washing in stale beer and stiffening with sugar or potato water.

Almost every kind of lace, including Irish crochet and Branscombe, in almost every age and every country, has been made in black, though it is commoner in bobbin than in needlepoint. Predominantly black, rather than white, laces were made at Bayeux, Grammont (Belgium) and the Erzegebirge (Saxony). Laces of the Chantilly and Spanish types were especially popular.

Blandford (Dorset). There is no record of this lace except in Daniel Defoe's *Tour through the Whole Island of Great Britain*, 1724, but he praised it so highly that it cannot simply be discarded as a figment of his brilliantly inventive genius — like his vivid 'eye witness' account of the Great Plague, published in 1720. He describes Blandford lace as 'exceeding rich, the finest bone lace in England ... I never saw better in Flanders, France or Italy ... they rate it above £30 a yard.'

In 1731, not only did Defoe die, but Blandford was destroyed by fire. The surviving inhabitants turned from lacemaking to the manufacture of Dorset buttons.

Bleaching and tinting of lace. The natural creamy ivory of flax thread predominated in the laces of the sixteenth and seventeenth centuries and much of the eighteenth. Then the rising popularity of muslins made a whiter lace more in demand, and they were bleached:

(a) By exposure to sunlight. This was called sun bleaching, or grass bleaching. Whiteness resulted, but the sunlight had a deleterious effect on the fibres – it seems in general to be harmful to all textiles – and it destroyed the waxes which gave the flax threads their pale lustre.

(b) Flemish laces had a general reputation for being of a slightly reddish or yellowish tinge. When this came to be disapproved of they were dusted with white lead powder, which was good neither for the workers nor for the lace, since on contact with wool, scent, sea air or a heated room it rapidly formed an irreversible sulphide of a distinctly sooty colour.

(c) Calcium oxide was also used. This, on contact with moisture, formed corrosive quicklime.

(d) A liquid chlorine bleach was first made in France in 1789 and known as eau de Javel.

The colour was said to be preserved, during storage, by wrapping the lace in blue tissue paper.

From time to time fashion required that lace should be of an 'antique' colour, or even darker. Such shades were called 'ecru' (French, un-bleached), but they were more than that. The first phase was in the 1820s when perhaps hand-made laces were tinted to distinguish them from the dazzlingly white products of the machines. Mrs Forrester in *Cranford* speaks of lace being washed in coffee to make it the right yellow colour. Mrs Palliser (1869) says that 'our coquettish grandmothers who prided themselves on the colour of their point, when not satisfied with the richness of its hue, had their lace dipped in coffee'. An infusion of tea might also be used, or crystals of potassium permanganate; or the lace could be boiled with saffron, chicory and lampblack. A writer of 1856 condemns the practice: 'There was a time when the dinginess of colour which of course necessarily characterises very old lace was esteemed so great a beauty as to be obtained by artificial means; and much of the modern lace was washed in a weak solution of coffee, and considered to have been greatly enriched by the operation. This perverted and unnatur-al taste has now happily passed away.' However, the fashion returned at the end of the nineteenth century, and Nevill Jackson (1900) also disapproved of it: 'It is not in good taste to affect the lace "Isabeau", a colour much worn recently; this is a greyish coffee colour, or in plain English the colour of dirt, the name of the queen who showed her devotion to her lord by vowing to change no body linen until his return from the wars ... '

Blonde. Originally a natural-coloured silk thread such as that imported into France from Nankin in the mid eighteenth century. The lace made from it was also called blonde. It became very popular and within a few years was displacing Mechlin as the main product of the béguinage. It was a delicately soft lace, admirably suited to the closely gathered trim-mings of this frilly period; a continuous bobbin lace, sometimes using a heavier silk for the repetitive floral design, with a fond simple ground, and made in strips like Spanish lace rather than in jigsaw shapes like Chantilly and nineteenth-century Maltese. It was patronised by royalty and is shown in portraits of Princess Charlotte (1817, daughter of George IV) and Queen Adelaide (1830).

As methods of preparing the silk improved, more of the gum could be got rid of (see *Silk*) and a lighter, softer yarn evolved. Before long confusion arose between the lace, the silk and the colour, and today we are faced with such terminology as 'silk blonde', 'white blonde' and 'black blonde'. Blonde lace was made extensively at Caen from about 1745, in parts of Flanders, in Barcelona and, in small quantities, in the East Midlands of England from 1860. It was one of the earliest laces to be copied by machine; both the Stocking and Warp Frames used silk thread. The Traverse Warp Machine (invented 1811) in 1833 produced a blonde, under the name of 'neige' (snow), marketed as real lace 'without detection during a whole season, it is said to the amount of £60,000, of which sum probably £40,000 was profit'. (Fig. 2c.)

Bobbins (French = fuseaux). (a) The boat-shaped shuttles in which the weft threads are carried for weaving cloth on either a hand or power-operated loom.

(b) The wafer-thin bobbins used to hold the 'weft' threads on Heathcoat's lacemaking machine and its derivatives such as Levers. They are similar to much compressed cotton reels, or spools, 1½ inches (38 mm) in diameter, but less than 1/16 inch (1.5 mm) thick. In their tiny grooves can be carried over 300 yards (274 m) of silk thread, and in a machine 216 inches (5,486 mm) wide there would be over four thousand bobbins. They gave their name to the machine and to its product, bobbin-net, a term not without ambiguity since bobbins also provide the name for a major group of hand-made laces.

(c) In bobbin laces, the bobbins serve the dual purpose of stretching the warp threads (passives or downrights) and providing handles for manipulation of the weaver threads, so that the yarn itself need not be touched. Bobbins take a variety of forms in different countries or regions, but in general each consists of a head, a neck where the thread is wound, and a shaft. The neck varies in length so that the thicker the thread the longer the neck, enabling an adequate amount to be held. The shaft may be straight or bulbous, plain or decorated in a variety of ways. The bobbin is usually made of fruitwood, but olive, spindle or yew may be chosen according to what is locally available. Bone appears to have been the original material (see *Fuller*). The use of more gimmicky substances, such as glass, brass, pewter or silver, is mostly confined to the East Midlands, an area notorious for the variety of its decorations (pewter inlay of tigers, leopards and butterflies, brass wire, beading, bitting, dyeing, the curious church windows, cows-in-calf and mothers-in-babe, and inscriptions of a loving or commemorative kind, of which the 'Hung' bobbins are keenly collected). These East Midlands bobbins alone bear the circlet of beads, or spangles, which, though decorative, appear to serve no very useful purpose. Even in the Midlands there is no reliable record of decorated bobbins before 1812. The earliest bobbins used in Italy are said to have been of lead, giving rise to the term 'merletti a piombini'. The name 'bone lace' may have come from the use of the narrow elongated bones from sheep's feet as bobbins. Bone bobbins appear in seventeenth-century portraits of lacemakers.

(d) Bobbins similar to the smoothly bulbous Flemish or Italian ones were used also for the making of braids (see *Gimp* (c)) and sometimes for knotted laces similar to macramé. This occupation almost certainly antedated true bobbin lace, and its representation in fifteenth-century paintings has sometimes been misinterpreted.

Bobbin lace, pillow lace, cushion lace, bone lace, dentelle au fuseau, merletti a piombini, trine a fuselli. A modified weaving process which takes its name from the way it is made – with bobbins, usually of bone or wood, on a pillow or cushion. Basically, the pillow is for sticking pins into. If the pillow is cylindrical it is supported on a stand to raise it to the right height and stop it rolling around. A pattern for the lace is needed, and this is called a pricking because holes are pricked with a sharp needle in a parchment or stiff card. The accurate placing of these holes is extremely important since through them, as the work proceeds, will be passed the pins which hold the threads which are attached to the bobbins which the worker moves to cross or twist the threads to build up the structure of the lace. Therefore everything hangs on the pins, and if they are badly placed, or if the pricking is 'worn', i.e. the pin holes have stretched or even run together with too much use, the design of the lace will be distorted. With Buckingham laces, where the point ground forms such an important part of the fabric, the pattern is drawn first on squared paper so that every mesh is precisely placed. In Mechlin and Valenciennes the ground is not pricked.

The origin of bobbin lacemaking lies in weaving, which goes back itself many thousands of years. The warp threads of the loom are represented by the threads which hang straight down, weighted by the passive bobbins or downrights. The weft threads, which on the loom are passed between raised and lowered warps by shuttle bobbins, are on the pillow held by worker or weaver bobbins, which are so crossed with the others as to produce a closely textured 'clothwork' which looks exactly as if it has been woven.

The two main groups of bobbin laces are the continuous, where the work goes right across from footing to heading, with ground and motifs in one; and the non-continuous, where the closed sprigs or motifs are made as one operation and the linking of them by brides or by mesh as another.

Evidence for early bobbin lacemaking may easily be misinterpreted, since bobbins are also used to make patterned braids (in which holes do not form an essential part of the design), to make macramé, as shuttles to make woven textiles (and, much later, as swinging discs to make bobbinet on the Heathcoat machine). The evidence for the beginning of bobbin lace, as we know it, rests on the documentary evidence of inventories and wardrobe accounts, on literature, on pattern books and on portraits. The earliest reference is in 1493 when the Sforza inventory lists a large quantity of household linen ornamented with cutwork and knotted lace worked 'with the needle, bobbins, bones, and other different ways'. It establishes the existence of bobbins, but not of bobbin lace.

1495. A painting at Lierre, Belgium, showing a girl making pillow lace, has been used as an argument for bobbin lacemaking in the fifteenth century. It was formerly attributed to Quentin Massys (1466-1530) but is now thought to be the work of his son, and considerably later.

1536. A book of patterns published in Zurich c 1561 by RM asserts that bobbin lace was introduced into Switzerland from Venice in 1536 (see *Swiss embroidery and lace* (a)).

1546. A passage in the third book of *Pantagruel* by François Rabelais (1483-1553) reads: 'Voudrais tu faire espoincter les fuseaulx, calumnier les bobines.' Mincoff and Marriage use this quotation as a heading for their chapter on the tools of bobbin lacemaking, but the translation 'Would you blunt the spindle, and slander the spinning quills' suggests a reference to spinning with a distaff; the further terms 'devidoir' (a shuttle winder) and 'pelotons' (balls made by winding thread) confirm a preparation for weaving cloth.

1549. A portrait of a lady by Lucas Cranach (see *Saxony* (a)) shows her twisting a handkerchief, edged with what appears to be bobbin lace, around her fingers.

1557. A book of bobbin lace patterns called *Le Pompe* was published in Venice by the brothers Sessa. Some of the designs were dentate edgings similar to a punto in aria; others were more like an openwork braid.

1561. Barbara Uttmann of Saxony (1514-75), according to her tomb-stone, invented lace in this year, reputedly bobbin lace.

1580-5. *The Seven Ages of Man*, a painting by the Fleming Martin de Vos (c 1534-1603), shows two girls engaged in some form of lacemaking: one twists sprang on a frame, the other works at a pillow with bobbins, but with such a meagre number that she is more likely to be making a solid braid than a holey lace.

1595-6. There are Bedfordshire records of children being taught to make bone lace.

1599. A bobbin lace coverlet was presented to the Archduke Albert, by Brabant, on the occasion of his marriage to Isabella (see *Brabant*).

1600. Shakespeare refers to 'the fair maids that weave their threads with bones'.

All this evidence places bobbin lace in Flanders, Switzerland, Germany, Venice and England in the sixteenth century. There is also reliable evidence that it was made in Genoa (Fig. 8). As a technique, opinions differ as to whether it derived more directly from weaving, from the hand twisting of braids, from plaiting or from knotting.

Bobbin net, bobbinet. A machine net invented by John Heathcoat in 1808, and improved in 1809. His 'two-twist bobbin net', later known as bobbinet, was a painstakingly accurate copy of the point ground of fond simple. He watched Midlands lace being made and was at first startled and bemused by the rapid tossing around of the bobbins 'like peas in a frying pan dancing about'. He observed that one set of threads, the passives, appeared always to lie straight, and that these might in a loom be put on a beam for warp threads. The more actively moving weaver threads could then be wound on swinging bobbins thin enough to pass between the warp threads. By a complex lateral movement of the warps, combined with a one-bobbin shuffle at the end of every twelfth swing, the wefts could be made to twist and lock around the warps, forming a row of meshes firm enough to hold their shape when removed from the machine. Because the bobbins are mounted in two rows, lined up one behind the other as they pass through the warps, an end bobbin can be exchanged between them as each row of meshes is made – and each completed mesh needs twelve swings. Thus if there are 2,000 bobbins, and one is moved along at every twelfth swing, at the end of 2,000 times 12 swings that one bobbin will have passed the whole way along the row from one end to the other. It is this 'moving on' process which enables the weft threads to pass diagonally instead of horizontally across the net, and so to be 'traversed' as in the hand-made form. The machine's advantage is that it can construct not one mesh at a time but an entire row of meshes – over 6,000 on a 216 inch (5,486 mm) wide machine using a high hole count (i.e. a small mesh size, many meshes to the inch). See also *Machine* (c), *Net* (d), and *Leavers*.

The early bobbinet machine was only 18 inches (457 mm) wide and worked by turning a handle, so that it could be accommodated as a cottage industry in the same way as the Stocking Frame and Warp Frame. A slightly wider form was known as the Old Loughborough because Heathcoat's workshops were sited at Loughborough, before he moved to Tiverton. An Old Loughborough, smuggled into France in

1815, produced its first lace there in 1816 – an entire dress of net, embroidered by hand, for the Duchesse d'Angouleme.

Bobbin winder, turn, wheel. Wooden machines, dating back to the seventeenth century, for the quick and even winding of thread on to the bobbins for lacemaking. A bobbin is placed in the spool holder, and the skein is arranged around pegs on the X-shaped arms. The end of the thread is attached to the neck of the bobbin and, as the flywheel is turned, the spool holder revolves and the thread is drawn from the skein on to the bobbin. When there is enough thread on the neck of the bobbin, a slip knot is made to prevent it unwinding. A similar principle is followed in winding the bobbins for the bobbinet machine, but here 198 bobbins, as opposed to one, can be wound, from a large reel instead of from a skein, and with up to 300 yards (274 m) of thread instead of a few feet. The speed is so rapid that with synthetic thread a static suppressor is needed to prevent the build-up of a high voltage spark. When the bobbins are full they are lifted out, and before their threads are cut off they are guided on to a new batch of bobbins, ready to start winding afresh.

Bohemia. An area of north-west Czechoslovakia, south of the Erzegebirge Mountains of Saxony, and formerly part of the Austro-Hungarian empire. It is associated with a rather flimsily worked bobbin lace of inferior flax made in the eighteenth and nineteenth centuries by peasants for the local markets. It often incorporated brightly coloured threads and was worn with black. The general design was marked with undefined coils and swirls. See also *Czechoslovakian lace*. (Fig. 27a.)

Bone lace. This is generally regarded as an early term for bobbin lace, but in some wardrobe accounts of the early seventeenth century they are listed separately as if there were some real difference between them. Bone lace appeared to be the fashionable thing to wear for being beheaded, for example by Sir Thomas Wyatt on a hat in 1554, and by Mary Queen of Scots on a gauze veil in 1587. The term 'bone' may relate either to the use of animal bones – traditionally the toe, ankle and wrist bones of a sheep – for bobbins, or to the use of fish bones or splintered chicken bones in lieu of brass pins, which were very expensive at that period.

Bonnaz. The first really successful chain-stitch embroidery machine, patented in 1865 by a French engineer called Bonnaz. Its method was very similar to tambour embroidery by hand, and its use became a peasant industry in Switzerland, the machines being small enough to be used in the home. Stoles, collars and shawls of Bonnaz embroidery on net were produced in large quantities, and also a form of muslin appliqué similar to Carrickmacross but with the shapes attached by chain stitch instead of a couched cord. See also *Tambour* and *Machine lace* (h).

Boot hose. The linings of the calf-high boots of the seventeenth century, with their folded-down, splaying tops, which were often filled in with lace.

Bourdon. See *Bullion* and *Gimp* (a).

Brabant. A duchy of Flanders, in which Brussels is situated. It is associated with lace from the sixteenth century, when, in 1599, a superb bed cover of bobbin lace was presented to Albert, Archduke of Austria and Governor of the Spanish Netherlands (which included Brabant) from 1596. He had married in 1598 Isabella, Infanta of Spain and grand-daughter of Catherine of Medici (through the marriage of her daughter Elizabeth to Philip II as his third wife). The coverlet depicts various biblical scenes; the word 'Brabant' is worked above the figures of the Archduke and his wife; and the kings and queens of Spain and of France are represented, together with the patron saint of Brussels.

Eighteenth-century Brabant lace has a strong resemblance to that of Brussels, being a non-continuous bobbin lace of rich and semi-formal design, the loosely textured flouncing depicting large floral bouquets supported from columns by ribbon swathes.

Brabant was famous also for its fine flax.

Braid. (a) A decorative tape woven on a loom or made with bobbins. (b) A lace made from these braids, for example Branscombe: see *Renaissance*. (c) 'Braid appliqué' referred to machine tapes which were not linked by a ground but were appliquéd on to net, e.g. *Princess*. (d) Plaited strands (cf a braid of hair), such as appear in the reseaux of droschel, Mechlin and Valenciennes: this is not general usage.

Branscombe. A Renaissance lace particularly associated with the village of Branscombe in East Devon, south of Honiton, and near to Beer. It is made in the same way as other *Renaissance laces* but it has distinctive features: the needlepoint fillings are many and closely worked (compare Battenburg); there are traditionally fourteen different fillings; the heading of the lace is purled with little picots oversewn with buttonhole stitches. (Fig. 44c.)

Branscombe lace is thought to have started about 1850; it was shown at the Great Exhibition of 1851; and in the 1860s there were dealers selling it by the yard, or as made pieces, in Sidmouth. Mrs Palliser, who lived there, says rather disparagingly: 'Among the various cheap articles to which the Devonshire workers have of late directed their labours is the tape or braid lace, and the shops of the country are now inundated with their productions in the form of collars and cuffs.'

With competition from the chemical laces in the late nineteenth century, its production became unprofitable. It has recently been revived: working patterns are made by taking rubbings on brown paper from a finished piece. This gives the outline for the tape to follow, and the fillings can then be copied from the original lace.

Breton lace. A needlerun embroidered net of rather plain unsubtle form made in Brittany between about 1860 and 1940, mainly as utilitarian pieces such as table runners, coverlets and simple collars. The embroidery was in silk or mercerised cotton, outlined with a heavier thread, and its designs were easily copied by the Schiffli. The machine could not of course take the threads in and out of the meshes in the same way as the running stitch done by hand, and so close examination can distinguish the two forms.

In the eighteenth century, drawnwork on muslin was made in Brittany and called 'Broderie des Indes' (Indian embroidery), after the translucent cotton scarves being imported from India at that time.

Brides (French, bridle or bonnet string). It is sometimes pronounced 'breeds' but is more frequently anglicised to 'brides'. For alternative names, see *Bars*. Brides are struts passing across the open spaces between one part of the design and the next, linking them together and holding them in position. They are often important diagnostic features in identification.

(i) In needlepoints in general they are oversewn with buttonhole stitches; in seventeenth-century Venetian they are in addition ornately picoted; in point de France they are arranged in large meshes and decorated with picots like tiny beads. The reseau of Argentan is some-times described as brides bouclées, and the heaviest form of Alençon reseau as brides tortillées.

(ii) In the better bobbin laces the threads are plaited, sometimes picoted (brides picotées), sometimes arranged as large meshes (eigh-teenth-century Flemish); in the less good laces the threads are twisted in a rather straggly manner; in some late nineteenth-century Belgian and Honiton laces a continuous plaited strand is taken like a zigzag between pieces of the design and caught there by a needle and thread – this reduces the labour of taking numerous sewings.

Until the late seventeenth century brides were the only form of ground. In the eighteenth century they were almost entirely replaced by reseaux and did not return until the 1850s, when they burst on the market with great aplomb. See also *Fond* and *Reseau*. (Fig. 6b.)

Laces with a ground of brides are sometimes given the generic name 'guipures'. Brides claires = undecorated brides; brides ornées = decorated brides.

Broderie anglaise. A form of white embroidery popular between 1840 and 1880 for underwear and children's wear. The design was formed of quite large holes decoratively arranged and pierced in the cotton material, with a stiletto or metal die before the embroidery, or with scissors after. The designs and techniques were copied identically by the Swiss hand-embroidery machine, from the 1870s. The designs were also copied in the 1890s by the Schiffli, but its long huddled stitches gave a fuzzy appearance to the white thread and so distinguished it. See also *Machine lace* (h), *Madeira, Richelieu* (b), *Swiss embroidery and lace* (c), *Whitework* (b).

Brodeur Isaac. An attachment for the patterning of machine laces which was used in conjunction with the Jacquard, in the 1840s, to produce silk laces, known as 'fancies', in imitation of hand-made blondes.

Bruges. A town in Belgium 50 miles west of Brussels. The lace named after it originated in the mid nineteenth century as a bold floral form (Bruges flower lace) made in a mixture of whole stitch and half stitch with no raised work, but a flat outlining gimp. Elongated trefoils and bulbous pods also frequently occur, and the quality varies enormously, the best having a ground of double plaited brides arranged like interlocking circles, the worst a single thread of poor cotton zigzagging irregularly from point to point (see *Brides* (ii)). The 'swing leadwork' is almost the only filling (see *Cutwork* (b)), but it may be formed with a needle. Occasionally the designs are remarkably like Honiton, but the thread is thicker and the flowers less delicate. The other form of Bruges (Russian lace) is the only one still made to supply the tourist and, because the demand is greater than the Belgian lacemakers can supply, prickings are sent to Taiwan for working.

Brussels. The capital city of Belgium and an important lacemaking centre since the seventeenth century. The wide variety of laces which bear its name are listed under *Belgian lace*. They include needlepoint, bobbin and mixed laces, as well as decorated nets. The bobbin laces are all non-continuous: in the seventeenth and eighteenth centuries they are grounded with droschel, in the nineteenth and twentieth centuries with brides. The eighteenth-century needlepoint, grounded either with Alençon-type reseau ordinaire (see *Alençon* (i)) or with droschel (Fig. 5b), is discussed under *Point de Venise à reseau*. The nineteenth-century point de gaze was at its best quite glorious and very expensive; the twentieth-century point de Venise was utilitarian. The decorated nets included almost overpoweringly lavish appliqués, like a dense whirlwind of spots and flourishes.

The most famous of the earlier forms was point d'Angleterre, sometimes called rather anonymously 'Brussels eighteenth-century bobbin lace'. Its strange pseudonym was used, according to the Venetian ambassador in 1695, 'to distinguish it from the others' (see *Point d'Angleterre* (ii)). Like them, it died out with the French Revolution, which exterminated Flanders's main export market. The nineteenth-century revival persisted into the 1930s, but not much beyond.

Some late nineteenth-century designs of Brussels duchesse and of good Honiton converge. Most likely some deliberate imitation was at work, but Honiton never quite loses its rustic quality: it lacks the sophisticated precision and urbanity, the profusion, the almost ubiquitous needlemade fillings of Brussels, while Brussels would never allow the shapeless forms of slugs and snails into its neatly cared-for grounds. In short, Honiton derives from a cottage industry, Brussels from professional establishments.

Brussels net, diamond net, three-twist net. See *Net* (e). Widths from 3 to 72 inches (76 to 1,829 mm) could be made, in cotton, rayon and silk-in-the-gum, i.e. before the gum was removed.

Buckingham (Bucks) lace, point ground, English Lille. A continuous bobbin lace in which the closely textured work and smooth ground give an impression of sylvan harmony. Its simplicity distinguishes it sharply from the intricately ornate products of Belgium. It has a silky gimp and a fond simple ground, though earlier forms may have had a wire, torchon or Mechlin reseau. Little is known, for certain, of Bucks laces before the nineteenth century, though they are recorded by Fiennes in the 1690s, and in 1698 a quarter of the total population of Buckinghamshire (about 30,000 people) were said to be occupied in making lace. The name 'Bucks point' is retained through long usage, confirming perhaps a French origin for this lace, which in its technique, and in some of its designs, so closely resembles Lille. Some two hundred designs are known, with names as ingenuous as those of other English laces: pretty dick, cat's face, honeysuckle and lover's knot. Fillings such as mayflower and honeycomb are commonly used. (Fig. 4.) See also *East Midlands lace.*

Bud, porte. Little openings in an expanse of closework. In Honiton, they are known as four-, five-, six-, seven- or eight-pin buds according to the number of pinholes which appear. In needlepoints they are made by leaving a gap in the dense buttonhole stitching and are more usually called 'portes'. See also *Pinhole*.

Bullet-hole net. A transition form between a plain and a patterned twist net, first produced in 1823. There was a simple repeat of round or oval holes at regular intervals. In a more elaborate form called Grecian net, each larger hole was surrounded by a circle of smaller holes, not unlike the honeycomb stitch of Bucks lace.

Bullion. A thread made by the winding of metal, silk or rayon around a cotton core, like the old gimp. It was sometimes used as a cordonnet for machine Alençon and was then called bourdon cord, but it did not wear well.

Burano. An island 5 miles north-east of Venice, part of the old Venetian Republic. The lace now known as Burano is a nineteenth-century needle-point, similar to a simple Alençon, with the rather thick reseau ordinaire worked over threads stretched evenly widthways on to give the impression of endless little ladders stacked side by side. The cordonnet was simply a couched thread; it was not buttonholed over, nor did it bear any picots. In the early twentieth century some good tourist pieces were made, showing the Doge's palace and barge, St Mark's and the Campanile. They were sold, fairly enough, as Venetian. See also *Venetian lace* (g).

Buratto (Italian, a sieve or sifter, from 'bura', a coarse linen). A silk or linen material woven with a single weft and double warp to give a gauze-like material with square meshes. There is thus ready made a ground for decoration which might with difficulty have been produced by drawnwork or filet knotting. Pattern books for burato (the antique spelling) were published by Paganino in 1518, 1527 and 1538 (*Il Burato, Libro de Recami* – i.e. 'Buratto, a book of embroidery'), and by Pagano in Venice in 1559. Designs in running stitch could be copied from the books using a counted thread technique, or they could be pounced directly on to the fabric. Buratto is far rarer than filet: seventeenth-century pieces were often embroidered with coloured silks which were in time rotted by the dye; the silk gauze itself tended, when tinted, to disintegrate. Nineteenth-century copies of older pieces occasionally come on to the market and are difficult to distinguish. See also *Lacis*.

Burial in lace. It was the custom from ancient times for people to be buried in their best clothes. The eastern Mediterranean coasts and islands were riddled with crypts and catacombs from which antique lace was extracted by avaricious dealers, in perhaps too large quantities, in the 1860s, when the collecting of lace was an innovation. In the sixteenth century the grand-daughter of King Gustavus Vasa of Sweden was buried in gold and silver lace (see *Swedish lace*). In 1625 Charles I spent £50,000 on a state funeral for his father. In England, in 1678, the Burial in Woollen Act was passed (see *Wool*); but in France, a little later Mme de Sévigné (1626-96) was exclaiming in horror at the pagan profanation of burying a fontange on its owner and recoiling at the thought of hairdresser and undertaker (encaser in lead) arriving together to deal with her lifeless body. On a more humble level, the Breton custom of preserving the bride's wedding dress to deck her corpse survived well into the nineteenth century. See also *Fremantle, Greek lace* (e) and *Mechlin* (d, iv).

Burnt lace, burned out or chemical lace. See *Machine* (h) and *Swiss* (c).

Butterfly. (a) A type of pewter inlay on the shank of East Midlands bobbins. (b) Lace butterflies were popular motifs for appliqué work and for brooches in the early twentieth century. (c) Papillon: the frill at the front of the cap crown worn by court ladies in the late seventeenth and eighteenth centuries.

Buttonhole stitch, scallop stitch, point noné, point de boutonnière, punto a festone, punto a ochiello, punto a smerlo. The basic stitch of all needlepoint laces. It is sometimes called a 'detached' buttonhole stitch since it was worked not into a woven material but over the previous row of loops or, at the border of the design, around a supporting thread. Some eighty variations are known, making possible a whole range of decorative fillings. Ten of the more commonly used forms are illustrated in Fig. 14. In (1), the simplest form, the stitches are worked first from left to right and then from right to left, forming open loops threaded through each other. In (2), often used for the point de gaze 'toilé', each row of loops is worked from left to right only; the sewing thread is then taken back to the left side in a 'straight return' and enclosed by the next line of stitches. In (5), the point de gaze reseau, the thread is twisted around the needle as the stitch is made. In (6), the reseau ordinaire of Alençon, the stitches are worked from left to right only, and the return thread is twisted around the previous row of loops.

Remarkably similar stitches have been analysed in relics of a woollen cap and jacket found in a bronze age tomb (c 2,000 BC) in Denmark.

Caen. One of the major centres of the Bayeux lacemaking area. Three kinds of lace were produced there from the early nineteenth century, under the management of Auguste Lefebure: (i) the original blonde de Caen, with its sprinkling of point d'esprit nestling in the cobwebby ground, and the suggestion of curved petals of shiny white silk hung along the border; (ii) blonde mate (as in matt, a smooth close texture) in Spanish style, made from 1829; (iii) the grillé blanc (French, a mesh or grill, half stitch), a form of white Chantilly, very fashionable between 1800 and 1820, with a fond simple ground, and with the floral sprays worked in half stitch, using silk or flax. From the 1850s mainly black lace was produced.

Calais. A flourishing centre for machine-made laces in the nineteenth century, and sometimes called the 'Nottingham of France'. The machines used initially were of English manufacture. The first, the Old Loughborough (Heathcoat's 1809 version of the bobbinet machine, little more than 36 inches or 914 mm wide) was, in spite of English export restrictions, smuggled into France piece by piece in 1815. It was set up and worked by twist-hand emigrés from Nottingham. In 1825 a Levers machine was imported from England, and copies of it were manufactured by a firm at Lille. By 1833 half the bobbinet marketed in France was of French manufacture and half of English. In 1834 the Jacquard apparatus, which automated the patterning of woven materials, was applied to lace manufacture; and in 1838 it was used for designs which imitated faithfully the old Chantilly but were never more than one-eighth of the price. With overproduction, and consequent reduction of wages and prices, the competition between England and France for the machine-lace market became fierce: they quarrelled as to who originated the designs; they pirated new ideas unscrupulously; and each claimed its own quality to be superior.

Camisole. A waist-length underbodice of cotton or fine lawn, worn over the corset in the nineteenth century, and frequently decorated at the neck and arm holes with lace.

Canons. In men's dress of the seventeenth century, a flouncing of lace around the lower leg, within the boot top, or attached to the garter on both the inner and outer side of the leg as a pleated or gathered fan, falling to mid calf.

Cantu. A town in the plain of Lombardy, 20 miles north of Milan, associated with the bobbin lace known as Italian rosaline. See *Rosaline*.

Cap crowns. The circular or horseshoe-shaped lace insets on a baby's bonnet; or the lace cap back of a court lady. See *Head*.

Carnival lace. The dowry lace of noble Venetian ladies, consisting of cutworks, drawnworks and reticellas, specially made for the bridal gown, and for the hangings and coverlet.

Carrickmacross. An appliqué lace associated with the town of this name in the north of the Republic of Ireland. It began about 1820, when decorations of the newly invented bobbinet were making the much slower bobbin and needlepoint laces commercially unsound. A stiffish woven muslin replaced the solid part of the design, and Heathcoat's net replaced the hand-made ground. The only handwork then involved was the drawing of the design on a backing cloth; the tacking on to this of an overlay of net and then muslin; the couching of the outlining thread which held together the net and its decoration; the cutting away of the excess muslin; and the embellishing of the flower centres with fancy needleruns. It was laborious enough, but still a saving of time and money, and it employed people who otherwise might have found it extraordinarily difficult not to die of starvation. In the late 1840s a guipure form was introduced, in which no net was used. The flowers and leaves were outlined as before and then linked by buttonhole-stitched bars, after which the excess muslin was cut away. Both forms had a border of rounded picots.

Though the quality had much deteriorated, small amounts were still available in the stores as yardages and shaped pieces in the 1920s. A machine imitation called 'net appliqué' was made on the Swiss embroidery machines. Here, the attachment of the muslin (batiste) to the net was usually without a cordonnet and could be performed over many repeats in one operation. (Fig. 35.) See also *Appliqué*, (d) and (f).

Carter, Sybil (d. 1908). Taught lacemaking to North American Indian tribes, from Minnesota to California, and also eastwards to New York. In 1904 she founded the Sybil Carter Indian Lace Association, which flourished until 1926. The laces were of renaissance, cutwork or bobbin types. Coverlets a little over 6 feet (1.8 m) square were priced at $600.

Cartisane, guipure, parchment lace. See *Gimp*, (b) and (c). In the sixteenth and seventeenth centuries 'cartisane' or 'guipure' were used on the Continent, while English accounts, from Mary I to Charles II, mostly refer to 'parchment lace'. (Fig. 1b.)

Catherine of Medici (1519-89). The Florentine wife of Henri II, and mother of three French kings: François II, Charles IX and Henri III.

Catherine, her daughters Marguerite de Valois (m. Henri IV) and
Elizabeth (m. Philip II of Spain as his third wife) and her daughter-in-
law Mary Queen of Scots (m. François II) were all keen needlewomen
and passed the hours in darning designs on filet grounds made by their
ladies-in-waiting. An inventory, made at Catherine's death, included
four hundred such pieces. She invited the ruff designer, Vinciolo, to stay
at the French court, and in 1587 his first pattern book was dedicated to
Henri III's wife, Louise.

Cellofas. A nylon chiffon fabric used in lace repair. See also *Crepeline*.

Cellulose. A carbohydrate of the polysaccharide group, insoluble in
water. It occurs universally in plant cells and so is an integral part of
textile fibres such as cotton and flax. Cotton is almost pure cellulose: flax
has an admixture of wood or lignin. The presence of cellulose in wood
pulp enables it to be used for making rayon of the 'reconstituted cellulose' type. See *Artificial fibres*.

Chain stitch. A simple looped stitch worked with a needle and thread
across the surface of a material. It was used extensively during the great
period of English embroidery, in the middle ages. Its connections with
lace are definite but not entirely clear:
(a) Sixteenth century. (i) The wardrobe accounts of Elizabeth I include
'Six caules (i.e. coifs or caps) of knot-work *worked with* chain stitch' and
'Six fine net caules *flourished with* chain stitch with sister's (nun's?)
thread'. It is uncertain whether 'worked with' means 'made of' or
'decorated with'. (ii) In 1568 references are made in the state papers to
frauds connected with the importation of 'cheyne lace'. (iii) English shop
inventories c 1570 note 'gold and silver chean lace' and 'chayne lace'.
(b) Sixteenth-century Spanish laces included a chain-stitch lace called
cadenetas.
(c) In 1755 the Dublin Society announced a prize for the making of
'cheyne lace'.
(d) In 1772 a bill from an upholsterer's in Clerkenwell Close and
Freemans Court, Cornhill, lists '86 yds white Thread chain lace at 2½d
... 17.11' for bed cover and hangings, and a further 30 yards for
curtains.
(e) Tambour work is chain stitch made not with a needle but with a
minute hook. When the end product is sufficiently openwork, for
example by being done on net, it forms an embroidered lace (see
Embroidered nets (b)).
(f) Crochet itself is an arrangement of chain stitches made not on
material, but 'in the air'. The name is derived from the French 'croc', a

hook, similar to the shepherd's crook, and referring to the implement used. As in embroidery, the chain stitches are made one at a time, to form a chain. A new row is made by working back along the previous one, looping through it at each stitch. The texture of solid crochet is rather inflexible, but by the creation of doubles and trebles a lacy form can be produced, and this was popular for tablecloths around 1900. An enormous number of stitch variations is possible, by catching loops together, making extra ones, and so forth, and their names include Idiot Stitch, Hollow Spot, Josephine Tricot, Double Knot and Raised Loop.
(g) Knitting is also related to chain stitch since it involves loops of thread being pulled through other loops; and stocking stitch, from the right side, looks very like rows of chain stitching. However, the horizontal progression of the work, with all the loops in each row being retained on a bluntly pointed needle, is quite unlike the one-at-a-time production of chain stitch in the usual sense.
(h) The looped laces of the Stocking and Warp Frames in the late eighteenth and early nineteenth centuries, and present-day Raschels, are made up of modified chain stitches.
(i) The Bonnaz was a chain-stitch machine used to imitate the hand-tamboured decoration of nets. The Schiffli, though technically using a lock stitch, presents the appearance of very elongated chain stitches on the reverse of the lace, and it is the proliferation of these which produces the overall fuzzy effect. (Figs. 29, 30, 31.)

Chantilly. A town in north-east France, best known for the black continuous bobbin laces produced there in the second half of the eighteenth century. The half stitch used, in place of the more solid whole stitch, for the delicate designs of flowers caught together by flowing ribbon bands, gave a fragile ethereal quality to a lace of fine flax with a gauzy trelliswork of fond chant. It was a favourite of Mme du Barry (mistress of Louis XV) and also of Marie Antoinette (wife of Louis XVI), both of whom were guillotined in 1793. The fury of the mob did not cease with the destruction of the aristocracy but spread to Chantilly itself and similar centres where the royal laces had been made. The laceworkers themselves were killed, and production ceased.

In the nineteenth-century revivals sponsored by Napoleon I between 1804 and 1815, Chantilly was made in Normandy, especially around the Bayeux area, and in spite of the different geographical origin the old name – along with old techniques and old designs – was retained. Only a small amount of white Chantilly was ever made: for the black there was a prodigious market in Spain and the Americas. After a period of decline the making of Chantilly revived once more, in the 1860s, again at Bayeux, but also at Grammont in Belgium. The ground was now a fond simple, the design – of strikingly natural tulips, irises, poppies and cornflowers – outlined with strands of flat untwisted silk. The quality and count of the thread varied, but the filmy fineness of the eighteenth-century products was quite gone. The very large pieces were made in oddly shaped sections invisibly joined, so that large numbers of workers could be employed. (Fig. 2a.)

Copies were made on the Pusher and Levers machines.

Chemical lace. See *Machine* (h) and *Swiss* (c).

Chemise (French, shirt). See *Shift* and *Underwear*.

Chenille lace (French, a hairy caterpillar). A silk yarn with a short pile standing out all round it. White chenille was sometimes used to outline the designs of French eighteenth-century needlepoints; green and gold for bobbin laces. Its place of origin is uncertain: a tantalising passage in a letter of Mme de Sévigné in 1676 reads: 'Have you heard of transparents? They are complete dresses of the very finest gold or azure brocades, and over them is worn a transparent black gown, or a gown of beautiful *point d'Angleterre,* or of chenille velvet like that winter *lace* you saw . . .'

In 1903 a chenilling device was patented in Nottingham. It made Chenille Spotting Veiling at the rate of 190,000 spots an hour.

Cheyne lace. See *Chain stitch*.

Chinese lace. Following the Boxer rebellion (1900-1), the craft of lacemaking was taken by nuns, missionaries and teachers to the Chinese mainland. Crochet, filet, drawnwork, bobbin laces and needlepoints were all taught, enabling the poorer people to earn a living. The bobbin laces were of the torchon, Cluny, Beds Maltese and Bruges varieties and were centred at Pakhoi, Tonkin and Shanghai. Some of them were made so cheaply that they could be marketed in England for less than the cost of machine laces. Penderell Moody, writing in 1907, complains: 'The work is already coming home in small quantities, and at a price for which no Englishwoman could work . . . If the copying of English lace grows to any real extent, this unfair competition must ruin the home trade. If our countrywomen abroad will pause for a moment's reflection, they will remember that charity begins at home . . .' The needlepoints, still made, are mostly of rather thickish thread and stiff, but useful for tablecloths and coverlets. See also *Bruges*.

Choker collar. A collar with a high neckband supported with wire or whalebone, and usually attached to a yoke. It was fashionable from c 1890 to 1910 and was made of contemporary hand or machine laces.

Christening gowns. See *Baby robes.*

Cinq trous. See *Reseau.*

Circular machine. See *Machine lace* (g).

Ciré (French, waxed). A lace made crosswise on the Levers machine, i.e. across the full width. It was popular in the 1920s and 30s for afternoon and evening dresses. Ciré is named from the highly lustrous finish, which makes it look polished, an effect achieved by heat treatment of the rayon threads which, against a background of silk, formed the design. A dull-finish lace of otherwise similar form, made of an acetate rayon, was called angel-skin (or peau d'ange). Bemberg was a rayon, also with a dull finish, used to make the so-called 'Spanish laces'.

Clothwork. See *Toilé.*

Cluny. A bobbin lace of simple geometric design incorporating circles, undulating 'divided' trails (see *Trail*), diamond blocks of half stitch and rosettes of wheatears arranged like the spokes of a wheel (Fig. 3d). It is said to be based on sixteenth-century Genoese laces preserved at the Musée de Cluny in Paris. Its mid nineteenth-century origin is attributed by Head to Le Puy, and by Thomas Wright to the East Midlands, as an offshoot of Beds Maltese. There is no doubt that Cluny-type laces from Le Puy and from Bedfordshire bear the strongest resemblance to each other. It is usually a heavy lace, more useful for furnishing than fashion, and was made extensively into the 1920s. The Barmen machine produces a form of Cluny almost indistinguishable from the hand-made; the Schiffli Cluny is distinguishable by the fuzzy look of its stitches, and the Levers by the two thicknesses of thread which are used, the thinner appearing to bind the thicker together.

Coggeshall. A town in Essex, noted for its tambour embroidery on net. The very successful industry was started in the early nineteenth century by a French, or Flemish, refugee named Draygo, who taught the cottagers how to stretch the net on oblong embroidery frames and work the decoration with a tambour hook. Draygo's son-in-law, Charles Walker, emigrated to Limerick and established a similar industry there, but using running stitches as well as chain. The Coggeshall manufactory remained productive into Edwardian times but then almost died out and has only recently been revived as a craft form, using old designs.

Coif. A close-fitting cap shown, for example, in portraits of Mary Queen of Scots. The linen was often decorated with cutwork and edged with a narrow upstanding border of punto in aria.

Col rabat, rabattu, rabato (French, a turned-down collar). A fashion which began in France at the time of Louis XIII (1601-43), and in England of Charles I (1600-49), replacing the ruff. An intermediate form where the ruff, still attached high around the neck, drooped downwards lower and lower until it rested on the shoulders as the 'falling collar' (qv) is sometimes called a rabat; but the more appropriate use is for the completely flat collar, made entirely of lace instead of being partly linen, lying over the chest like a two-sided bib, held in place by a narrow band behind the neck (c 1665) (Fig. 48b). Powys equates the rabat with the cravat, but this is incorrect. Rabato, or rebato, in the sixteenth century, was either the underpropper or supportasse of the millstone ruff (cf Shakespeare, *Much Ado About Nothing*, c 1596), or the separate wired structures worn with the ruff, but standing out on either side of the head like gauzy wings, the forerunner of the Medici collar.

Colbert, Jean Baptiste (1619-83). Minister of Commerce to Louis XIV, and successor in 1661 to the powerful Mazarin (see *Sumptuary edicts*). Colbert attempted to remedy the near bankruptcy of France by encouraging home manufactures. Contemporary French laces – from Paris, Lyons, Normandy and the Auvergne – had long failed to satisfy the discriminating tastes of the court, and rivers of gold cascaded year after year into the coffers of Italy and Flanders. Under Colbert's direction some thirty Venetian needlepoint lacemakers were smuggled into France; workshops were set up at Arras, Le Quesnoy, Sedan and Alençon; and in 1665 a shop was opened in Paris to sell the new 'Points de France'. These were meant to include bobbin laces, but even with the fashion triumph of the fontange and lappets, just a few years before Colbert's death, the Flemish laces could not be ousted, and it was another fifty years before the development of the silk blondes and of Chantilly made French bobbin laces à la mode in France.

Commode, fontange (French), **cock-up** (Scottish). A high-rise head decoration of fluted lace mounted on a scaffolding of buckram and tiffany. It developed from the simpler fontange and was fashionable in both France and England from c 1679 to 1710. It soared to 18 inches (457 mm) in height, dwarfing the normal proportions of the ladies of the court and, like the exaggerated ruff of a hundred years before, arousing extreme ridicule. Pinners, or lappets, were attached to the commode. (Fig. 20).

Commonwealth (1649-60). A time between kings in seventeenth-century Britain, when, under the directorship of Oliver Cromwell, a fairly puritanical regime was established, at least among the plebeian folk. At court – if it could so be called – officials still appeared in coats so thickly laden with braid and lace that the material to which they were attached could scarcely be seen. The court ladies, including Cromwell's mother, still indulged their fancy with lace-trimmed gorgets (see *Whisk*), which, edged with Flemish lace, cost £50 apiece and were ordered by the half dozen.

Continuous laces, fil continu, straight laces. Bobbin laces which are worked straight across between footing and heading, the ground and the denser parts in one. It includes French, Spanish, Genoese and East Midlands, as well as most Flemish laces. The ground is a reseau or more rarely brides.

The opposite is 'non-continuous' laces. The terms 'cut thread' (fil coupé) and 'attached thread' (fil attaché), though applicable to non-continuous, are not exclusively so, as sometimes in continuous laces the number of threads between the solid part and the ground has to be adjusted by increase or reduction, and bobbins then have to be added in or cut out (Fig. 28). Hollie point is the only continuous needlepoint lace, but then it is simply lace which is all 'solid' part, with no open ground at all. See also *Fil, Fond, Non-continuous, Free.*

Coralline. A rare form of Venetian flat point consisting of minute irregular fragments held by starry brides. Its firm delicate tracery is reminiscent of the complex fretting of Byzantine metalwork. Some forms, however, are quite crude and unbeautiful.

Cording. See *Imitation laces.*

Cordonnet, trolly, gimp. An outline to the motifs of lace, giving them a sharper definition. It may be made by:
(a) A single thickish thread, or gimp, e.g. in Bucks, Mechlin and Lille.
(b) Several untwisted silk strands, e.g. Chantilly.
(c) A padded wreath oversewn with buttonhole stitches and extended outwards into a coronet of picots. This occurs particularly in Venetian and, to a lesser extent, French needlepoints.
(d) Chain stitch. (i) in some needlerun nets, e.g. Lunéville; (ii) in Brussels

muslin appliqué, where it may be tamboured by hand or worked by a chain-stitch machine such as the Bonnaz.
(e) Couching the outlining thread, e.g. in Carrickmacross, where the thread also holds the muslin to the net (Fig. 35b and e).
(f) Machine. (i) The cordonnet is run in by hand after the patterned lace has been taken off the loom (Pusher). (ii) It is outlined by the hand-operated Cornely machine, which uses a lock-stitch mechanism. This, like (i), is slow, working only one pattern at a time, and so is expensive. (iii) It is added, by the machine, as the lace is made. The cordonnet threads have then to be carried across the back from one part of the design to the next, leaving 'floats' which have later to be trimmed away by hand (Levers). (iv) Some of the Levers machine designs are arranged to form a continuous pattern over the ground, so that the outlining thread can pass from one to the other without floats. Because there is no need for hand finishing this is a cheaper product; it is also more durable as there are no clipped ends to fray with wear. See also *Gimp*.

Cork, County. A nineteenth-century centre for lacemaking in southern Ireland. It was noted for: (a) Irish crochet, produced at the Ursuline Convent, Blackrock, in the early nineteenth century; during the famine years (1846 ff) it spread to a much wider area (see *Irish lace* (e)); (b) an unusual needlerun of black silk on a white net ground; (c) Youghal needlepoint, first made at the Presentation Convent in 1840 (see *Irish lace* (d) and *Youghal*).

Cornely. A hand-operated lock-stitch machine sometimes used to attach the cordonnet to machine-patterned laces. See *Machine* (k).

Cost of lace. The cost of living from the sixteenth century to the present day might be represented by a steadily steepening incline. The cost of lace, in relation to this curve, has shown, after a peak in the seventeenth century a fairly steady decline. Today, since hand lace is no longer made on a commercial scale, except perhaps in the Far East, or is made out of thick yarn so that the time taken to produce it is relatively small, it is very difficult to put a price on fine old lace. By far the most expensive part of its making was the time: a Honiton flounce, 5 yards (4.6 m) long, shown at the Great Exhibition of 1851 had taken forty women eight months to complete. At a modest annual income of say £4,000, this would make the cost of the flounce in 1982 £100,000. At market value in 1982 it would fetch less than £1,000. The lavish spending of past ages is shown by comparison with the general cost of living:
1685. £36 for a cravat when a good servant was paid £8 a year, a bushel of wheat cost 3s 2d, and a quart of strong beer 1d.

1760. One order of Mechlin and Brussels laces, for one lady, cost £1,500, and Mme du Barry spent £200 on a 'head-sute' of lace, while meat cost between 1d and 6d a pound.

1815. An 18 inch (457 mm) square of droschel cost £15, a bushel of wheat 13s 6d, and factory workers earned 7s a week.

See also *Alençon* and *Earnings*.

Costume. See *Fashion*.

Cotton. The floss surrounding the seeds of the cotton plant, contained within a boll. The fibres around each seed are about 1½ inches (38 mm) long, 1/1,000 inch (0.025 mm) in diameter, and 4,000 in number (Fig. 23b). The differences in appearance and natural function between cotton and flax fibres give rise to different chemical and physical properties which are reflected in the properties of the fabrics which they make. Cotton is pure cellulose; flax has some lignin deposited in it. This makes it stronger, cooler, heavier, more pliable (though less elastic) and more absorptive of water.

Cotton fabrics were first introduced into England by the East India Company in the early seventeenth century, and by 1700 cotton was being spun in Manchester. The materials made were flimsy gauzes and muslins, and it was not until 1805 that a cotton yarn strong enough for use on the Warp Frame was developed, in Nottingham. When Heathcoat's machine was invented, in 1808, the same cotton yarn was found to be suitable for bobbinet. 1833 is the generally accepted date for the first use of cotton for bobbin laces. Prejudice against cotton continued for some time – in favour of flax for hand-made lace, and silk for machine lace – but the advantageous properties of cotton (that it was warmer, more elastic, lighter in weight, brighter in colour, and above all cheaper) enabled it gradually to supersede the more luxurious fibres. Its main disadvantage of fluffiness, resulting from its 1½–3 inch (38–76 mm) staples (up to 48 times shorter than those of flax), was overcome by a process of gassing the thread, invented in 1817. It involved passing it rapidly through a flame which singed away the fluff to leave a smooth yarn (see *Gassed cotton*).

In the 1860s cotton machine lace was being bleached to achieve 'perfect whiteness'. It was then dried in a kind of spin drier, passed through a hot gum and starch mixture, squeezed by revolving cylinders like an old-fashioned mangle, stretched up to 120 yards (110 m) in length, winched out to its proper dimensions, pinned to hold it, blotted to remove excess gum, fanned to dry it, and the selvedges were run in along the sides. The amount of dressing could be varied according to the weight and stiffness required. Felkin says that a piece weighing 15 pounds (6.8 kg) when it left the loom would increase to 60 pounds (27.2 kg) when 'Paris dressed' and 'the edges will cut through the skin like a saw'. See also *Fibres* and *Mercerised cotton*.

Count, lea, slip. A measurement of the relative fineness of threads used for lacemaking. A count is the number of skeins of flax, each 300 yards (274.32 m) long, required to make up a pound weight (0.4536 kg). The finer the thread, the less will each skein weigh, and so the more will be needed to make up the pound, and the higher will be the count. The flax threads used for lace in the sixteenth and early seventeenth centuries were of counts less than 100. From the mid seventeenth to the mid eighteenth century, counts of 1,200 were used for many Venetian needlepoints and for Flemish bobbin laces. These threads were hand-spun and had a diameter of no more than 45 thousandths of a millimetre. The highest count that can be made by machine is 300, but the highest currently (1982) available is 180. The 300 yard skein is sometimes called a lea. For silk threads and synthetics measurements are more usually in deniers.

Thomas Wright uses 'slips' to indicate the fineness of cotton. The cotton was done up in 2-ounce (56.7g) packets, each containing four parcels. Each parcel held between 3 and 14 slips. Thus a '3-slip' cotton would have 3 x 2 slips to the ounce, or 3 x 2 x 16 = 96, to the pound. Without knowing the precise length of a slip, it is not possible to equate slip and count with certainty, but it seems likely that they are the same. See also *Spinning*.

Counted thread work. Sixteenth-century pattern books, for example by Vinciolo, show blocks divided up into squares like graph paper, with the number of meshes clearly stated: 'This Goddess of flowers representing the Spring contains in height 69 meshes, and in length 64.' The design is printed in white on the squared ground, so that by counting the squares the embroiderer or lacemaker can reproduce every detail of the pattern before her. Counted thread designs are equally applicable to drawnwork, filet and buratto.

Couronnes (French, crowns). (a) The additional ornaments to the raised cordonnets of needlepoint laces, especially the Venetian. They are variously known as crowns, spines, thorns and flying flowers (fleurs volantes). (b) A filling in needlepoint laces (see *Stitches* (e, ii)).

Craft lace. (a) Lacemaking carried on as a hobby rather than as a livelihood, i.e. amateur rather than professional. (b) Laces where practical utility predominates over artistic delight. Craft laces include the nineteenth- and twentieth-century knitting, crochet, macramé, tatting,

Tenerife work and renaissance laces. In some museums, even the professional antique laces which took years to make and cost fortunes are regarded as 'craft'.

Cravat. A scarf of linen intended to be tied, more or less elaborately, around the neck in such a way that its lace-decorated ends, sometimes as wide as 18 inches (457 mm) across, could be displayed to advantage across the chest. It succeeded the col rabat about 1670, when Charles II started the fashion for huge periwigs which completely hid the shoulders and back of the neck. A less formal version of the cravat, tucked with studied nonchalance through a buttonhole, or into a lady's decolletage, was called the Steinkirk after the battle of that name in 1692. By 1730 the cravat was being replaced by the jabot, but it continued to be worn by older people for another forty years.

Crepeline. A silk chiffon used for repairing or remounting lace. See also *Cellofas.*

Crochet. A form of lace worked with a crochet hook from a continuous thread. It is thought to have originated in the sixteenth century and may perhaps be equated with the chain lace ordered from Italy by Elizabeth I and her contemporaries (see *Chain stitch* (a)). The hook was of varying sizes; the threads were of cotton, mercerised cotton or silk, and the stitches all combinations of the basic chain stitch.

Crochet was introduced into Ireland by French nuns in the 1830s and formed an important occupation of the poor during the desperate times of the Potato Famine (1846). The main centres were at Cork (qv) in the south and Clones in the north of the Republic. Some excellent pieces with elaborate raised work, in imitation of the Venetian needlepoints, were produced; but unfortunately the cheaper machine laces drew away their custom, and before long they were forced – except for special commissions – to make quantity more important than quality.

The chemical laces in the 1880s chose Irish crochet as their first lace to imitate. During the early twentieth century crochets imitating attenuated Irish designs proliferated in China, France, Belgium, India and Australia. This depleted form is still made as tourist pieces and sold at Shannon. See also *Chain stitch* (f).

Crochetage. See *Sewings.*

Cross. One of the movements of bobbin lacemaking, the other being twist (Fig. 24C). Quite simply, whole stitch is a repetition of cross-twist-cross, and half stitch of cross-twist only. According to some experimentalists, any manipulation of threads incorporating these two movements, even when it is 30 feet (9 m) high and made of rope, is a bobbin lace.

Cuffs. Decorations of the sleeve ends, usually matching the collar in design and in type of lace. In the sixteenth century they were ruff-cuffs, or rufflets, like tiny millstones; in the seventeenth century cones expanding gently from wrist to elbow, ending with starched scallops of lace, and matching the falling collar; in the late seventeenth century, for women, broad ruffles clinging around the upper arm and elbow, or spiking outwards to complement the little fence of lace standing upright around the decolletage. In the eighteenth century, the soft lace of the lappets was matched by tiers overflowing like waterfalls from the ends of closely fitting sleeves. 'The ruffles must be tripple very full and deep' says the *Ladies' Complete Pocket Book* for 1761. By 1800, straighter styles had almost demolished cuffs as such. Later they reappeared as straight or pouched undersleeves emerging at the wrists, embroidered with whitework, or with narrow decorations of Bucks or Lille. In the 1860s, the wide openings of the pagoda sleeves were filled with a froth of lace and tulle. (Figs. 11, 20, 21.) See also *Engageants*.

Cutwork. (a) An important form of embroidered lace which in its simplest form consisted of holes cut in linen, embroidered around with thread, and decorated with buttonhole-stitch bars. The sixteenth- and early seventeenth-century cutworks were obviously very splendid things: Flemish cutwork was received by Mary Tudor as a New Year's gift in 1556. It was so prized that her Sumptuary Laws forbade its wearing by anyone below the rank of baron. Cutwork is known also to have been made in Italy and Sedan (France). The earliest pattern book entirely concerned with it was published in 1542 by Pagano of Venice; it appears in portraits of the 1550s; and in 1559-60 a cutwork ruff is recorded 'garnished with small sparks of rubies and pearls'. Cutwork was expensive: Elizabeth I paid 55s 4d for one yard, a quarter of a yard wide. She purchased too 'a mantle of lawn wro't thro'out with cutwork of pomegranites, roses and honeysuckle, with crowns'. (Fig. 6a.) See also *Drawnwork, Reticella*.
(b) Cutwork, leadwork, woven plait, tally. See *Plaits* (b). Variations of its use in Honiton lace are the swing leadwork, diamond leadwork and brick filling.

Czechoslovakian lace. Formerly a part of the Austro-Hungarian empire, Czechoslovakia became an independent republic in 1918 and has had a chequered career since. Its modern lace is a torchon edging with strong red and blue colours. See *Bohemia, Design* (ix).

Dalecarlian. A peasant bobbin lace of geometric design, often made of unbleached linen thread, or with a different coloured gimp. See *Swedish lace*.

Danish lace. (a) In the seventeenth and eighteenth centuries the town of Tönder in the Schleswig-Holstein area, ceded to Germany in 1866, was famous for white surface embroidery and drawnwork on lawn and muslin. It is regarded as second only to the superlative Dresden work of Germany. Sewing schools were established in the mid eighteenth century to teach 'Tönder', and some twenty varied filling stitches decorated the designs.

(b) Hedebo is a heavier form of this work, severely geometric, and used mainly for household linens. The designs are made with a combination of darning and buttonhole, chain and satin stitch.

(c) A bobbin lace was, and is, sometimes also called Tönder. It has some similarity to simple Normandy, Saxony and Bucks laces. The shirt collar of King Christian IV (1588-1648), from the castle of Rosenborg in Copenhagen (Fig. 10 a and b), has been quoted as an example of Danish lace, but trade with the Low Countries was so extensive that, in the absence of any very distinctively national characteristics, it is impossible to be certain. Also, it is known that lacemakers from Brabant and Westphalia, c 1647 and 1712, were encouraged to settle in Denmark to improve the quality of the local lace. Thus Danish bobbin lace might well have been Flemish, or German, lace, made by Flemish workers on Danish soil.

(d) Relics of clothing from bronze age tombs show work very similar to the buttonhole stitches of a needlepoint lace. See *Buttonhole stitch*.

Darned netting. A decoration, made with a needle, in darning or run stitch, on a knotted (filet), woven (buratto) or machine-made (net) ground, to form a geometric or representational design. (Figs. 17a, 19 d and e.)

Dating of lace. The dating of any individual piece of lace cannot be done by reference to theoretical considerations alone but requires a wide experience of lace types, over the whole range of geographical and temporal origin. The main relevant factors to be considered are:

(a) Design. Basically this follows the time sequence: geometric, baroque, rococo, neo-classical, romantically naturalistic, art nouveau, art deco, abstract, passing from the sixteenth century to the present day. However there are many overlaps and throwbacks – in the last quarter of the twentieth century 'traditional' and 'advanced' exist side by side. (Fig. 17.)

(b) Technique. A few points of technique may be used as date fixers e.g.: the form of the ground (broadly, up to 1700 brides, 1700-1850 reseaux, after 1850 both brides and reseaux); the brides tortillées of Alençon are a nineteenth-century form preceded by the eighteenth-century reseau ordinaire; the timing of raised instead of completely flat laces cannot at present be condensed into a generalisation; the precise type of buttonhole stitch used, or the precise spinning method (S or Z twist) may prove to be important in dating after more extensive research has been done.

(c) Pattern books. These set out, visually or verbally, types of lace in manufacture at the time they were printed. The patterns could of course be copied at any later date. (Fig. 6a.)

(d) Portraits. In England the Tudors (1485-1603) were the earliest monarchs to employ superb artists to paint their portraits in an intensely realistic manner, with an inspired attention to the minutiae of jewels, silks, velvets, gold and lace. Thanks to such artists as Holbein and Hilliard, we can tell not only when lace was being worn but even, with a high degree of probability, what lace it was. Thus the portrait of Anne of Cleves, sent on approval to Henry VIII about 1538, shows her coif to be clearly of drawnwork and to bear the message 'A bon fino' (see *Messages in lace*). Similarly, portraits of Mary I and Elizabeth I and their entourages show cutwork and punto in aria almost as vividly as if the material itself was at hand. Lace was represented in stone effigies or by carvings in wood. Remarkably, even here its technique may be identified, though the inevitably raised appearance of carved or sculpted laces has sometimes led to strange conclusions. (Figs. 9a, 11.)

(e) Wardrobe accounts. These may be regarded as eminently reliable sources for what lace existed at varying times. They establish Mechlin in 1657, point de France in 1665, point d'Angleterre in 1678, Alençon in 1717. Other reliable histories date Carrickmacross at 1820, Maltese at 1833, and so on. The only real problem lies in understanding the words used: cheyne lace, Ragusa, punto a groppo, punto avorio, all valuable laces according to the accounts, have never yet been matched precisely with actual surviving pieces of lace.

(f) Literature. This must be treated with more caution. Writers might well be tempted by an over-lively fancy away from the truth; or sheer ignorance might blur their judgement. See *Blandford*.

(g) Fashion. The shapes of lace pieces worn at different times were all determined by fashion. Ruffs, fontanges, lappets, aprons, engageants, cravats, rabats, all had their time span. But shapes could be and were modified, as by the nineteenth-century cannibalisation which turned flounces and huge old collars into fichus, fall caps and chokers. (Figs. 20, 21.)

(h) Dates worked into lace. Dates of birth may appear on baby's caps, dates of completion on a length of lace, and commemorative dates, e.g. for Queen Victoria's diamond jubilee. They are not reliable enough to be considered in isolation.

(i) Types of thread. All hand-made laces up to 1800 were made of gold, flax or silk. How long after 1800 cotton was first used is difficult to determine. 1832-3 is the generally accepted date. Mercerised cottons and art silk date from the early 1900s, and synthetics from the 1960s.

(j) Fineness of flax or cotton thread. Between approximately 1650 and 1750 a count of 1,200 was used for the finest Venetian and Flemish laces. This has never been available since. Before and after, the thread was coarser. In the twentieth century 200 was the maximum fineness generally available.

(k) Spinning of thread. Until 1766 there was only hand-spun thread. The use of machine-spun thread (more tightly twisted) in a hand-made lace therefore dates it as after 1766. See *Spinning*.

(l) Weaving of linen. Hand-woven linens or muslins were the background of all embroidered laces until after 1780. Machine weaving is recognisable by its greater regularity. See *Loom*.

(m) Net. Twist nets (as opposed to the loop nets of the Stocking and Warp Frames) were first invented in 1808. Therefore any decorated nets – embroidered or appliquéd – which use them must be after that date. The three-twist or diamond net first appeared in the early 1830s.

Dawson wheel. A method of patterning materials or nets, which was superseded by the Jacquard. See *Lyons*.

Denier. A measurement of thickness or fineness of a yarn, applied especially to filament fibres such as natural silk or synthetic nylon. It represents the weight in grams of 9,000 metres of filament. Thus 15 denier means that 9,000 metres weighs 15 grams; 30 denier means that 9,000 metres weighs 30 grams, and so on. It is a measure of the variable weight of a fixed length, unlike the count or lea used for cotton and linen yarns, which measures variable lengths of a fixed weight of thread. For this reason a low denier represents a fine thread a high denier a thick one, while a low count represents a thick thread and a high count a fine one. The silk used by Heathcoat's machine for tulle illusion is measured in denier.

Dentelle. A general term for lace, but obscure. In France, 'dentelle' now includes all laces, with bobbin lace rendered by 'dentelle au fuseau', needlepoint by 'dentelle à l'aiguille', and machine lace by 'dentelle mécanique'. 'Dentelle' however did not appear as a noun until 1549, when it meant 'little teeth' or 'ornamental ironwork'. Its earliest use in reference to lace is as an adjective describing a passement: 'Passement of fine black silk, dentellé on one side' (1557). In 1577 Marguerite de Valois (see *Catherine of Medici*) owned 'two ells of silver passement haute dentellé', i.e. deeply toothed.

The first usage of 'dentelle' as a noun meaning lace was in 1598 when Montbéliard produced a book of designs for 'dentelles'. In 1633 'dentelle' appears to exclude cutwork, and therefore perhaps all embroidered laces. This is indicated in a seventeenth-century engraving where a distressed lady is described as 'nayant plus pour paraistre bel, ny dantelle ny point coupe' (no longer having either lace or cutwork to make her appear beautiful). By 1663 'dentelle' had completely replaced the older term 'passement'.

Dentellière (French). (a) A maker of bobbin lace. (b) A machine invented about 1860 which was able to plait strands of threads where all previous machines had only been able to loop them (Stocking and Warp Frames), twist them (Heathcoat) or weave them (Levers). Droschel, Mechlin and Valenciennes grounds could be made on this machine, but the cost of producing them was greater than in making them by hand. The process was called 'platting'.

Design. (a) The more solid parts of the lace as opposed to the ground of brides, or reseau.

(b) The overall impression of the lace, which is of great importance in placing it in time and space (see *Dating* and *Geography*). Design is visual, and a purely verbal description, however detailed, leaves too much to the imagination and so can be misinterpreted. The larger pieces of lace (Fig. 17) show the impact of design on the eye, the way in which the pattern hangs together, repeats, flows or portrays. Generalisations are difficult, but some of the important trends are given below:

(i) Geometric forms: characteristic of the embroidered laces which are based in a woven linen or knotted square-meshed ground, where the design is controlled by the straight lines of warp and wefts. Also found in sixteenth-century bobbin laces and reticellas.

(ii) Scalloped or vandyked borders: early seventeenth-century bobbin laces of Flanders and Genoa, and the needlepoint punto in arias.

(iii) Baroque, c 1660-1712: a period of prodigal beauty with the magnificent blossoms of Jacobean crewel work embroideries and the intricate 'bizarre' silk brocades vying with the laces to produce bold, rich and overflowing designs. In some Venetian raised points and Flemish bobbin laces such as Mechlin, Binche, Valenciennes and point d'Angleterre almost the entire space is filled with the solid parts of the design, with little left open to be crossed by brides. Such laces, though often of extreme delicacy, are because of the paucity of holes sometimes described as 'opaque'.

(iv) Rococo, c 1712-70. Gradually, sharply drawn scrolls, shells, garlands and ribbons replaced the burgeoning foliage. Their formal gracefulness and stylised forms brought a static, and eventually stagnant, element into lace design. Flemish laces remained horticultural but the French, under the influence of masters of decor such as Bérain (1640-1711) and his followers (see *Points de France* (a)), became more architectural, with an overcrowded regimentation of small motifs, including the orientally orientated 'fairy people', beautifully garbed and turbaned, and not more than an inch (25 mm) high, almost lost in a miniature forest.

(v) Short repeats: during the second half of the eighteenth century designs became progressively smaller. The ground was now entirely in the form of reseau, rather than brides. It encroached upon the solid elements, which became sparse and weak, producing a lightweight insubstantial lace. This trend was fostered by a change in fashion from sculptured dresses of heavy silks to filmy muslins and gauze. The design of the lace was no longer displayed but gathered closely together so that what appeared visibly was not the pattern, but the frilly texture. Blonde, Mechlin, Valenciennes and Alençon all mirror this debilitation, while in point d'Angleterre the ground took over to such an extent that entire veils were made of it, without any design at all (see *Point d'Angleterre* (a)). Finally, the French Revolution (1789-92) made lace a disgrace; and the neo-classical fashions which followed made it demodée.

(vi) Nineteenth-century revivals: the late eighteenth century, with the French Revolution and the industrial revolution, marked the end of a commercial era for lace. In the nineteenth century remarkable individual pieces of superb quality were produced, for example the coverlet of Brussels appliqué on droschel designed for Napoleon I by the court painter Jacques Louis David (1748-1825) with a spectacular representation of the legend of Diana and Endymion in a pastoral setting beneath a sky powdered with stars. The Lefebure brothers introduced the 'fleurs ombrées', or shaded effect, where marked variation in density of flowers and leaves brought sunlight and air to the naturalistic clusters of blooms. In England the wedding of Queen Victoria in 1840 produced an unusual Honiton lace made to an old design (Fig. 46b, and cover). The Great Exhibition of 1851 stimulated Thomas Lester of Bedford to produce a charming range of animal forms. But these are like rare pinnacles in a mundane landscape: the demand for perfection was almost gone, and the lower end of the market strengthened continually.

(vii) Imitations: few could afford the productions of the creative professional designers. Others, lacking originality, looked back to seventeenth-century Italian baroque for inspiration. Milanese was copied by tape (renaissance) laces, and Venetian raised point by crochet as well as by relatively coarse French, Irish and Burano needlepoints, in the second half of the nineteenth century. See also *Imitation laces.*

(viii) Machine designs: the aim of the machine, as the manufacturers openly declared, was to produce copies of the hand-made (especially bobbin) laces so faithful to the original that no one could tell them apart. Their success spelt financial failure for the hand productions. As they failed, so fashion disparaged them and, with the emergence of the art nouveau movement at the end of the century, machines gave up the imitations and began to produce designs adapted to their own unique abilities.

(ix) Modern: the design trend is now closely linked with the need for speed. Traditional hand-made laces are excruciatingly slow (see *Hours of work*), but the use of coarse thread, such as synthetics, chenille, heavy wool or hemp, enables infinitely quicker results to be achieved. Naive designs of children or figures like paper cut-outs eerily dancing have a dramatic impact as 12 foot (3.6 m) high wall-hangings; and relatively little time or skill is required for their making. Much of this work has originated in Poland and Czechoslovakia. The more totally abstract rope and steel constructions, many yards across, whatever their claim to art, inventiveness or beauty, come only disputatiously within the usual definition of lace.

Devon lace. In the past the lacemaking area of this name extended westwards to Torbay. To the east it may have included the recorded centres of Blandford (Dorset), Downton (Wiltshire) and Bath (Avon). These three may, on the other hand, have represented a kind of eighteenth-century lost Atlantis of lace, Bath Brussels resembling Brabant, and Downton Lille, while the nature of Blandford lace is unknown.

(a) Devon trolly. (Fig. 44a.) Devon laces differ from the other major English centre of the East Midlands in both design and technique, being non-continuous instead of continuous. However, Palliser (1910 edition) illustrates as Devon trolly a continuous lace of Tulip design, outlined with a gimp thread and with a fond simple ground similar to Bucks point. An almost identical piece, claimed as Old Bucks, was donated to the Buckinghamshire County Museum at Aylesbury, in the Burrowes collection (see *Trolly*). Other samples in the Treadwin collection at Exeter Museum also look very like Bucks. Since Palliser and Treadwin both lived in Devon at a time when the making of trolly lace had only just been discontinued, it seems unlikely that they would have blundered.

Devon laces of the seventeenth and eighteenth centuries are not reliably provenanced, but the following are thought to have been made there (b-d):

(b) A seventeenth-century vermiculate collar lace similar to some produced in Flanders, but loosely worked. See also Fig. 45.

(c) Flounces of mid eighteenth-century Bath Brussels, not unlike a Brabant, but with a less concentrated design, and very typical Honiton fillings. The droschel ground covering the open spaces follows in varied directions the curves of the design. In the contemporary Brussels lace, the droschel ground would have been made in narrow parallel strips, joined by point de raccroc.

(d) Point d'Angleterre. There is no evidence that this lace in its most perfect form was ever made in Devon, but late eighteenth-century corrupted forms distorted by exhausted parchments, inexperienced prickings or misinterpretation of pinholes are attributed to that county. They have imprecise Honiton shapes, pretty fillings and a meandering droschel ground. In some even more decadent types, referred to as 'eighteenth-century Devon', all that remains of the pattern are intertwined tortured segments like chopped-up arms and legs. But the raised and rolled work, the Devon rose and the leadwork fillings presage the typical nineteenth-century Honiton lace. See also (c).

(e) Honiton is the generally accepted name for nineteenth- and twentieth-century Devon lace of a non-continuous type. The separate sprigs often represent patriotic flowers. In the early nineteenth century they were appliquéd on to droschel, then on to two- or three-twist bobbinets. Later the sprigs were linked by a hand-made net-stitch ground, and after the 1850s by brides, i.e. as a guipure. It was often made by a number of different outworkers, so that proportions are not always consistent.

(a-e) are bobbin laces.

(f) A braid or renaissance lace, made of a machine tape linked by buttonhole stitches. It had the advantage that it could be carried around by the worker and stitched at in odd moments, which would not be possible with a bulky pillow and bobbins. It began in the 1860s and is now called Branscombe lace. (Fig. 44c.)

(g) The establishment of Heathcoat's bobbinet factory at Tiverton in 1816 to some extent encouraged the making of Honiton sprigs since bobbinet could be used as a basis for their application. By 1822, however, the factory workers' wages were discouraging to a bobbin lacemaker, who earned thirty times less. Of the 2,400 lacemakers in Devon before 1816, only 300 remained six years later, while Heathcoat was employing 1,500 people. By 1910 the Honiton lace industry was regarded as defunct.

Devonia. A form of Honiton lace in which separately made pieces, e.g. butterflies, were attached so that they appeared to hover over a border of flowers. Devonia began in 1874, in imitation perhaps of the layered petals of the commercially successful Brussels point de gaze.

Dickel lace. A form of tape lace designed in the twentieth century by Franziska Dichtl. Four widths of Dickel braid were available, and about 150 designs, all involving close sinuous contortions so that, apart from tacking the braid on to the pattern, the only handwork necessary was the making of buttonholed bars to hold it all together.

Dieppe lace. See *Normandy*.

Downright. A Devon term for the 'warp' bobbins, or passives.

Downton. A village in Wiltshire associated with laces both of Bucks point and of torchon design at least since 1880. It might be postulated that it provides the missing link between the very disparate laces of the Midlands and Devon: its bobbins are like Honiton ones, but its laces are continuous like those of the Midlands. On the other hand, it is worked with the footing on the left in the Continental manner. Conceivably Devon trolly (of which we know so little) was also worked in this way.

Drawnwork, punto tirato, fil tiré. A distinction is often made between: (a) Drawn threadwork (in USA, 'withdrawn element work'), in which selected warp or weft threads are drawn out and cut off, the raw edges stitched over, and the remaining threads decorated with buttonhole or other stitches in a variety of designs. Extensive use of this technique could result in *Cutwork*, i.e. the creation of large holes by the removal of whole blocks of warp and weft. In Ruskin work the square of linen to be removed is marked out by the withdrawing of single warp and weft threads around the perimeter. (Fig. 47b.)
(b) Pulled threadwork or drawn fabric (in USA, 'deflected element embroidery'), in which threads are not actually removed but instead are pulled together by tightened stitches to make small perforations. Confusion between them arises because 'drawn' and 'pulled' in everyday English can have the same meaning, for example a horse-drawn carriage means a carriage pulled by horses. Although pulled threadwork requires a loose weave, and drawn a firm one, the two techniques not infrequently occur together, i.e. they do not often have any real significance in distinguishing laces. A sensible compromise would therefore seem to be the use of a comprehensive term such as 'drawnwork', which can then be defined as 'the creation of holes, or an openwork pattern, in a textile, either by drawing threads out of the material in restricted areas, or by drawing them together so spaces are formed between them'. (Fig. 18.)

Drawnwork has an ancient origin and has been identified from Egypt well before Christ. It was probably made in every country in Europe and is known from England, Germany, Scandinavia, Sicily, Sardinia, the Philippines and South America.

The pattern was usually formed by that part of the original fabric which was left untouched, and it was usually over-darned, or strengthened with shadow stitch, to give it greater intensity. From this laborious technique only a short step had to be taken in order to *begin* with an openwork ground, as in filet and buratto, to which the design could then be added. See *Spanish lace* and *Pattern books*.

Dresden work. Drawnwork produced from Saxony in the mid eighteenth century using almost transparent lawn or muslin. The minute threads were counted and rearranged, to produce a delicate mesh ground and many beautiful varieties of fillings. It was made into fichus, caps, aprons and lappets, the exquisite whitework giving a simple pastoral quality to the less formal dresses of the day. It was sufficiently highly valued to be smuggled (see *Smuggling*) and also to be remounted – an advertisement in 1772 publicised the grafting of old Dresden on to new muslin 'so as not to be perceived where done'. Similar, though inferior, forms were made in Sweden, Scotland and New England. One version used two thicknesses of muslin, outlined with chain stitch. (Fig. 18c.)

Dressed pillow. The bobbin lacemaking pillow when it has all the necessary parts attached, i.e. pricking, pins, threads, bobbins, pincushion and slider, ready for working.

Droschel, drochel, drossel, vrai reseau, Flemish reseau, point d'Angleterre net (rare). A form of reseau characteristic of Brussels bobbin laces from about 1690 to 1815 and also of the eighteenth-century English Bath Brussels and Devon. The meshes were hexagonal, two sides being made of four threads plaited four times, and four of two threads twisted twice; and they were tiny – 1 square inch (6.452 sq cm) of the finest held as many as 900 meshes. In Brussels laces they run straight and parallel to the long axis of the lace; in English laces the sewn-in droschel fills the ground piece by piece in irregular shapes and in different directions in the way that a child with a picture book fills, inconsistently, the scattered patches of sky (see *Devon lace* (d)).

In the late eighteenth century plain veils were made of ¾-inch (19 mm) wide strips of droschel, invisibly joined (see *Design* (v) and *Point d'Angleterre* (a)). It died out soon after bobbinets came on to the market, but one last swan-song piece was made to special order in Devon in 1869. (Fig. 5c.)

Dublin Society. See *Anti-Gallican Society, Chain stitch* (c), *Irish lace, Knitted lace* and *Tambour.*

Duchesse, indicating a good quality Belgian lace, is usually associated with Brussels, though occasionally with Bruges. The thread is relatively thick, giving a dense appearance to the closely textured clothwork, and a dignified formality to the symmetrically floral design. Richness is added by raised work and rolling, gimp threads and small lightly attached sprigs caught on the surface of the arc-like festoons. Though non-continuous, the motifs are linked as the work proceeds so that the pattern is never haphazard and never presents that appearance of an oddly put-together jumble of pieces varying in size, quality, tension and even colour of thread which characterises so much Honiton.

   Duchesse was copied on the Levers machine, and also in chemical lace.

Dutch lace. Although Holland and Flanders are situated so close to each other, the histories of the two countries vary considerably, Holland becoming independent in 1648 while Flanders remained under the domination of Spain and then Austria until 1831. Their skills differed too, Flanders being supreme in bobbin lace production for at least a hundred years, c 1660-1760, while there seems some doubt whether Holland ever produced any lace at all (see *Netherlands*). Travellers of the late seventeenth century record that Dutch houses were full of lace, even brasses and warming pans being muffled in it. That is not to say that it was made there: the revocation of the Edict of Nantes in 1685 brought floods of Huguenot refugees to Protestant Holland and must have carried in its wake a vast flotsam of salvaged lace.

   However, there are two distinctive laces in need of a name, and to date they have generally been known as 'Dutch':
(a) A thick, closely made bobbin lace almost like a strong woven damask, with a design of great clusters of rounded flower heads spilling out of minute vases, and flanked by cornucopia.
(b) An equally closely worked needlepoint lace, almost solid and of extremely compact design. A piece in Aylesbury museum bears a two-headed eagle, and another, in the USA, a Madonna and child. The eagle does not much help to identify the piece: the lace could have been made to special order for anywhere in the Holy Roman Empire; it could have been pre-1648 while Holland was owned by Spain, but this early date is unlikely; it could have been made in Flanders or Spain. The piece with the Madonna and child was identified by Margaret Taylor Johnstone (1926) as Ragusa.

Dykeside. A term for a vandyked, scalloped or dentate heading.

Eagle, two-headed. A symbol of imperial power, associated traditionally with the Holy Roman Empire (800-1806) and later for a short time with Russian imperialism, which appears in a number of bobbin, needlepoint and embroidered laces. Its geographical significance is still obscure: in the seventeenth century the Empire included not only Spain and Austria, but the lacemaking centres of the Spanish Netherlands (Flanders), Milan, Bohemia and Sicily. Its appearance in the 1661 so-called 'Devon' lace (Fig. 45) is an argument for questioning whether this piece was in fact made in England. See also *Dutch lace* (b).

Earnings of lacemakers in the nineteenth century in England were on a par with those of an agricultural worker – and most of them were cottagers. In 1810, before machine nets were really established, they were earning 9s to 10s a week. In 1840, if Queen Victoria's wedding lace was indeed made by 200 workers over an eight-month period, the £1,000 which it is said to have cost, split between them, would provide only 2s 6d per head per week, not allowing for overheads. In 1860, Devon workers making sprigs for application to net earned 7s a week, while East Midlands workers making less popular laces earned no more than 3s 6d a week for a ten-hour day. Also, they were often not paid direct but by the truck system, in spite of this being made illegal in Acts of 1831, 1887 and 1896. Earnings of machine lacemakers over the same period varied from £10 a week in 1818 (blonde, on the Traverse Warp Machine), to 35s in 1865, following a trade depression. See *Cost*.

East European, Slavic laces. Laces made in the eastern part of Europe, and having in common the use of coiling trails, threaded with colour. See *Bohemia, Czechoslovakia, Hungary, Russia* and *Vienna*. (Figs. 26 and 27.)

East Midlands laces. A type of continuous bobbin lace associated with the counties of Buckinghamshire, Bedfordshire, Northamptonshire, Oxfordshire, Wiltshire and East Anglia. The first two names are used generically to cover all the varieties. Their early existence is established by references in Shakespeare, who would have seen the lacemakers at work on his journeys between London and Stratford-upon-Avon (c 1596-1613). Cottagers at their pillows were seen by Celia Fiennes in Stony Stratford (Buckinghamshire) and in Bedford. What kind of lace they were making is not known, but it is generally regarded as bearing a close resemblance to Lille and Mechlin, being influenced by French and Flemish Protestant refugees. The French influence was certainly strong in the late eighteenth century when lacemakers, fleeing from the guillotine, settled there; and the simpler nineteenth-century Bucks and Normandy laces are closely similar.

Their disadvantage was that they could not be used in conjunction with the machine laces, except perhaps as borders to wedding or bonnet veils; also their fond simple ground was the very one which Heathcoat had so perfectly copied in his two-twist bobbinet; and the naive short-repeat designs made them ideal for copying by the Jacquard apparatus. Their designs could also be copied, very closely, by run or tambour embroidery on net.

All the East Midlands laces are regarded as having been, until the mid nineteenth century, of similar type, known now as 'Bucks point' or 'Bucks point-ground'. In the 1850s, when the industry was in danger of being submerged by patterned machine laces, a splinter group was established, imitating the successful continental laces of Malta, Cluny and Le Puy. Though still continuous, they had a ground of brides and used thicker thread, and so they were quicker to make and cheaper; also their bolder form was more acceptable to the heavy fashions of the mid nineteenth century, on which the lightweight Bucks was inconspicuous. This splinter group of 'guipure' laces came to be known as Beds, though neither it nor the parent form is strictly localised. The term 'East Midlands laces', then, covers Bucks point, black and white silk laces (blondes) and Beds, which includes Maltese, Cluny and Le Puy types, as well as a few imitations of Honiton. The more utilitarian torchon and yak laces were also made. (Figs. 3 and 4.) See *Bedfordshire, Buckingham, Devon.*

Eches. The cotton or linen tabs stitched to either end of a parchment pricking. They are used to stretch it taut and pin it tightly to the pillow, for bobbin lacemaking.

Ecru. See *Bleaching.*

Egyptian lace. Various relics were found during the excavations of the pyramids and catacombs of Egypt: a network similar to filet, made of knotted squares and fringed at both ends (Louvre); a piece of coarse network which appears to have been made with bobbins and was taken from a Coptic tomb (Cluny Museum, Paris); twisted and plaited threadwork in the manner of sprang, from a mummy case in Ehnasya (Victoria and Albert Museum, London); mummy cloths decorated with drawnwork (British Museum).

These pieces are sometimes taken as proof of the very early existence of lace, and certainly no one would dispute that embroidered lace, like embroidery itself, goes back into the mists of time, perhaps as far as 1000 BC or earlier. Whether plain networks should be regarded as lace is debatable. An important part of the definition of *Lace* is that it should be patterned or should decorate something, while the first three examples appear to be as exclusively functional as a fishing net or a shopping bag. If plain netting is to be regarded as lace, then bronze age relics from Denmark must be included. See also *Sprang*.

Ell. A measure of length, now obsolete. Cottage lacemakers were formerly paid by the ell. Its actual length varied in different countries: England 45 inches (1,140 mm); France 54 inches (1,372 mm); Flanders 27 inches (680 mm); Scotland 37.2 inches (945 mm).

Embroidered laces. Laces worked with a needle and thread on a woven linen or cotton. They are all characterised by extensive openwork.
(a) Holes are cut in the material to form the design (cutwork, broderie anglaise, eyelet hole work), while the solid material forms the 'ground'.
(b) The solid material forms the design, and a holey ground is created by: (i) drawing threads of the material out, or pulling them together (drawnwork), the untouched parts of the material making the design (Figs. 13b, 18); (ii) knotting threads into a network or square-meshed background, on which the design is embroidered (filet) (Fig. 17a); (iii) an open gauze weave characterised by double warp and single weft threads, on which the design is embroidered in darning stitch (buratto).

These are the earliest laces and must considerably antedate the sixteenth-century pattern books which record them: 1524 drawnwork, Schönsperger; 1532 filet, Vavassore; 1542 cutwork, Pagano; 1559 buratto, Pagano.

Embroidered nets. Nets produced by machine, and then decorated by hand or machine embroidery. The looped nets of the Stocking and Warp Frames were both decorated with chain stitch from the late eighteenth century, but much the most widely used was Heathcoat's two-twist bobbinet, invented in 1808. It was decorated from the 1820s by two main techniques:
(a) Needlerun, run net, darned net. The design was pounced on the fabric, which was stretched on a large embroidery frame so that two or more 'runners' could work on it at the same time. The stitches passed in and out of the meshes at regular intervals, usually in one direction only for the more solid parts; for the fillings over fifty stitch variations are known. The work began in Nottingham but spread to Ireland, France, Belgium, Spain, Sicily, Sardinia, India and the USA. The best was produced before 1850. After that, patterned machine laces developed and rapidly achieved an astonishing dexterity, with the result that hand-worked laces in general suffered a severe decline.
(b) Tambour work, i.e. chain-stitch embroidery done with a tiny hook. It

is said to have originated in France and been brought to Coggeshall, from where it was taken to Limerick. See *Tambour.* In the later nineteenth century a great deal was made in Belgium: the thread was generally thicker, the design more lavish and luxuriant, and the ground showered with a snowstorm of tamboured spots. The Bonnaz machine also produced chain-stitch embroidered nets in the 1890s, mainly in Switzerland. (Fig. 19a-c.)

While muslin and net appliqués (see *Appliqué* (d)) can be regarded as forms of embroidery, the application of bobbin and needlepoint sprigs is a distinct form of decorated net.

Enchainette. A type of filling found in needlepoint laces, e.g. Alençon. See *Stitches.*

En coquille. Lace trimmings the shape of cockle shells, laid on a dress.

En eventail, godet. A shaped lace trimming hung to a skirt by its narrow end so that it flares out like a half-open fan.

Engageants. Long, asymmetrical, closely tiered and gathered ruffles especially fashionable (in blonde and Dresden) in the mid eighteenth century. See *Cuffs.*

English lace. (a) England was never in the top rank of lacemaking countries, and the opinion abroad of English laces was far from high. England did, however, in the Renaissance period excel in embroidered laces such as cutwork, drawnwork and filet. Also in 1629 the making of 'Venice gold and silver lace within the kingdom' (i.e. Britain) had been brought 'to that perfection' that it was thought unlikely that any would need to be imported.
(b) Both the continuous bobbin laces of the East Midlands and the non-continuous bobbin laces of Devon began in the sixteenth or early seventeenth century and were throughout a cottage industry. They seem never to have been chosen by British royalty for their beauty or splendour, but only from a sense of duty and the need to support the often impoverished makers. Levies against the import of foreign laces were needed again and again to enable English laces to hold any part of the home market, and there are few records of English lace being exported. Nevill Jackson speaks of 'the beautiful point d'Angleterre, which is erroneously supposed to have originated in Belgium', being given by Henrietta Maria to her sister-in-law Anne of Austria, Queen of France, in 1636, but the term was not in fact used at that time, and no one else regards the 'beautiful' point d'Angleterre as having been made

in England.

(c) English needlepoints were less localised and do not bear place names. Most were ecclesiastical, seventeenth-century, and made by nuns. Cutwork or reticella samplers of fine quality are known, dating from c 1600. Miniature pictorial scenes, only a few inches square, with biblical characters dressed in Jacobean clothes, were worked entirely in buttonhole stitch, with the petticoats and cravats, pavilions and leafy trees raised three-dimensionally, and the all-white gowns enriched with tiny pearls or minute black beads. Larger pieces, similar to Venetian flat points, though coarser, were sometimes worked with initials, or dated, e.g. 1689. They were less vital and less well designed than the Venetian and were described in 1680 as 'an ill sort of lace which serves no national or natural necessity'. Hollie point resembles a single motif of 'point plat' with its decorative 'portes' arranged like a pin-pricked outline to designs of symbolic significance such as a shepherd or the Garden of Eden. (Fig. 43a.)

(d) England's pièce de resistance was perhaps the machine laces. The industrial revolution originated in England, and most of the lacemaking machines were invented there, though they were soon copied, and sometimes improved on, elsewhere. See *Calais, Nottingham* and *Machine lace*.

Engrêlure. See *Footing*.

Erzegebirge. See *Saxony*.

Exhibitions of lace. See *Great Exhibition*.

Experimental laces. See *Continuous, Design, Free* and *Cross*.

Eyelet embroidery. See *Broderie anglaise* and *Embroidered laces* (a).

Falbala. See *Flounce*.

Fall, fall cap, fall piece. A fall was a piece of lace hanging loosely from a garment, or in Scotland a shawl. A fall cap was a head covering, popular through most of the nineteenth century, with a diamond-shaped cap crown nestling on top of the hair and extending down either side as a lappet resting against the cheek. Other caps were wedge-shaped, the point projecting on to the forehead, the lappets suspended over the nape of the neck or tied decoratively under a twist of hair. They were the derivatives of the seventeenth- and eighteenth-century 'heads' (qv). (Fig. 44c.)

Falling collars were worn in England by both men and women, following on from the *falling ruffs* of the early seventeenth century (Fig. 11). The fashion is said to have been brought to England from France by Henrietta Maria when she arrived in 1625 to marry Charles I. The falling collar was usually made with a wide linen foundation, but sometimes entirely of lace; it passed high round the throat and then softly down over the shoulder line, sometimes in two or three tiers. It was matched by broad cuffs extending upwards from wrist to elbow. Both collar and cuffs – edged with Flemish or Genoese bobbin lace, scalloped or broadly dentate – were attached to the shirt (or smock), which at that time was worn very full. The *falling band*, or col rabat (qv), developed as a reorientation of the falling collar: the back of the collar was reduced to a narrow band, while the front spread downwards like a paired breastplate. It was often made of Venetian gros point or, in the post-1665 court of Louis XIV, of point de France. (Fig. 48b.)

Fans of lace. Lace fans are recorded in the mid seventeenth century. A portrait by Rembrandt c 1640 shows a lady wearing a falling collar and holding a fan opened to reveal a leaf indisputably of lace; and Palliser quotes a reference of 1668: 'Flanders lace is still in high estimation, and even fans are made of it'. Earlier non-folding 'stick fans' are shown in sixteenth- and seventeenth-century portraits and engravings as banded with narrow lacings of silver and gold. However, it was not until the late nineteenth century that fans with lace leaves – as opposed to painted or printed ones – became part of the grand occasion ensemble and had invariably to appear at weddings, balls and court gatherings. From about 1900, patterned machine laces were also used, for example around the edge of the fashionable bisque-coloured chiffon fans, painted with whimsical fairies and butterflies.

Fan, eventail. See *Shell*.

Fashion in lace. The despotic tyranny of fashion from the sixteenth to the early twentieth century is now hard for us to credit. It was essentially and intentionally undemocratic, a discriminating agent between the haves and the have-nots. That the type of clothes in favour should change as the years went by was one thing: that anyone with society pretensions should be forced to wear highly elaborate and inordinately expensive clothes, even when it necessitated their selling or mortgaging everything else they possessed, was quite another.

The coif, and then the millstone ruffs, were the earliest garments on which lace was exhibited. With the seventeenth century there followed open ruffs, falling ruffs, falling collars (Charles I), the col rabat, the cravat, and by 1692 the Steinkirk. Women had, in addition, the option of a lace bertha worn straight around bare shoulders.

In the mid seventeenth century men wore, on the whole, more lace than women. An engraving of Louis XIV in 1670, by Gagnières, shows him with lace at his neck, waist, arms, wrists and knees, on his tunic, petticoat-breeches and shoes, all mixed in with hundreds of yards of looped silk ribbons (galants). (Fig. 21a.) Women also had lace on caps or bonnets with the pinners, streamers or lappets which depended from them. In 1679 the fontange took the French court by storm. The fashion spread to England and continued into the reign of Queen Anne and the early eighteenth century. Also from about 1680 aprons of lace – point de France, point plat, Milanese and Argentan – replaced even more expensively the fine linen aprons trimmed with punto in aria which had graced skirts and petticoats for almost a hundred years. (Figs. 1a, 21b.)

The fontange went out about 1710, but lace caps and lappets remained in. The Watteau style followed from 1725 to 1775: the elbow-length sleeves were trimmed with tiered ruffles (engageants) made of blonde lace or of Dresden work, while the low square necks were edged with matching lace standing upright, in a slightly gathered manner.

The War of the Austrian Succession, in which Britain opposed France, and the Seven Years War of 1756-63, reduced the influence of French fashion, and by 1780 the English court under the tutelage of the Prince Regent had taken the lead. Within a very short time, however, the plain lace-less fashion of the neo-classical period came in, and lacemaking was on its way out. The simplicity of dress, the French Revolution and the machines came together to cast the centuries-old lacemaking skills into oblivion.

Lace crept back in the early nineteenth century in the guise of a veil 'à l'Iphigenie', named from the Greek legend, and of a lace-frilled stole-like pelerine. But it appeared only for women: for men clothes became, and remained, lace-less. For women, there were lace-trimmed tunics, fichus and aprons, and again the very low-cut bodice with its little frilled border of lace slanting upwards, starched stiff as a barricade.

From 1820, embroidered nets were being made into stoles, veils and gowns. Then, by 1831, exotically rich dresses were appearing again, with huge sleeves and tiny waists, and with lace accessories swarming busily all over them in flounces, tuckers, berthas, pelerines, fall caps and poke bonnet veils of Chantilly, blonde or decorated net.

Queen Victoria, at the time of her wedding in 1840, was regarded as the leader of fashion, but really only because France's internal affairs were in such a mess. By 1854 the Empress Eugenie was occupying that position, and with the death of Prince Albert in 1861 Queen Victoria lost her interest, never very acute, in haute couture. Lace shawls were fashionable from the 1840s to the 1860s, either triangular or square, black or white, hand-made or machine. Soon after, complete dresses and jackets began to be made of lace. In 1863 the very first ready-to-wear clothes appeared, from Germany, at much the same time as the couturier Worth was rising to the height of his influence. High-priced and low-priced laces marched side by side, with the line of social demarcation becoming progressively blurred. France was now a republic, and the dwindling number of royalties which still survived in Europe could no longer afford to be the dictators of fashion.

Fashion plates. Prints which instructed people what they should wear during the coming season. They were quite distinct from the records of current fashion provided by the engravings of Bosse and Bonnart. Both these and the fashion plates provide invaluable records of how lace was worn. The Ladies' Pocket Books of the earlier eighteenth century gave prints of the fashion of the previous year, while forecasting in words what should be worn in the months to come (see *Cuffs*). Shortly afterwards, instructions on being à la mode appeared in *The Lady's Magazine* (1770 ff) and *La Gallerie des Modes* (1778 ff). Before that time, only model dolls or sketches showed the customers what there was in store: they were, after all, a very small and select clientele. The fashion plates, once established, continued after the Revolution, with Heideloff's *Gallery of Fashion* (1794 ff) indicating the failing power of the dwindling courts to retain the monopoly of what was to be worn, and by whom. This dissemination of at least a knowledge of fashion was reinforced in the mid nineteenth century by mass production, which gradually was to bring a near uniformity of dress within the reach of almost everyone. By 1914 the output of magazines had multiplied enormously, making the fashion plates themselves superfluous. Meanwhile the great couturiers – pioneered by Worth, who from 1860 advised the Empress Eugenie on what she should wear – were recreating the fashion hearts of the courts in their own expensive and exclusive salons.

Fibres. (Fig. 23.) Long thin hair-like structures used in the making of lace and other textiles. They must be of adequate flexibility, fineness, length and strength and may be obtained from naturally occurring animal, vegetable or mineral sources or may be manufactured by a synthetic process.

Animal fibres are made of protein and are of two main kinds, wool from sheep and silk from silkworms. Mohair and alpaca are fibres similar to wool; angora (from a rabbit) and human hair are chemically similar to wool, but much smoother. Silk can also be obtained from other caterpillars and from the spinnerets of a spider, but neither is available in commercial quantities.

Vegetable fibres are not made of protein but of cellulose, a carbohydrate found only in plants. The two main kinds used in lace are flax from the stem and root of the flax plant and cotton from the fibres surrounding the cotton plant seeds. Mercerised cotton is cotton treated to make it look like silk. Fibres from the leaf of the pineapple plant are woven to make pina cloth, which is used in the Philippines as a basis for drawnwork; various forms of aloe (qv), plantain, Solomon's seal, grasses and coconut occur in experimental and tourist pieces. Lace bark is not a textile fibre as such but a complete network of bast fibres forming a mesh on the inner side of the bark of the tree.

Mineral fibres, such as gold and silver, either in pure form or alloyed with base metals, when they were known as cliquant, were most commonly used. There is one record of glass lace and one of asbestos.

Synthetic fibres include the acetate and viscose rayons, acrylics, polyamides and polyesters. See *Artificial fibres.*

Apart from their origins, fibres can be distinguished by:

(a) Structure. Wool is scaly, cotton twisted, flax segmented and minutely pitted, while silk and synthetics simply look endlessly long and very smooth. A high magnification is necessary.

(b) Length. (i) Staple fibres are short, a maximum of 3 inches (76 mm) for cotton, 8 inches (203 mm) for most wools, and 36 inches (914 mm) for flax. They must be spun into continuous lengths of yarn before they can be used. See *Spinning.* (ii) Filament fibres are produced in the first place as a continuous thread of great length – silk between one and two miles (1.6-3.2 km), and synthetics to infinity. If they are spun it is not to lengthen them, but to thicken and strengthen them.

(c) Diameter. These vary, but on the whole cotton is thicker than flax, and wool than cotton.

(d) Other physical characteristics such as weight, strength, pliability and temperature (dependent on water-absorbing properties) are important in distinguishing linen laces from those made of cotton (after 1830).

(e) Chemical and other tests. (i) The staining of fibres with some coloured lignin detector, since cotton is pure cellulose, while flax contains wood. (ii) Burning: the animal protein fibres, silk and wool, will smell like singeing hair and then go out, leaving black charcoal blobs where they have burnt; the plant fibres cotton and linen burn right away without a smell, leaving almost no ash; synthetics will melt and then burn. (iii) Warming with dilute sulphuric acid: the cellulose fibres (cotton, linen, rayon) will turn black, while the animal fibres will be unaffected.

Fichu, neckerchief, kerchief, half handkerchief, neck or breast cloth

(sometimes also called a gorget or whisk). A triangular cloth, or a square cloth folded into a triangle, used at various times between 1650 and 1850 to cover the shoulders or to conceal an extensive decolletage. See also *Pelerine* and *Tippet*.

Fiennes, Celia (1662-1741). The daughter of a Parliamentarian (Roundhead) colonel, and related to the third Viscount Saye and Sele, she travelled on horseback through much of England between the years 1685 and 1703 and left in her journal a marvellously observed record of the atmosphere of the time. She refers to French refugees making silk at Canterbury after the revocation of the Edict of Nantes; to the growing of flax in the Midlands; to the method of spinning 'some wth ye Rock and fusoe as the French does, others at their wheels out in the streete and Lanes as one passes' (a rock was a distaff, and a fusoe a kind of spindle – see *Spinning*); to the prevalence of knitting as an occupation 'through Lanes where you meete ye ordinary people knitting 4 or 5 in a Company under the hedges'; to the localisation of bobbin lace in Buckinghamshire and Bedfordshire – 'At Stony Stratford they make a great deal of bone lace and so they do all here about, its the manuffactory of this part of ye Country, they sit and worke all along ye streete as thick as Can be'. Referring to Bedford itself, she explains the change of usage of the rooms, originally set aside for public business, to the spinning of wool: 'The Lord Russell that built it, by his untimely death, being beheaded, put a stop to its ffinishing'. Referring to a 9-mile radius around Bedford, she writes 'They make much bone lace in these towns' and she confirms the derivative nature of Honiton lace: 'Here it is they make the fine bone lace in imitation of the Antwerp and Flanders lace and indeed I think its as fine – it only will not wash so fine, wch must be the fault in ye thread.'
    It is on evidence such as this that most of our knowledge of when and where English laces of the past were made depends. Inventories and wardrobe accounts almost never mention it.

Fil (French, thread). (a) Fil attaché (attached thread): a bobbin lace technique where additional threads are attached or sewn in during the making of the lace. This happens in all non-continuous laces and also in the otherwise continuous nineteenth- and twentieth-century Belgian Valenciennes, and in some Bucks, where the difference in number of bobbins required at times between clothwork and ground means that adjustments have to be made by adding or taking away threads.
(b) Fil coupé (cut thread) has, of necessity, to go along with fil attaché, as the unwanted threads in any particular part of the work are cut off. Fil coupé and fil attaché, together, must occur in all free, non-continuous or à pièces rapportées (with pieces brought together) laces: the parts of the

design are made as separate pieces, the threads used to make them are *cut off*, the pieces are then *brought together*, and sewings are taken around their edges so that threads can be *attached* in order to link them together by brides or reseau. (Fig. 28.)

(c) Fil continu (continuous thread), straight lace. Design and ground are made in one, *straight* across, by a *continuous* process. Since (a) and (b) occur occasionally in continuous laces, as well as forming a separate category, 'non-continuous' is a better opposite to 'continuous' than either of them.

(d) Fil de crin and fil de trace for heavy outlines of the design are no longer used.

(e) Fil tiré = pulled threadwork. See *Drawnwork*.

Filet (French, a safety net, a drag net), **filet brodé** (French, embroidered net), **filet guipure, guipure d'art, Modano.**

(a) The 'filet' refers to the knotted mesh on which the pattern is darned. The mesh, sometimes known as punto a maglia quadra, or square hole stitch, is made like a fisherman's net using a mesh stick (lease, spacer or gauge) to keep the holes of even size, and a netting shuttle (needle) to carry the thread. A fisherman's knot is most commonly used (Fig. 40c). The design is worked with punto a rammendo, a running stitch in one direction only, often covering two meshes at a time, and punto a tela, linen stitch, closely darned in both directions so that several crossing threads occur within each mesh. A denser punto a stuova, or matting stitch, is sometimes used.

Patterns for filet work were printed by the Venetian Vavassore in 1532. In the sixteenth and seventeenth centuries, covers and coverlets were made in alternating squares of filet and reticella. It was produced in Germany, France, Italy and Sicily and, in the twentieth century, also in China. These latter were so low-priced as almost to put European filets out of production. Apart from price, they could be distinguished by thread, the Chinese using cotton and the Europeans linen: if the knots were pressed between finger and thumb, the linen left a deeper impression. Levers produced a faithful machine copy, but without knots. Crochet copies of the designs were made in America in the 1920s, and their texture was copied by the Barmen. A filet-like plain ground made by machine was sometimes used for hand darning.

(b) Point de filet, or passée de filet (= half stitch), is a continental term, and confusing.

See also *Buratto, Embroidered lace, Lacis.*

Fillings, à jours, ajours, jours, modes. Stitches that fill the enclosed cavity of a lace shape representing flowers, fruits, people or animals.

Fillings are essentially ornamental, and varied, as opposed to the ground, which serves the practical purpose of holding the design in place and is of uniform appearance. In continuous laces, such as Bucks, the fillings are made at the same time as the rest of the lace; in non-continuous laces such as Honiton, they are made after the outline of the shape has been completed, by the sewing in of new threads. (Fig. 4a.)

Finger. A measure of length used by lacemakers of the past. It was equivalent to 4½ inches (110 mm).

Fining, Bobbin. One of the principal Levers machine set-outs. It produced a sheer texture by a twisting technique involving three sets of threads: an alternation of stationary and moving warps, and the bobbin threads, which were twisted around by the moving warps. The V-shaped zigzag which resulted is quite unlike anything found in hand-made laces, and therefore 'fining' is one of the easiest machine techniques to identify. See *Leavers.*

Five-hole ground. See *Reseau.*

Flat point. A needlepoint lace with no raised work. It is associated especially with Venice and with England in the last two decades of the seventeenth century. See also *Point plat.*

Flax. (Fig. 23c.) 'Flax' is used of the plant and of the fibres obtained from it, 'flax' or 'linen' of the thread spun from the fibres, and 'linen' of the material, or lace, made from the spun thread.
    Commercial flax is obtained from the bundles of bast fibres which run lengthwise from the tip of the stem to the tip of the root of the flax plant, *Linum usitatissimum,* and which may be as much as 3 feet (914 mm) long. The fibres in their original role were intended to give elasticity to the stem to spring back as the wind swept over it, and this accounts for the supple texture of linen laces. The bundles are made of closely packed cylindrical cells, each cell having a thick wall of cellulose strengthened with lignin, for additional resilience. The preparation of flax is expensive since the plants have first to be hand-pulled to get the longest possible length of fibre. Then, before the bast can be exposed and separated, the softer tissues of the plant have to be rotted, or retted, away. This was always a laborious process taking several weeks, first of drying, then of exposure to dew or damp; it was also skilled since with insufficient care the flax fibres themselves would disintegrate or lose their lustre. From the evil-smelling mess were extracted the bundles, split apart into long strands in which the unit cells were held together by a gummy substance.

These strands had then to be spun so that the whole length remained together instead of shattering into the microscopic slivers of individual cells, which it would be impossible to handle. According to Henneberg, only seven of these strands, each barely 1/150 of a millimetre in diameter, were spun together to produce the almost invisibly fine thread which composed the gossamer bobbin laces of Flanders in the second half of the seventeenth century (see *Count* and *Spinning*). The enduring and beautiful qualities of fine flax, its lustre, strength and cool supple firmness are easily endangered by a careless preparation process. The superb quality of the old flax threads has long since been unobtainable, and no doubt the various attempts to save time and money have contributed to this: the introduction of chlorine bleaching in 1789, the practice of boiling the thread in caustic soda to remove impurities, the tight machine spinning and the flax-hackling machine of 1838 combined to corrupt the fine qualities of antique flax.

The finest flax of the past came from the Low Countries; Italy's was good, but thicker; England grew a little of poorish quality in Devon and the Midlands; and flax was of great commercial importance to Ireland in the nineteenth century.

Flax is, on the whole, too soft to take the strain of the mechanical tension in machine laces, but it was sometimes used by the Barmen.

Flemish lace. A general term for laces of that amorphous geographical and political unit known from the sixteenth to the early nineteenth century as Flanders. They are listed under *Belgium*. The supreme epoch of Flemish lace lasted from c 1550 to 1750, but its early development is obscure:

(a) Cutworks appear frequently in English, French and Spanish wardrobe accounts and inventories of the sixteenth and early seventeenth centuries. (Fig. 6a). See also *Cutwork* (a).

(b) Flemish bobbin laces were made in the towns of Mechlin, Binche, Valenciennes and Brussels and in the province of Brabant (Fig. 7 a-c). Each had its distinctive characteristics and is described under its own heading. Their date of origin is uncertain, but there seems no doubt that they revealed a marvellous degree of perfection by the mid seventeenth century, becoming progressively more ethereal until they achieved the translucency of patterned rice paper. In 1661, Louise de la Vallière, mistress of Louis XIV, is described as wearing gloves of 'cream-coloured Brussels lace'. Fuller, in 1662, speaks of Devon lace as saving thousands of pounds yearly formerly 'sent over Seas, to fetch Lace from Flanders' (see *Fuller*). The sumptuary edicts of Louis XIV in 1660 and of Charles II in 1662 were strongly, though not exclusively, directed against Flemish laces. They appear to have sprung, like the incredibly fine threads of which they were made (1,200 count), almost out of nothing, since precise sixteenth-century references to Flemish bobbin lace are very sparse indeed:

(i) The Holy Roman Emperor Charles V (reigned 1519-56) is said to have encouraged lacemaking at schools and convents in the Spanish Netherlands (see *Dutch lace*), but this most probably would refer to cutworks.

(ii) An engraving by Collaert after the Flemish painter Martin de Vos, c 1580, shows some work with bobbins in progress. But even if this were bobbin lace, which is doubtful, de Vos had lived for some years in Italy and may therefore have been representing not a Flemish but an Italian scene (see *Bobbin lace*).

(iii) In 1591, according to Paulis, bobbin lacemaking (minuteyten and spellework) was being discouraged by the authorities as a waste of time.

(iv) A pattern book was published in Liège in 1597 by Jean de Glen. However, it was not of bobbin lace and was basically a plagiarism of Vinciolo.

(v) In 1599, the existence of bobbin lace (of thickish thread) appears irrefutable, in the large and beautiful coverlet worked for Albert and Isabella of Brabant (see *Brabant*). Thirty years later 'Flemish collar lace' was being worn by Charles I and Henrietta Maria in the Van Dyck portraits which depict the form and design of the lace so minutely that even the texture and quality seem apparent.

Apart from the familiar place names (see *Belgian lace*), there are also the general names of 'Flemish seventeenth-century vermiculate' and 'Flemish peasant'. Another unlocated form is 'eighteenth-century Flemish bobbin', qualified either by picoted brides or by a round Valenciennes ground. They lack any sharp design, and the latter is very similar to the decadent Milanese of the later eighteenth century.

The Italian and Flemish laces, excluded from their natural markets of England and France on the grounds of expense, became extremely attenuated. By the end of the eighteenth century much simplified Mechlin, Antwerp, French Valenciennes and a plain droschel were all that remained of the riotous blooms, leafy fronds and trailing sprays of a hundred years earlier.

(c) Flemish needlepoints. See *Point de Venise à reseau* and Fig. 5.

Flanders was also famous for its flax, its spinning and its damasks.

Fleurs volantes. See *Couronnes*.

Floats. The long threads of the design carried forwards by the Levers machine from one of the more solid parts of the lace to the next. They have to be cropped by hand after the web is off the loom. The heavier outlining threads (cordonnets) also have to float across the surface in this way, and their cut ends on each side of each motif are a sure indication of machine origin (see *Cordonnet* (f, iii)).

Florentine knots. Another name for raised plaits (see *Plait* (b, iv)). They are found in seventeenth century Milanese lace, in Thomas Lester's intricate designs for Beds Maltese and in some French Le Puy laces.

Flounce, flouncing, furbelow, falbala, volant. A broad edging of lace worn gathered around a skirt, sometimes in two or three tiers, so profusely frilled that the wearer looked like a large bird shaking its feathers. The transition from edgings (from ¼ inch, 6 mm) to flounces (up to 36 inches, 914 mm) occurs at about 6 or 7 inches (150 to 180 mm). The Levers machine makes flounce lengths across its width, i.e. up to 15 feet (4.6 m). As each depth, say 27 inches (686 mm), is completed a short gap of plain warp is left before the patterning begins again. These gaps can later be cut, releasing separate flounces each 5 yards (4.6 m) by 27 inches (686 mm). Their lower edges will show a fringe of cut warp threads instead of picots. Such laces are said to be made 'cross-wise of the loom'.

Fond (French, ground), **background, champ, entoilage, treille, open part.** This is the background of the lace against which the design is displayed. It surrounds and supports it, in both bobbin and needlepoint laces, and is one of the main criteria for distinguishing one type of lace from another.

Palliser distinguishes three main types of ground: fonds clairs = the reseau, mesh or net grounds; brides claires = plain brides; brides ornées = decorated brides. However just two types, reseaux and brides, are more usually distinguished.

The ground may be worked in one with the design (see *Continuous* laces), or the fragments of the design may be worked separately and subsequently linked together by the ground (see *Non-continuous*). Examples of these arrangements are: continuous with reseau = Binche, Mechlin, Valenciennes; continuous with brides = Beds Maltese, Le Puy; non-continuous with reseau = point d'Angleterre, some Honiton, some Milanese, Alençon, Burano; non-continuous with brides = Brussels duchesse, some Honiton, some Milanese, point de France, Venetian raised points.

Bobbin laces usually have bobbin-made grounds but some may have a needle-made ground, e.g. some early nineteenth-century Honiton grounded in net stitch (see *Net* (1)), and the late nineteenth-century point d'Angleterre where the bobbin design is bedded in a point de gaze ground.

Needlepoint laces usually have needlepoint grounds, but some may have bobbin, e.g. some very delicate mid eighteenth-century Brussels needlepoints grounded in narrow strips of droschel. (Fig. 5c.)

The following terms are sometimes used of reseaux: fond à la mariage = honeycomb, mostly used as a filling; fond à la vierge = virgin ground, rose ground, cinq trous; fond d'armure, in Mechlin c 1725, see *Armure*; fond chant = Chantilly ground, six-point star, point de Paris; fond clair, used specifically for Bucks point or Lille; fond simple, also used for Bucks point ground, Lille and tulle (qv); fond de neige = snow ground, oeil de perdrix.

See also *Brides, Reseau*.

Fontange, commode, cock-up. An erection of tiered lace worn above the forehead to a height of 12 inches (305 mm) or more, projecting slightly forwards like the horn of a unicorn and decorated with hair, flowers and ribbons. The fashion was launched in 1679 by a young lady who had set her heart on catching the eye of Louis XIV. She was created Duchesse de Fontanges but soon fell from favour, and she died in 1681 aged twenty. In spite of ridicule and the king's disfavour, the style named after her persisted, in all types of lace from elegant point de France to wispy Flemish bobbin. In England it lasted through the reign of four Stuarts to disappear finally in 1710. (Fig. 20.) See also *Commode, Head-sute, Lappets*.

Footing, foot, footside, engrelure. The straight edge of a length of lace by which it is attached to the material it is to decorate. It is often attached indirectly, through a strip of linen or narrow beading, to minimise the pull on the lace itself. The free border is called the heading.

Machine laces have entirely their own language: a footing is a length of plain net, 1 to 3 inches (25 to 76 mm) wide.

Foreign terms. Discussions of lace in English are frequently hampered by the vocabulary being cluttered with foreign terms. These are mainly French or Italian – see the many entries under 'point' and 'punto' – and the fact that many of the laces being talked about are French or Italian (or Flemish laces, to which French terms are now commonly applied) does not greatly help.

For some of these foreign terms there are now comprehensible English equivalents, such as fillings for ajours, bars for brides, partridge eye for oeil de perdrix, and ground for fond. The usage, however, is inconsistent. Others have passed into the English language, e.g. droschel, ecru, guipure, lacis, filet, cordonnet. Yet others such as reseau, toilé and mezzo punto, perfectly lucid in their original tongue, have no completely satisfactory English equivalent and are at the same time difficult to define concisely. See *Tulle, Point*, and *Point d'Angleterre* for other muddles.

The profusion of these foreign terms, combined with the paucity of English ones, might argue the small importance of English laces compared with those of the Continent. However, it must be borne in mind that the prime market for lace was the court, that French was for a considerable time the language of the court, that even in the nineteenth century it was the language of gentility, and for a long way into the twentieth century the language of diplomacy. Such foreign terms, to the people who wore the lace, would have seemed perfectly natural. See also *Naming of laces.*

Fowler, Mrs Ann. She kept the lace shop in Honiton in the late nineteenth century. She had many employees, who specialised in putting together the tiny sprigs made by the outworkers. She held the royal warrants as lacemaker to Queen Victoria, Queen Alexandra and the Princess of Wales, later Queen Mary. She started lace classes in schools c 1906, was a skilful designer of lace and rediscovered how to make droschel.

Frame knitters. The people who worked on the Stocking and Warp Frames making hosiery and lace.

Free lace. (a) Non-continuous laces where the motifs are made separately and then linked into a design by brides or reseau, since considerable freedom of arrangement is made possible by this method. See also *Fil.* (b) Free lace may also refer to freedom of expression, where the maker is not bound by traditional patterns and techniques but explores new combinations of colour, line and texture. 'Their aim', says Pfannschmidt in *Twentieth Century Lace*, 'is structure, not ornament'. (See *Design* (b, ix) and *Lace* (a, iv)).

Fremantle. A Bucks design said by Thomas Wright to have been copied by machinery in the early twentieth century and exported in huge quantities to Russia, where it was used for lining coffins. The Heathcoat product made for this purpose was Meklin. The Levers product was a warp net, i.e. made of warp threads only, and so used less yarn and was less expensive than ordinary twist net. See *Mechlin* (d, iii and iv).

French lace. See *Points de France.*

French ground. Point de Paris *Reseau.*

Frizette (French, friser, to curl). A gathered edging of lace. The fashion became extreme in the second half of the eighteenth century: lappets were broadened by the addition of matching frills, and multiple frilling over the dresses and around the head gave an impression of being feathered. A *Receipt* (recipe) *for Modern Dress* of 1753 recommends 'frizzling the elbows with sixteen ruffles'. *The Ladies' Pocket Book* setting out the 'Directions for the Manner of Dressing in the Year 1761' advocates 'for the head ... chevaux de frize lappets'. (Fig. 5b.)

Fuller, Thomas (1608-61). Chaplain extraordinary to Charles II, and a prolific writer. His *Worthies of England*, published posthumously in 1662, contains important references to lacemaking and confirms both the existence of Flemish laces in the sixteenth century and the huge sums of money spent on them. Referring to bobbin lace, he says: 'Much of this is made in and about Honyton, and weekly returned to London ... Bone lace it is named, because first made with bone, since wooden, bobbins ... Modern is the use thereof in England, not exceeding the middle of the Reign of Queen Elizabeth (i.e. c 1580) ... it saveth some thousands of pounds yearly, formerly sent over Seas, to fetch Lace from Flanders.' See also *Flemish Lace* (b).

Fuselli (Italian, bobbin). Trine a fuselli is bobbin lace.

Fuseau (French, bobbin, spindle). Dentelle au fuseau is bobbin lace. Its second meaning is in spinning: Fiennes (qv) c 1690 speaks of spinning 'wth ye fusoe as the French does', and Rabelais, 1546, of 'espoincter les fuseaulx', i.e. blunting the spindles (see *Bobbin lace*). However, the English second meaning of bobbin – the weaving and lacemaking machine shuttle – is rendered in French by 'la navette'.

Galants. Little knots of gold or silk ribbon worn all over men's clothes from the 1640s onwards. As many as six hundred might be found on one suit, or 250 yards (229 m) on a pair of petticoat-breeches.

Galon, galloon (French, stripe, braid). Lacy ribbons woven in silk or metal and applied flat to material in the manner of braid in the seventeenth century. In the early twentieth century, 'galon' was used of metallic straight-edged insertion or for laces having a scalloped edge on both sides. Fashion advertisements, c 1908, illustrate 'Real Point de Flandre Galon, 2½ inches wide, at 5s 6d a yard'.

Gassed cotton. A defect of cotton thread, as compared with linen, is its fluffiness. In 1817 the gassing of thread, and of manufactured lace, to singe away the fluffiness was invented by Samuel Hall. The process involved passing the thread, net or lace through flames of hydrogen drawn up to a height of about ½ inch (13 mm) by a vacuum above so that the flame surrounded the material to be cleared. The process was improved and patented in 1823. Hall in several popular magazines advertised not only his gassed thread, under the name Urling, but inserted actual samples of the product, so publicising both his de-fluffing process and the bobbinet which he had treated. A rapid expansion of Heathcoat's industry followed – from a total of 700 bobbinet machines in 1817 to 2,500 in 1826 and 4,500 in 1831. Hall's charge for gassing was ¾ d a square yard, and he gassed some 5,000,000 square yards a year. G. F. Urling and Co were appointed manufacturers of British lace to Queen Victoria in August 1837, and she bought some £72 of lace from them in 1839. Gassed cotton is still used for bobbin lacemaking.

Gauge. (a) In bobbinets, the number of bobbins working per inch width of the machine, e.g. 10-point gauge is ten bobbins per inch. See *Machine lace* (c). (b) In Raschel machines, a times two multiple of the number of needles working per inch width. See *Raschel*. (c) A spacer used in the making of filet. See *Filet* (a).

Gaze quadrillée. See *Stitches* (e, ii).

Genoese lace, poynt Jean. This originated from the city of Genoa on the coast of north-west Italy. The earliest were the gold and silver laces, either in pure metal or in that adulterated form known as 'faux (false) galon'. They were extremely dear and forbidden by sumptuary laws to the local populace. Almost none have survived, having been melted down to realise their mineral value. In the late sixteenth century silk laces, both black and coloured, were ordered by Queen Elizabeth. Around 1600, Genoa produced her imitations of punto in aria: the thin supple skeletons of plaited lace; the broader, stronger frettings of strawberries and carnations; and then the collar laces, deeply scalloped, garnished with wheatears, and made with stout flax in close even workmanship. This last was a non-continuous bobbin lace, the very short brides being sewn in as the work proceeded. Macramé, also made in Genoa, formed an important part of the trousseau of a Genoese lady.

Addison, in 1764, called it a decayed city. It was still making lace, but not profitably. (Figs. 8, 9.)

Geography of lace. (Fig. 22.) In origin, lace is European. Its extension to other parts of the globe was by refugees (the Pilgrim Fathers from Holland to New England via Plymouth), by conquest (the Spanish in

Paraguay and the Canary Islands), by settlers (the English in North America), or by missionaries (to India and China).

Within Europe, lace production from the sixteenth to the early nineteenth century was centred in three main locations: Italy, Flanders and France. Its export all over Europe was a major source of wealth for the countries of origin. Fashion favoured first one and then the other, but when a lace was in fashion all Europe – or all the closely intermarried courts of Europe – wore it. Embroidered laces from Flanders and Italy dominated the sixteenth century, scalloped Flemish bobbin laces the early seventeenth century, encrusted Venetian needlepoints the following decades, until the ethereal Flemish surpassed them and excluded them in the early eighteenth century. The stouter French Alençon came in first to withstand the turbulent winter weather, while the diaphanous cobwebs of Flanders were relegated to summer laces. French bobbin laces found their place at last in the tightly gathered frills of the later eighteenth century. England's time was the nineteenth century, but then it was her clever machine productions which were exported: her hand-made laces remained commercially unsuccessful.

Laces are on the whole – by technique, design and texture – distinctively from their country of origin. In spite of extensive pirating of designs over more than three hundred years, in spite of the kidnapping or enticement of workers – from Venice to France, from Flanders to Denmark, in spite of the rash of forgeries brought on in the nineteenth century by any commercial success, the laces of Venice, Milan, Mechlin and all the other towns, cities and provinces maintain their regional integrity.

For embroidered and craft laces the geographical origin is less easy to determine. The embroidered laces were made over wide areas, mostly by nuns, and convents hundreds of miles apart could produce identical pieces. Drawnworks such as Dresden, Tönder, Hardanger and Hedebo are exceptions; but the craft laces Tenerife, Modano and Madeira, though named after places, refer more accurately to widely disseminated techniques.

German lace. See *Saxony* and *Venetian lace* (e).

Ghent. A city rich in béguinages, which has made a kind of Valenciennes (qv) since the mid eighteenth century. The reseau was diamond-shaped (à mailles carrées), the bobbins being twisted 2½ times. Production almost ceased with the French Revolution and was not revived until 1852 when Sister Mary Joseph, director of two lacemaking schools for orphans and poor children, invented a new form of Valenciennes called 'Ghent lace with varied reseau'. This lace was non-continuous and sported a wide selection of Flemish grounds and fillings which, combined with the closely textured whole-stitch flowers and foliage, gave the appearance of a herbaceous border in bloom. Production of this lace ceased in 1867 (Fig. 28). Ghent also imitated the 1840s Limerick work of tambour embroidery on net (Fig. 19a). See also *Fil* (a) and *Valenciennes*.

Gimp. (a) The thick thread outlining portions of the design in most bobbin laces except Binche and Valenciennes. In East European laces, the gimp may run through the centre of the trail instead of around the outside. (Fig. 4c.) Where the outline is padded, as in Spanish and Venetian raised points, it is called a cordonnet. 'Cordonnet' is also applied to a completely surface thread, as in Carrickmacross. In machine laces, the outlining thread is a cordonnet, whatever form it takes. In French, the terms bourdon, fil de contour and fil d'ornement may be used.
(b) A thread formed of a core of silk or parchment wound with gold or silver foil or silk.
(c) A braid or lace made from thread (b) in the fifteenth and sixteenth centuries, sometimes using a needle and thread, and sometimes bobbins to facilitate handling. But it was not a bobbin lace: the gimp threads were simply held together to form a flat braid, up to ¼ inch (7 mm) wide, with the binding threads twisted at the edges into looped picots. This braid was then sewn down into designs and connected by corded bars. See *Guipure* (b). When thread (b) has a parchment core the product is sometimes called a parchment lace (cartisane). Palliser identifies it as Ragusa (see *Ragusa* (vii)). (Fig. 1b.)
(d) Palliser defines gimp as 'the pattern which rests on the ground or is held together by brides'.
(e) A large heavy bobbin which carries the outlining gimp. It is also called a trolly bobbin and is associated with trolly lace.
(f) Gimping. A Levers machine product in which the solid parts of the lace present a woven appearance, as in a bobbin-made toilé.
(g) A narrow Honiton braid called ten-stick, which has pinholes along one side only. See *Raised work* and *Stem stitch*.

Gingles, jingles. The loose pewter, wood or bone rings found on the shank of the trolly or gimp bobbins used in East Midlands lacemaking.

Godet (French, an ornamental curve, in relief). (a) About 1900, a short dress flounce in which the lower edge was longer than the upper so that it fluted outwards without any gathering or pleating. (b) The fourteenth-century word 'godet' in its later form of 'godron' (gadroon) was frequently applied to the complex flutings of the millstone ruffs, which were also called 'collerettes gaudronnées'. Blaise de Viginière describes them as 'gadrooned like organ pipes', while Henri III, intent on fixing not only his own ruffs but those of his intimate friends, was derided as a 'gaudronneur des collets'.

Gold lace. The thread for gold lace was a gimp of thin metal strips wound around a flexible core. The lace was made by men using giant bobbins 7¾ inches (200 mm) long to weight the threads and to prevent tarnishing. Pattern books of 1549 (Lyons) and 1559 (Venice) were for laces of 'gold, silver, silk and other threads'. Gold laces do not antedate the sixteenth century, but gold embroidery did, and the relics of openwork gold decoration left in tombs after the material they were worked on had rotted away have been used erroneously to date gold lace as early as AD 800.

Solid braids of precious metal lace were lavishly worn in the sixteenth century. In France, in 1577, Henri III had one suit weighted with 4,000 yards (3.66 km) of pure gold. In England the currency was debased by the massive influx of Spanish gold and silver (largely as braids), and prices trebled. When import restrictions, e.g. of 1562 and 1573, cut down these supplies, the edges of coins were clipped by those determined to provide themselves with gold lace, and it was not until 1662 that the milling of coins introduced by Blondeau finally defeated this practice. Gold laces came also from Venice, and Elizabeth I's wardrobe accounts contain many entries for 'Venice sylver' and 'Venys gold'. However, by 1629 the 'Venice gold and silver lace' being made in England was so perfect a copy that a lady granted the customs dues on importations was finding herself without income (see *English lace* (a)). It was still being made in 1743 when a proposed Bill to tax English gold and silver lace was opposed as likely to ruin a flourishing home manufacture.

In spite of a flood of sumptuary edicts and import restrictions, and the raging of reformers, the extravagant wearing of gold lace continued to drive the aristocracy more and more deeply into debt. The fashion passed, almost suddenly, in the mid eighteenth century as lighter finer fabrics rejected any heavy decoration. Very little of the early gold lace survives: the ladies of the court unravelled the metal from its base core and sold it as scrap.

Small quantities of gold lace continued to be made for church use, and for military and other uniforms. In the late nineteenth century some was made at Newport Pagnell, but the workers complained that it twippered (curled up), a tendency which would presumably have been corrected by the use of heavier bobbins. At this time also, gold lace was being made in Valencia (Spain), in Mexico, and, as a combination of gold thread and white silk, in Ireland and Germany.

Golilla, gorget (French = gorgerette, a collar or tucker). See *Whisk*.

Grammont. A town in Belgium which produced, in the late nineteenth century, an imitation Chantilly of black silk, which was much exported to America.

Great Exhibition, 1851. The first of the international exhibitions, it was held in Hyde Park, London, in a huge glass emporium, which was later removed to Sydenham as the Crystal Palace. The Exhibition, initiated and chaired by Prince Albert, was a great stimulus to both hand-made and machine-made laces and succeeded in making £186,000 profit in six months. Beds Maltese and Beds plaited laces appeared for the first time. A pair of Nottingham lace curtains was shown, each 5 yards (4.6 m) long and 2 yards (1.8 m) wide, entirely covered with one elaborate design which had required 15,000 Jacquard cards. Another exhibit was of a novel method of displaying lace samples, by 'nature printing', in which an impression was taken of the actual piece of lace on a light-sensitive plate. This replaced the tedious method of mounting dozens of pieces of lace in a book, with handwritten descriptions, to show customers.

Later exhibitions, in 1855, 1862, 1867, 1874, 1884, 1889 and 1900, encouraged superb hand-made pieces, as well as intricate machine laces of excellent design, such indeed as have never been seen since.

Grecian net. See *Bullet-hole net*.

Greek lace. There is no evidence that any lace of commercial importance was ever made in Greece, so 'Greek' may be without geographical significance. However:
(a) Palliser says of reticella, 'This point is *identical* with what is commonly called "Greek" lace'. Hudson Moore is of the same opinion.
(b) Powys illustrates Greek lace by a stiff coarse type of reticella, similar to that associated with the tourist trade in twentieth-century Cyprus.
(c) Thomas Wright illustrates a lace not unlike a sixteenth-century Venetian bobbin, known to have been made at Winslow (Buckinghamshire) in the early twentieth century, and called by him 'Old Greek Pointed Lace'.
(d) The term Greek lace may have originated from the time when the Ionian Islands were a possession of the Venetian Republic, from the fifteenth to the eighteenth centuries. Much Italian work was then imported into the islands and perhaps subsequently sold as if made there.
(e) During the nineteenth century, when the islands were a British protectorate, shrouds and burial cloths were unearthed in vast quantities as rare souvenirs. They were evil-smelling and discoloured enough to be authentic but too coarsely crude to bear any resemblance to the supple lightness of Italian reticellas, and therefore conceivably they were made

in Greece, by a cording method, and not so very long ago.

Grillé, Point (French, a grating). See *Half stitch.*

Groppo, Punto a (Italian, knotted stitch. Also spelt gruppo, gropo, gropari). (Figs. 40, 41.) This Italian term covers a narrower field than the English term 'knotted lace'. Some rather heavy pieces of edging, frequently with a dentate border, are regarded as sixteenth-century and Italian. They are rare, study of them is hampered by lack of material, and their exact technique is uncertain. Also they are often so shrunken, crushed and stiffened by washing, ironing and starching, over hundreds of years, that the course of the threads is difficult to follow. They have in general a heavy look, with a trace of geometric design and very few holes.

(i) Knotted buttonhole stitch (point noué), made with a needle, is postulated as the most likely technique. Professor Lotz, who made a study of sixteenth- and seventeenth-century pattern books, was of the opinion that Pagano's designs in 1542 for 'ponti gropposo' were only for this stitch and could not be adapted for macramé.

(ii) Macramé has its own typical knots, the arrangement of which gives it quite a different appearance from the form described above. Also it uses threads of limited length and is worked downwards so that the unknotted residue appears as a fringe. However, in the small-scale sixteenth- and seventeenth-century macramés, the fringed ends are often pulled together into little picots, making the border look mildly dentate, and concealing its origin. A needle is not used in macramé: the threads are knotted by hand, either without any implements or using bobbins. Sharp, however, speaks of 'Punto a groppo, now known as macramé', and Lowes of 'Punto a groppo or macramé ... the earliest form of woven lace', while Hudson Moore, under the heading 'Punto a Groppo' describes only macramé; and Jourdain (1908) has a caption 'Modern macramé' below two photographs of fringed macramé and unfringed puncetto.

(iii) Puncetto, produced in the nineteenth and twentieth centuries in the mountain valleys of Tuscany, may be a descendant of the antique punto a groppo, though it is much lighter in texture, and more open in design. It was also made in a labour-saving corded form. Hungerford Pollen uses a photograph of puncetto to illustrate punto a groppo.

(iv) 'Groppi moreschi' (Moorish knotting) is used by Tagliente in his 1527 pattern book. During the nineteenth and twentieth centuries North Africa, Cyprus, Syria and Palestine all produced a fine knotted lace varying in form from the flower garlands of bebilla to the tiny regular teeth of Moroccan handkerchief borders. It is possible, however, that the sixteenth-century reference of Tagliente is not to a technique but to the interweaving knot-like arabesques of his Byzantine designs. On the other hand, Moorish influences were powerful in Spain, and Spanish knotted laces (see below) may have been linked with Adriatic and Middle Eastern forms.

(v) Date and place of origin: the Sforza inventory of 1493 lists 'Pecto uno d'oro a grupi' (one breast cloth of knotted gold), and 'Lavoro uno de rechamo facto a grupi' (one work of embroidery made by knotting). If this referred to punto a groppo, it would place it in the fifteenth century and in Milan, but we have no means of resolving the 'if'. Gold and silver, as well as flax threads, may have been used, and punto a groppo may have come from Spain, with its records of randas and redicellas (see *Spanish lace* (a and f)), or indeed from that near mythical city of the Adriatic, Ragusa (qv).

(vi) Alternative names for punto a groppo used by various authorities – with or without justification – are 'punto di Ragusa' (Nevill Jackson and Pfannschmidt), 'knotted point' (Palliser) and 'punto avorio' (Powys). This last seems particularly inappropriate since the lace is too corrugated by the rounded hillocks of the knots to look anything like carved ivory, except perhaps for the crystalline morse ivory from sea animals. See *Avorio*.

(vii) Crochet. Although the general appearance of the early knotted laces sometimes closely resembles the raised double stitch or hollow spot stitch of crochet, nothing like a chain stitch is visible.

Gros point. A bold form of Venetian needlepoint, much worn by men in the mid seventeenth century, as collars, cuffs, garters and canons. Jourdain puts its beginning at about 1620, and it was certainly still being made in 1685 when James II bought a Venetian cravat for his coronation. Gros point was characterised by spacious flowers with heavily padded borders. The padding was made of a bundle of flax or wool thread, covered with buttonhole stitches, and extended into crowns of spines and other intricate embellishments. The smooth solid texture of the petals was lightened by minute windows pierced in lozenge and chevron designs. The sheen of the flax made it look as firm and lustrous as carved ivory, and some forms were for this reason called 'punto avorio'. It was also sometimes known as 'punto tagliato a fogliami' (cutwork with foliage) (see *Pagano* and *Reticella* (ii)). In the better pieces the whole luxurious effect was of spreading blooms whose petals touched each other. Where brides were present they were ornately picoted.

Unfortunately in the nineteenth century many old pieces were cut up and reconstituted, with inferior joining threads and garbled pattern, to be worn as berthas, plastrons and choker collars. See *Venetian lace*.

Ground. The background of the lace linking and displaying the more solid parts of the design. The term 'grounded' is often used, e.g. 'grounded with droschel', or 'grounded with brides picotées'. 'Regrounded' means that the original ground has been replaced with a new one, which may or may not be similar to it. See also *Brides, Fond, Reseau.*

Gueuse (French, beggar). A poor quality bobbin lace, similar in design to torchon, made in France especially near Paris in the seventeenth century. It was perhaps related in some way to Les Gueux (The Beggars), a Protestant group who opposed Catholicism in the Netherlands in 1565 but were suppressed by the Duke of Alva in 1568. More probably, however, its general dish-rag appearance earned it that name. It may also have been made and sold by beggars.

Guipure (French, guiper, to roll). It is also spelt guiper, cuipure, gimpeures and gumpeures.
(a) It is used in the sense of a thread (*Gimp* (b)) and also of a braid (*Gimp* (c)). Inventories of Mary Queen of Scots list 'guimpeure d'or' and 'guimpeure d'argent' (gold and silver guipure) in 1597.
(b) The simple braid developed in the late seventeenth century into a bobbin-made or woven tape. Such tapes were treated in the manner of gimp threads but, as they were less flexible, the result was rather awkward. The straight tapes had to be bent, folded or gathered to surround the floral designs. Buttonhole stitches held them together and filled up the empty spaces enclosed by the tapes. Such work is also called 'seventeenth-century tape lace', or sometimes 'mezzo punto' (Italian, mixed stitches, or mixed techniques).
(c) In the seventeenth century, 'guipure' referred to a lace, either bobbin or needlepoint, where the design units were held in position not by a reseau but by brides. Brides disappeared in the eighteenth century but reappeared in the second half of the nineteenth century in a whole range of 'new guipure laces' such as Brussels duchesse, Bruges, Honiton, Beds Maltese, Irish crochet, Youghal, Carrickmacross and French Le Puy – in fact far too wide a category to have any sensible meaning.
(d) Machine guipures were made on the Levers machine in the 1850s. They were described as having 'leg-work as opposed to net' (legs being synonymous with brides), and they were made as edgings, insertions, or in an all-over form for blouses and dresses. The chemical laces of the Schiffli machine were also given the generic name 'machine-embroidered guipures'. See *Machine* (h), and *Swiss* (c).
(e) 'Guipure d'art' was in the nineteenth century applied to filet work, either on a hand-knotted or a machine-made mesh. It is still used in this sense today.

Haarlem. A town in Holland, near Amsterdam, famous in the seventeenth and eighteenth centuries for its fine flax thread.

Hainault. A province of Belgium in which the town of Binche is situated. So-called Hainault lace was a late nineteenth- and twentieth-century production not unlike a coarse Beds Maltese, with loosely attached wheatears which clung to its surface like pastry leaves superimposed on a pie.

Hair lace, point tresse. Human hair was occasionally made into lace by either a bobbin or a needlepoint technique. Its smoothness and springiness made it difficult to work, and the products were mostly intended as sentimental reminders (Fig. 43b). A little square of point tresse was sent to Mary Queen of Scots by the mother of her second husband, Lord Darnley. Nets of hair were made as a foundation for wigs. Louis XVI is said to have worn a cravat of silver hair at his coronation; and lacemakers in Bedford and on the Continent are known to have used their own white hair. Human hair is also said to have been used to support, during the making, the extremely fine picots of Venetian and French needlepoints, where the more commonly used horsehair was too thick. See also *Messages in lace.*

Hairpin crochet. A form of lacy crochet worked over an implement resembling a large steel hairpin or two-pronged fork.

Hairpin stitch. A Buckinghamshire name for six-point star ground. See *Reseau.*

Half stitch, grillé, gauze stitch, point de filet, passée de filet, half linen, net ground. (Fig. 24a.) In bobbin laces there are two main stitches used to make the solid parts of the design: whole stitch and half stitch. Whole stitch is more closely worked and gives the appearance of woven linen. Half stitch is more open, looking like a grill of intersecting stars. In working it, only one thread passes across the passives instead of two as in whole stitch, i.e. only one worker bobbin is used. In some laces, notably Chantilly, half stitch alone is used to create the sprays of naturalistic flowers, and it gives them a lightness and delicacy which might otherwise be lacking in a black lace. Half-stitch lozenges occur frequently in Cluny and torchon, but its most skilful use was in the nineteenth-century silk laces of Bayeux and Caen where alternations of whole and half stitch give a vivid impression of sunlight and shade.

The list of alternative names given above shows some of the problems of nomenclature: 'filet' misleadingly suggests a knotted mesh, while 'net ground' suggests a machine product.

Half wheels. An ornamentation of the brides of seventeenth-century Venetian needlepoint laces.

Hamilton lace. A Scottish lace said to have been started c 1750 by the Duchess of Hamilton after she had seen bobbin lace being made on the Continent. By 1752 she had a small school going with a dozen girl pupils between the ages of seven and fourteen. In 1754 the girls presented the Duke and Duchess with sets of ruffles they had made, and these were worn on the Duke's birthday. The *Edinburgh Amusement* remarked that 'The yarn of which the ruffles were made weighed only 10 drops each hank' (1 drop = 1/16 ounce, or 1.8 grams). In the same year was founded the Select Society of Edinburgh, the Scottish equivalent of the Anti-Gallican Society. Its aim was to encourage home industries and so reduce imports. It was headed by the Duke, and prizes were offered for, among other things, the best Hamilton lace. The lace appears to have been a light and loosely worked torchon, used for trimming small articles of dress, the Scots being too impoverished by the unsuccessful Jacobite rising of 1745 to afford anything more elaborate. There are no records of this lace, or of any commercial bobbin lacemaking in Scotland, after 1788. See *Ayrshire work* and *Scottish lace.*

Hand-embroidery machine. See *Swiss embroidery.*

Hand-run. Thread worked by hand in a running stitch. It can refer to darned net, filet and buratto, and also to the outlining thread (cordonnet) of machine laces. Before 1840 all cordonnets had to be hand-run, but a few years later all machines could do it except for the Pusher, which always needed this hand finishing. For other laces, a hand-run instead of a machine-made cordonnet was regarded as a sign of good quality. See also *Breton lace, Embroidered lace* and *Limerick.* (Fig. 19d and e.)

Hardanger lace. A type of geometric cutwork embroidery named from the town of Hardanger, and made in Norway in the nineteenth and twentieth centuries. It was based on reticella designs, though with a flavour of the art nouveau. The work usually included needle weaving, drawnwork and loop stitch. An even-weave ecru linen, in which the threads could be counted, was used. (Fig. 38b.)

Head, head-suite. The suit of lace worn on the head by court ladies from about 1680. It comprised a pair of long lappets, a cap crown and, at the front, tiered ridges of lace rising to a great height, and intertwined with gold and silk ribbons and jewels (Fig. 20). All this valuable lace took a lot of arranging. To save repeated effort, it was mounted on a wig so that it could be used day after day. Such 'heads' were often a target for thieves. See *Fontange*.

Heading, headside, turnside. The free edge of a length of lace, not attached to the material. See also *Footing*.

Heathcoat, John (1783-1861). A lace manufacturer, first established near Nottingham, where he invented the Bobbin-net machine in 1808. It was 18 inches (457 mm) wide and worked by turning a handle. His great success aroused the anger of the Luddites, who felt he was putting the frame workers out of business just at a time when silk Warp Frame lace was becoming commercially successful, and the workers were being offered very high wages. In 1816 fifty-five of his machines and goods to a total value of £10,000 were destroyed. Heathcoat transferred his business to Tiverton, where it still produces bobbinets, including those used for royal weddings. He set up a steam-driven plant in Paris in 1818, but this French branch was closed down in the 1860s when Calais had developed as a rival centre. The thread first used was cotton, but silk net was made in addition from 1824. See also *Bobbinet, Machine lace* (c), *Net, Illusion,* and *Spinning.*

Hedebo (Danish, heath-dwellers, referring to the area between Copenhagen and Roskilde). A combination of drawnwork and surface embroidery probably dating back to the fifteenth century. It was extensively worked by the peasants for hangings to decorate their homes, for sham towels and pillow cases, and traditionally for the linen wedding shirt given by the bride to the groom. It had no commercial value until the mid nineteenth century, when a revival occurred, and by 1900 instructions for making Hedebo had found their way into women's magazines. See *Danish lace.*

Hitch, half-hitch. The knot holding the thread around the head of the bobbin so that it will not unwind while the lace is being made.

Hole count. The mesh size of a machine net, measured by the number of meshes along two sides of a 1 inch (25 mm) square. For example, a 40 hole count could be made up of 20 meshes horizontally and 20 vertically, or 24 horizontally and 16 vertically. The horizontal count (across the warps) is always a times two multiple of the number of bobbins per inch width of the machine, i.e. of the gauge. The vertical count (up the warps) can be varied as required by adjusting the tension. The numerical relationship of horizontal to vertical count determines the shape of the mesh, though this is to some extent adjusted when the net is stretched out during the finishing process.

Hollie point, holy point. A form of needlepoint lace, made c 1690 to 1810. It is found only on baby clothes and, rarely, associated garments such as a nurse's cuffs or apron. The pinprick designs, made by spaced buttonhole stitches, show a religious influence in lilies of the annunciation, the dove of peace, the crown of glory, the tree of life and the star of Bethlehem (Fig. 43a). Even the fashionably dressed shepherd and shepherdess on a dated (1739) piece may be regarded as symbolic. Another piece, dated 1744, reads 'May the boy for whom this cap is designed live to be an honour to his parents, friends and country'.

Collars of 'hollie work' appear in the inventories of Mary Queen of Scots (1542-87), but it is unlikely that they refer to the same technique. It probably means simply work done by nuns, i.e. holy work, which at that time would have been a cutwork or other embroidered lace. In 1640 another inventory lists 'two pairs of Holland sheets, whereof one pair sewed with hollie work'. Again, the identity of this work is scarcely likely to be hollie point as we know it: it was far too slow a process, as well as being in larger pieces not particularly decorative – its beauty lies in the minuteness of its portrayals. Palliser calls her illustrations of hollie point 'needle-made Brussels', but this lace is generally regarded as being exclusively English.

Honeycomb. (a) A bobbin-made ground or filling, e.g. in Bucks. (b) A machine net produced in 1832 by Freeman and in 1835 by Crofts. Though more like point de Paris (qv) it was called 'honeycomb net' and was used as a basis for needlerun embroidery on fichus, shawls or pelerine collars. A similar mesh, known as 'Ariston', was on show in four grades at the *Daily Mail* Exhibition of Lace in 1908.

Honiton. (a) A town in East Devon which has been an important lace-making centre since the seventeenth century. In 1697 it had 1,340 lacemakers compared with 326 in Beer and Seaton.
(b) A non-continuous bobbin lace of the nineteenth and twentieth centuries. At its best, as in Queen Victoria's wedding lace made in 1839 (see *Earnings* and Fig. 46b), and in the productions of Tucker, Treadwin and Fowler, it is superb; at its worst it earns John Jacoby's scathing dismissal of it as 'a melancholy soup'. It has typical fillings such as diamond, toad in the hole, blossom, and swing and a pin; and typical design units called bullock's hearts, turkey tails, Devon rose, pear border, beetle-head sprigs and orange blossom. The rural flavour is unmistakable, but in poorer specimens the ground is overgrown with unidentifiable weeds and plagued with 'snails'. In the later

nineteenth century, when Brussels duchesse and point de gaze were pre-eminently successful, Honiton tried to capture a little of the market by copying Brussels designs.

(c) A tape lace was made at Branscombe, 10 miles south of Honiton, from about 1860. Unfortunately the machine braid used for it was called 'Honiton braid', and thus the term 'Honiton lace' came, especially in America, to be extended to all tape (renaissance) laces, to the exclusion of the 'real' Honiton bobbin lace.

(d) The Levers machine produced some deceptive imitations of both black and white Honiton.

As with other English laces, indisputable evidence for the early existence of Honiton lace is bewilderingly scarce, though apocryphal romances abound:

(i) Church records or parish registers show that in 1617 James Rodge, bone-lace seller of Honiton, was rich enough to leave a bequest to the poor. He is said to have brought back lace designs from Brussels, for local use. The burying of many male and female lacemakers is recorded between 1654 and 1692. In 1756 and 1767 severe fires destroyed a great deal of the town, including no doubt most of the lace and its history.

(ii) Literary references to Honiton are found in the writings of Thomas Fuller (qv), c 1662; of Westcote, c 1630, who refers to the bone lace of Honiton as 'a pretty toy now greatly in request'; of Cosimo de Medici, 1669; of Celia Fiennes (qv), 1698; of Dr J. Yonge, who, describing the celebrations of the coronation of Queen Anne in 1702, refers to 'bone lace, the great manufacture'; and of Daniel Defoe, who in his travels of 1724 comments on 'the valuable manufactures of lace for which the inhabitants of Devon have long been conspicuous'.

(iii) Social history: in 1698 the lace manufactures of Devon were regarded as second only to the wool trade, and Devon lace cost £6 a yard. However they were still in fear of foreign imports, and a petition was sent to Parliament for continued protection against Flemish lace.

(iv) Lack of evidence: the general consensus is that a lot of lace was made around Honiton, and that it was in general of good quality. What is lacking is any description of its design or technique, any portrait known to show it, or any wardrobe account which commissioned it.

(v) Its resemblance to Flemish lace of the eighteenth-century point d'Angleterre type seems generally well established, and it is very likely that both Flemish and French refugees settled in Devon at many times between the Duke of Alva's persecutions of 1598, which drove out Protestants, and the French Revolution of 1789, which drove out lacemakers. See *Trolly*.

(vi) Effigies: two effigies in the Honiton area show lace which was almost certainly imported. In Exeter Cathedral, Lady Doddridge (1614) wears punto in aria, or possibly Genoese plaited lace (Fig. 9a). In Colyton church, Lady Elizabeth Pole (1623) wears a triple-tier falling collar, a cap and cuffs, all edged with a scalloped lace similar to seventeenth-century Flemish (Fig. 11). There is no reason to assume that the lace which they, or any other local effigies, wear was made in Devon. The difficulty of accurate attribution is also demonstrated by a collar preserved at the Art Institute of Chicago (Fig. 45).

Because Honiton is a non-continuous lace, 'sewings' have to be taken (Fig. 24c). This involves the drawing of a thread through the fine pinholes bordering the sprigs, so that pairs of bobbins can be attached, which will then be used to work the fillings of the design, and in some cases to make the ground. Honiton bobbins therefore have to be slender and spindle-shaped and are often polished with beeswax to make them glide more smoothly. They do not have any encumbrances such as spangles. See also *Devon lace*.

Horsehair, le crin. In needlepoint laces the constructing of the tiny loops or picots within the fillings or around the motifs or cordonnet is made easier by supporting the thread over a horsehair, which can be withdrawn when the picot is completed. It also helps to keep the picots of even size. Black hair is most often used as it shows up clearly against the thread. In coarser nineteenth-century Alençon laces, white horsehair was used to support the larger picots of the cordonnet and was left in the lace, though its sharply cut ends tended to tear the reseau when the lace was folded. Jourdain says that 'Horsehair was introduced to give firmness and consistency to the cordonnet in the latter period of Louis XV and during the reign of Louis XVI', i.e. c 1760-89. However, the unravelling of broken fragments of cordonnets reveals only a slight padding of some other fibre such as flax, cotton or even wool, and it seems certain that horsehair was never used to raise the cordonnet, only to support its picots.

Hours of work. For the individual professional lacemaker, either directly employed or paid by the piece, the hours of work were always long – twelve, fourteen or sixteen a day. The making of lace by hand is extremely slow, and the finer the thread the slower the work. A few figures for the total time needed to complete individual pieces are given below: (i) Honiton guipure flounce, 5 yards (4.57 m) long, Great Exhibition 1851: 40 women, 8 months, or about 27 years for one person; (ii) a dress of Alençon needlepoint, Paris Exhibition 1855: 36 women, 18 months, cost £2,800; (iii) a Bucks stole worked in three strips, later invisibly joined, late nineteenth century, bought by Queen Victoria: 3 women, 18 weeks; (iv) Alençon flounces for a dress, Paris Exhibition of 1867: 40 women, 7 years, cost £3,400; (v) Valenciennes flouncing, 10 inches (254 mm) deep, Paris Exhibition 1867: 60 hours for ⅓ inch (8.5 mm), i.e. 2 years per metre, cost £80 a metre.

Long hours were not unique to lace. Dressmakers in 1843 worked from 8.30 a.m. to 11 p.m. in winter, and 8 a.m. to midnight in summer, with a total of forty-five minutes a day for meals.

Huguenots. A name first used for French Protestants c 1550. It persisted into the nineteenth century. See *Refugees.*

Hungary. An East European country known for its production of peasant embroideries and for its bobbin laces, which, like those of Russia, Czechoslovakia and Austria, often incorporate colour and spread like an underwater pageant of coiled sea shells and arboraceous worms over a ground of rippled sand. (Fig. 27b.)

Illusion. An almost invisibly fine silk net appearing like a shimmering mist around the head and shoulders. It was produced on a bobbinet machine at Lyons in 1828 and, in its plain, slightly stiffened form, was very popular. 'Tulle illusion' was revived in the 1940s on Heathcoat's machine at Tiverton and specially made for the royal weddings of Queen Elizabeth II (1947), Princess Anne (1973) and the Princess of Wales (1981) (Fig. 33). See also *Machine* (c) and *Net.*

Imitation laces. (Fig. 37.) A general term for laces which copy the appearance of other laces, using a different technique. In commercial laces, the motive is to cut down time and therefore cost. In craft laces, the motive is to recreate the designs of several centuries ago in a manner geared to the skilled amateur rather than to the professional lacemakers.
(a) The earliest imitations might be regarded as sixteenth-century: the bobbin lace copies of the needlepoint punto in arias.
(b) Mezzo punto, or mixed lace, was a copy of flat needlepoint, using narrow woven tapes or braids to make the shape of the design. The fillings and the brides were then worked in buttonhole stitch. Mezzo punto was made in Italy in the seventeenth century and was revived in northern Europe and in America in the second half of the nineteenth century, under the name 'point lace', from its original inspiration. The term is open to misinterpretation, and the alternative names of tape, braid or renaissance lace are to be preferred.
(c) Intagliatela is basically a seventeenth-century imitation of Venetian gros point using a woven linen as a substitute for the toilé. The design is embroidered in outline, sometimes with a raised cordonnet, which may be edged with gold thread. Minute drawnwork fillings replace the original fancy buttonhole stitchings, and when the excess material is cut away, leaving the bold flowers linked by brides, the general appearance has all the rich exuberance of the raised-point original. Intagliatela has technical similarities to some sixteenth-century cutwork and to the nineteenth-century Carrickmacross guipure and Richelieu work, which copied it. It was also copied c 1900 by the Schiffli machine.

(d) Cording was a nineteenth- and twentieth-century method of copying reticellas and the closely knotted Italian work known as puncetto. The more tedious stitches were replaced by the binding around of linking bars as in *Gimp* (b) except that the binding thread was linen around a flax or cotton core. The solid part, or toilé, was formed by closely textured darning. Although cording was done by hand the finished product has, rather confusingly, the appearance of chemical lace (see *Swiss* (c)).

(e) Crochet copied the appearance of Venetian rose point and coralline; embroidered nets that of Brussels bobbin and needlepoint appliqués and of Bucks bobbin laces.

(f) Patterned machine laces imitated everything, up to the art nouveau period, when they developed original designs of their own (Fig. 17c).

(g) Trompes l'oeil: pierced paperwork, line etchings or white gouache might imitate the design of a lace so closely that at a glance, or from a distance, they would appear as such. This technique is especially common on fan leaves (Fig. 38a).

(h) Copies of old laces using the same technique are not included in this definition, for example Alençon made at Burano, Argentan at Bayeux, punto in aria at Bologna, and so forth. These are late nineteenth-century tours de force taking just as long as their prototypes – allowing for an increase in the thickness of the thread – and of equivalent virtuosity.

Import restrictions. Their main function over the centuries, apart from providing revenue and saving the country from bankruptcy, was to protect home industry. In the time of Henry VII England was largely an exporter, her population of less than four million was self-supporting, her wool trade extremely flourishing: all she could import in exchange were luxuries such as silks, velvets, precious metal braids and, later, laces. As early as the 1480s it was necessary for an importation Act to be passed to prevent short measure (e.g. 12 ounces of gold or flax being palmed off as 1 pound) or cheating (a top layer of precious metal 'lace' covering layers of inferior quality). In 1504 all foreign 'lace' was prohibited. Queen Elizabeth I (reigned 1558-1603), though she was strongly against extravagance in the people and issued sumptuary edicts sternly suppressing it on pain of public whipping, made an exception of herself and her court.

Contemporary edicts and import restrictions in France were equally ineffective. There were ten between 1549 and 1583, but the courtiers continued to carry 'their mills, their lands, their woods, their meadows and their income' on their bodies in a hazardous investment of ornament: everything was mortgaged for sartorial splendour. In 1594, 1600, 1601 and 1606 Henri IV repeated the prohibitions and even tried the unprecedented – and unsuccessful – experiment of dressing simply himself. The main effect of these and other import restrictions was an increase in smuggling.

In 1635, in England, the home manufacturers were 'brought to great want and necessity, occasioned by the excessive importation of these foreign wares', and Charles I placed restrictions on the import of cutworks, bone lace and similar items. In 1662 Charles II passed an Act prohibiting bone lace and cutworks to protect the home industry 'made by many poor children'. However, Flanders still provided the best bobbin lace, and Venetian gros point was much prized, so in the same year Charles granted a licence to a merchant, John Irwin, to import freely all the lace required for the dressing of the royal family: his excuse was that they would serve as patterns for English manufacturers to copy.

In 1698 William III restricted the importation of bone lace, loom lace, needlework point and cutwork from Flanders, with a penalty for smuggling of 20 shilling a yard and forfeiture. However, this was repealed in the following year, since Flanders threatened to close the export market for English wool. In 1778 the Irish Parliament passed an Act prohibiting the import of English and other foreign goods, since Ireland's own lace manufactures, especially those of the 'famishing children' of the Dublin workhouse, were adequate for its needs.

To show that lace was not uniquely discriminated against, records of 1784, 1787 and 1789 list candles, bricks, felt hats, horses, silk handkerchiefs, linen, ribbons and gauze as having duties levied against them, not to mention human hair for wigs, on which the duty of 2 shillings to the pound amounted to a customs total of £1,640 in 1788.

By 1860 Queen Victoria had removed all duties on foreign lace since the competition to English hand-made lace from English machines was much more serious than that from importations. See *Sumptuary edicts.*

Increase widths. A term used in bobbin lacemaking when it is necessary to work the pattern on a larger scale.

Indian lace. Lacemaking was introduced into India by European missionaries in the nineteenth and twentieth centuries. Torchon laces were made and marketed at Travancore and in Sri Lanka; a simplified Irish crochet in white or ecru mercerised cotton was used for sets of table mats; and needlerun patterns on net for baby gowns and handkerchief borders were made in convents. A form of white embroidery with drawnwork, sometimes known as Lucknow or Delhi lace, was made into vestees and christening gowns: superficially like a coarse Ayrshire, it was angular and undetailed and often incorporated botehs, elephants and tropical palms. Some flat, rather coarse needlepoint is still made in Indo-China. Its manufacture is said to have been introduced by the French in the 1920s and is centred at Tonkin.

Indes, Broderie des. See *Breton lace.*

Industrial revolution. The general name given to a series of technical inventions of the eighteenth century which revolutionised the textile and other industries by speeding up production and reducing manpower. It is regarded as having begun in 1733 with John Kay's Flying Shuttle, which made easier and faster weaving possible. Both this and James Hargreaves's Spinning Jenny of 1764, by means of which one person could spin a number of threads instead of only one thread as on the spinning wheel, could be used at home. So could the Stocking Frame, the Warp Frame and Heathcoat's Old Loughborough (1809). But with the invention of Cartwright's Power Loom in 1785 centres of industry began to spring up, and the factory-governed life of the towns gradually split apart from rural England with its waning cottage industries.

Inishmacsaint (County Fermanagh). Fine Irish imitations of Venetian and Spanish-type needlepoints began here c 1865, using the local flax thread. In 1869 substantial orders were obtained for it, which lasted for several years. It was still made to some extent in the early twentieth century, when a length was used to tie a small bouquet of flowers for Queen Alexandra, and when simplified instructions for making it were included in a book published by *The Girl's Own Paper and Woman's Magazine*.

Inner pearl. Ornamental loops, pearls or picots in Honiton lace, worked round the central cavity of a motif. See *Stitches*.

Insertion. A length of lace in which the two edges are straight and parallel to each other. It is used to join two pieces of material together so that neither of its borders hangs free. Cf *Galon*.

Intagliatela. See *Imitation laces* (c).

Iphigène. A gauzy neo-classical drapery which covered the head and fell forwards over the face, fashionable in the 1810s, and named after Iphigenia, a heroine of Greek legend. See *Fashion*.

Ipswich (Massachusetts). (a) A centre for bobbin lacemaking at the end of the eighteenth century. Surviving examples are of fairly coarse continuous laces of white thread, or of black silk, of no particularly distinctive design, but with some similarity to the point de Paris laces of France, or to the black Erzegebirge laces of Saxony. Production ended in the 1820s.
(b) Twist net of the Heathcoat type was made on bobbinet machines smuggled in from England. The industry was dependent on good imported thread, and the two companies (Boston and Ipswich Lace Co, and New England Lace Co), penalised by a heavy import tax imposed by Great Britain, survived only a few years (1824-7, 1827-33).

Irish lace. Eighteenth-century references include the records of the Dublin Society, which c 1739 was offering prizes for Irish work, including lace, and a little later prizes for 'cheyne' lace (1755) and for tambour work (1760) – possibly the same thing.

Jonathan Swift had campaigned in 1721 for the Irish to use goods of their own manufacture and so save themselves the great expense of importations, for example £90,000 on silk and £30,000 on cotton and linen materials. He continued: 'What the price of the lace amounts to is not easy to be collected from the Custom-house book, being a kind of goods that, taking up little room, is easily run (smuggled); but, considering the prodigious price of a woman's head-dress at ten, twelve, twenty pounds a yard, it must be very great.'

After the 1770s there is no record of Irish lace except for an Act of 1778 prohibiting the importation of foreign laces, including English, into Ireland (see *Import restrictions*), and no lace appears to have survived from that early flowering. The Irish became anarchic, inspired perhaps by the French Revolution. A rebellion broke out in 1798, and during the next few years a great deal of eighteenth-century achievement was destroyed.

In the nineteenth century the following types of lace are associated with Ireland:

(a) Carrickmacross. Two forms are known: a muslin appliqué on machine net, and a muslin guipure. They began c 1820 and are thought to have been inspired by intagliatela.

(b) Limerick tambour: a chain-stitch embroidery on net which began commercially in 1829.

(c) Limerick run (needlerun) came from Nottingham and was at first made for the upper end of the market, but after the 1840s it aimed at a wider public.

(d) Youghal: a flat needlepoint lace which began in a County Cork convent in the 1840s. A lace school for teaching it was opened in 1852.

(e) Irish crochet was not heard of before the 1840s, but the distress of the famine years accelerated and brought to the fore as commercial products a number of occupations which had been no more than a pastime until then. Cork in the south and Clones (County Monaghan) in the north were the main centres, but production was soon widespread, and by the late 1860s 12,000 women were employed in and around Cork alone. In the 1930s a good deal of inferior Irish crochet was made in China and used to trim underwear, children's dresses and jabots. The width, and price, were measured not only in inches but by the number of 'beans', the little kidney-shaped arcs around the roses.

(f) Some slightly raised needlepoints called Inishmacsaint were made, and, according to Cole, some bobbin laces in imitation of Honiton.

Tatting proliferated, in 1847, for famine relief and raised £5,000. The tiered rose petals, the shamrock and the harp frequently figure in Irish lace, perhaps with an eye to the tourist. For more detail, see the various heads.

Isabeau, Isabelle. A colour of lace. See *Bleaching*.

Isle of Wight lace. An embroidered net, possibly of ornate tambour work in thick thread. It was for a time under the patronage of Queen Victoria, who loved the island. She had a dress and train of Newport lace made for the Princess Royal in 1856, and several tippets for her other daughters. Her favourite pattern was said to be roses in the Mechlin style. The industry, never very large, did not survive her death. (Fig. 29b.)

Italian laces. The famous seventeenth-century centres were Venice, Genoa and Milan, and here professional lacemakers produced the magnificent raised and flat needlepoints, the costly gold and silver braids and the closely textured bobbin masterpieces. More run-of-the-mill laces, mainly openwork embroideries and peasant bobbins, were made throughout Italy for home use up to the 1950s. The main types of Italian laces are listed below, and details are given under their separate heads:
(a) Venetian needlepoints, fl 1620-1710.
(b) Genoese, including bobbin imitations of punto in aria and bobbin collar laces, precious metal laces and macramé. Sixteenth and seventeenth centuries. (Fig. 8 and 9.)
(c) Milanese bobbin, seventeenth to mid eighteenth century. After that it became nondescript. (Fig. 25.)
(d) Sicilian peasant laces, bobbin and filet, seventeenth to nineteenth centuries.
(e) Italian rosaline (qv), twentieth-century bobbin lace.
(f) Embroidered laces of no precise location and made through all the ages, including drawnwork, filet and buratto. The use of hand-spun and hand-woven linens makes accurate dating almost impossible.
(g) Knotted lace: puncetto (sixteenth to twentieth centuries); and imitation puncetto made by cording (nineteenth and twentieth centuries). See *Groppo*.
(h) Point de Milan (see *Mezzo punto* (d)) and point de Venise (see *Venetian lace* (h)) were twentieth-century laces made in Belgium.

Ivory stitch. See *Avorio*.

Jabot. A decorative frill worn at the base of the throat, fastened in place by a pin or by a narrow band passing around the back of the neck. It was worn by men from c 1725, replacing the cravat, which was basically a lace-ended linen scarf. Jabots for women were fashionable in the 1920s and 1930s as a foam of 'real' lace at the neck of a silk evening jacket.

Jacquard, Joseph (1752-1834). A Frenchman who invented a preselection principle for the patterning of woven materials. His invention consisted of a series of punched cards linked to steel bars which, for each row of the material as it was made, controlled the warp threads. The fixed sequence of the cards guaranteed identical reproduction for every repeat of the design. The technique was first applied to the patterning of silks at Lyons in 1801, and in 1834 fine copies of black Chantilly lace were produced. By 1851 patterned machine laces were well established. There were several experimental prototypes of the Jacquard system, such as Bouchon's perforated paper of 1725 and Falcon's Pattern-weaving Loom of 1728, but Jacquard's was the first to dispense with the need for a drawboy. One card was required for each row, or course, of the design and, depending on its complexity, the number of cards needed could vary from a dozen to several thousand. The Jacquard was also applied to lace-embroidery machines such as the Schiffli. See *Calais, Leavers, Lyons.* (Fig. 32 b.)

Javelle, eau de; Javel water. A solution of sodium hypochlorite, used as a bleach. It was invented by Berthollet in 1785 and was first manufactured in the village of Javel, on the outskirts of Paris. By 1789 Javel water was being used for the whitening of cotton and flax fibres in place of the protracted and unreliable sun bleaching. See *Bleaching.*

Jean, point de. A sixteenth-century term for Genoese lace.

Jingles. See *Gingles.*

Joanna the Mad (1479-1555). See *Lacis, Samplers.*

Jours, ajours. See *Fillings.* The term is sometimes used to mean, imprecisely, openwork and thus to include the tiny decorative holes like pinpricks in the solid part of a bobbin or needle-made design. These are more correctly called 'portes' since they do not fill a space but create one.

Kat stitch. See *Reseau.*

Kerchief (French, couvre-chef, cover-head). Hence, a square of cambric used as a head scarf. See *Fichu.*

Kitty Fisher's eye. The large bottom bead of an East Midlands spangle, when it was made of greyish glass indented into shallow saucers like eye sockets. These were filled with white paint, and a centre spot of blue was added, to give the appearance of the white and iris of an eye. Kitty Fisher was a well known actress who died in 1767. The centre spot was sometimes red instead of blue.

Knitted lace. The craft of knitting, using a series of loops on one or more needles and a continuous length of thread, may date from the twelfth century, but at what point openwork patterns were introduced, which would allow it to be considered a form of lace, is uncertain. Fourteenth-century paintings show ladies knitting, and Mary Queen of Scots is recorded as having knitted cuffs, collars and nightcaps for Queen Elizabeth I, as well as coifs of 'gold reseille'. A widespread occupation of knitting is recorded by Fiennes, in East Anglia, c 1698. In 1767 in Ireland prizes were offered to workhouse children by the Dublin Society for 'thread laces made with knitting needles'. Baby caps of that period were often minutely knitted, made of flax thread and light as down. One is said to have been worn by Horatio Nelson (born 1758) (Fig. 29a). During the nineteenth century knitting revived, along with other crafts, and many lacy forms were produced, with such patterns as horseshoe, pine tree, open star and wave. The finest of all were the Shetland shawls (see *Scottish lace*) made of singled lamb's wool, and worked on number 18, or finer, needles so that each 5 foot (1.5 m) row took an hour to complete. When finished, they could be passed like springy gossamer through a wedding ring.

Other wispy knitting, in the Azores, used the fibres from the century plant (see *Aloe*). More tourist-orientated than practical, it produced innumerable small mats a few inches across of many different designs.

Machine knitting, on the Stocking Frame, dates from the sixteenth century, and on the Warp Frame from the late eighteenth. Their techniques are sometimes referred to as weft knitting and warp knitting, the loops progressing in the first case horizontally, and in the second vertically (Fig. 30). See also *Chain stitch*.

Knotted lace. (Figs. 40, 41.) (a) Lace trimmings made in the countries along the eastern and southern sides of the Mediterranean, and variously known as Smyrna (Turkey), Armenian (Turkey, now USSR) and Rodi. They were also made, until recently, in Syria, Palestine and North Africa. (b) Bebilla is associated with Cyprus, but also with the Greek and Turkish mainland. (c) Puncetto was made in north Italy. (d) Punto a groppo (see *Groppo*) is a name given to the ancestral form of the sixteenth and seventeenth centuries, said to have originated in Ragusa.

(a) to (d) were probably made with a needle and a short length of thread. (e) Filet and netting use a gauge and shuttle (sometimes called a needle, but the thread is wound round it instead of being threaded through it). (f) Macramé is knotted by hand, though bobbins may be used to make manipulation easier. (g) Tatting is made with a tatting shuttle, using a lark's head knot.

Lace. (a) A textile patterned with holes which are created by the manipulation of threads. This definition can be reworded in many ways, but the four essential features are: that to be called lace the fabric must be made of *threads,* it must have *holes* which form an essential part of the *design,* and which are deliberately made by *special movements* of the threads. The precise nature of the special movements, i.e. the technique, though of prime importance in the classification or identifying of laces, is not a vital part of the definition itself.

These four main criteria together include all the main groups: embroidered, needlepoint, bobbin, and the large variety of craft and imitation, as well as machine, laces. At the same time they exclude:

(i) Textiles without holes, such as surface embroidery, woven materials and braids.

(ii) Textiles with accidental holes, where threads have not been deliberately manipulated to create them, e.g. moth-eaten, burnt or ripped holes.

(iii) Textiles in which the relation of holes to design is not an essential one, i.e. the holes are introduced solely for artistic effect, to create a dramatic nuance, as in some modern tapestries.

(iv) Textiles in which the holes, though deliberately created by the manipulation of threads, do not form a pattern or design, i.e. they are completely plain and of uniform openness. This is a controversial field since design, like beauty, is likely to be in the eye of the beholder, i.e. to be subjective. In traditional laces, there have always been more dense and less dense areas, which usually take the form of closely worked motifs separated by open spaces in which holes are enclosed by a reseau or by a latticework of brides. Undecorated machine nets are then not lace; neither is the plain droschel, waiting for its applied decoration ... But here the argument begins: some experimentalists claim that completely undecorated holey textiles, if made by traditional techniques, should still be called lace. By this point of view gigantic nets, wall-hangings and free-standing or free-swinging thread sculptures, with no areas of varying density, are still decorative in themselves because of their shape and the space which they occupy, being often three-dimensional, curiously twisted and patterned by shadows. A separate category, e.g. sculptural lace, is obviously needed to contain them.

(v) Non-textiles, i.e. patterned holey structures without threads (see

Fibres). Examples are ornamental ironwork, filigree, pressed and cut ivory, and pierced paperwork often forming a trompe l'oeil of lace as in paper doyleys and occasional fan leaves (Fig. 38a). The piercing of woven material so heavily starched that it has the texture of glazed paper is also not lace since the holes are not made by the manipulation of threads.

(vi) Points of view. Some people would exclude from the definition laces made with coloured threads, for example all East European (Slavic) laces; others would exclude buratto (though not filet) because it is worked on a woven ground. There is certainly room in the definition, as in the whole field of lace, for some difference of opinion. But the latitude is limited: the object of a definition is that other people shall understand what we are talking about. Without this agreement communication becomes meaningless.

(b) Cords or tapes for tying things up or together, for example shoe or boot laces, laces uniting doublet and hose in the fourteenth to early seventeenth centuries, and the laces of stays or corsets. In the sixteenth and seventeenth centuries corsets of wood, leather or steel were worn by both men and women: those who did not wear them, such as certain Venetian ladies, were said not to 'lace' themselves at all (see *Underwear*).

(c) Braids, stitched flat on the surface of the material, were often called laces. As they did, technically, merge into true laces, by becoming holey instead of solid, it is almost impossible to distinguish between them in wills, inventories and wardrobe accounts, unless they are additionally qualified.

Lace bark. A brown gauzy net obtained from a Jamaican tree, *Lagetta lintearia.* Lace bark represents the bast fibres of the tree and so is precisely the same as the flax fibres which are extracted for the manufacture of linen, except that whereas the flax fibres are formed in straight lines, those of *Lagetta* separate and rejoin to form a natural mesh, an arrangement characteristic of tree-ferns. Charles II was presented with a cravat and ruffles of lace bark by a governor of Jamaica; and at the Great Exhibition of 1851 a lace bark dress was presented to Queen Victoria. (Fig. 39a and b.)

Lace Curtain machine. See *Machine lace* (f).

Lace lamps. These were glass lamps about 9-12 inches (229-305 mm) high, intended to provide light for several workers at a time. The open bulbous top was filled with vegetable oil and fitted with a wick. The light from this rayed out in all directions through three or four spherical globes filled with water that were placed around it. These refracted the light and concentrated the beams on the lacemakers' parchments so that they could see clearly the movements of the threads and where to place the pins. Globes of this kind are recorded as far back as the 1770s. They were filled where possible with snow water or rain water, to obtain a near-distilled particle-free liquid which would not cast shadows from its own impurities. Quite frequently a candle with an adjustable nozzle was used instead of a lamp. (Fig. 24b.)

Lacemakers. Our information about this largely anonymous body depends mostly on the evidence of travellers and contemporary writers: (a) Professional lacemakers:

(i) Nuns. The Reformation of the sixteenth century and the nineteenth-century disestablishment of the Spanish convents disclosed some superb embroidered and needlepoint laces, made by nuns (see *Alençon, Spanish lace*). Mrs Forrester in *Cranford* expresses the hope that her beloved lace 'made by nuns abroad' and which 'cannot be got now for either love or money' may be obtainable again following the Catholic Emancipation Bill of 1829. In 1756 the town of Mechlin was 'full of convents; Mechlin lace is all made there' but 'they talk of giving up the trade as the English upon whom they depended have taken to the wearing of French blondes'. In the strongly anti-Catholic England of the eighteenth century the money spent on foreign laces (£2 million c 1760) was bitterly resented: 'As lace in particular is the manufacture of nuns our British ladies may as well endow monasteries as wear Flanders lace, for these Popish nuns are maintained by Protestant contributions.' The Presentation Convent at Youghal started a needlepoint lace manufacture soon after the potato famine of 1846 (see *Irish lace* (d) and *Youghal*). About 1907, Belgian nuns were blamed for undercutting the prices of English lace since they employed children who worked unpaid in return for their training in lacemaking: in Bruges and Ostend lace could be bought for 10 francs which had taken a full two weeks to make working twelve hours a day. Today, Argentan lace is made only at that town's Abbaye Notre Dame.

(ii) The cloistered seclusion and freedom from distraction of the convents extended also to the béguinages. These, peculiar to Belgium and French Flanders, were a sort of commune for pious women and also for single ladies of the upper classes. Mechlin lace is recorded from béguinages in 1681, Antwerp in 1698, and Brussels in 1756. The Ghent béguinage incorporated a lace school and in 1756 employed nearly 5,000 women. In the late nineteenth century Valenciennes lace was made at béguinages in west Flanders, for example at Ypres.

(iii) Similar set-ups, perhaps more commercially orientated, must also have existed in Venice, producing with equivalent diligence the six thousand stitches to the square inch of the Venetian gros points. In France from c 1708 to 1780 the family Guyard employed 1,200 women, making Argentan. These included many names of noble families, and no doubt poor people too, spending their entire lives at the work.

(iv) In both France and Spain men were employed to make the highly profitable gold and silver laces.

(b) Non-professional lacemakers:

(i) The rich: lacemaking was a popular pastime for court ladies, who were able to spend many hours a day at it and between whiles did not have to dirty or roughen their hands with other work. Familiar examples are filet and knitting by Catherine of Medici and Mary Queen of Scots; needlepoint lace, cf Le Paultre's engraving of 1676 (Fig. 21a); and the tatting or knotting of Marie Antoinette.

(ii) The poor: as early as 1596 the 'pore children' of Bedfordshire were promised a weekly wage to 'worke bone lace'. In 1662 Thomas Fuller writes of bone lace in England: 'Hereby many children, who otherwise would be burthensome to the Parish, prove beneficial to their parents: Yea many lame in their limbs, and impotent in their arms, if able in their fingers, gain a lively-hood thereby.' About 1740 it was said: 'some ladies now squander away all their money in fine lace because it sets a great many poor people to work.' In 1778 lace was being made by the 'famishing children of the Dublin workhouse' (see *Import restrictions*).

(iii) Cottagers: references to lacemakers sitting in their cottage doorways to catch the best of the light abound from the time of Shakespeare, through the travellers of the seventeenth and eighteenth centuries (see *Honiton*), to Cowper in 1782; and there are also the chroniclers and the commissions reporting on rural and urban occupations. Much English lace and many continental laces were produced by cottagers, but only bobbin or craft laces of the speedier kind could be so made: finer bobbins, needlepoints and embroidered laces would suffer too much from hands roughened by household chores.

Skilful and painstaking as the lacemakers must have been, the real creative artistry of the lace must have lain with the designers, some of whom were very eminent people (see *Design* and *Point de France*).

Lace men, merchants. 'Lace men' was a general term for wholesalers and retailers in the lace trade. In the sixteenth century pedlars carried laces from door to door. They achieved an established status in 1699 and in 1705-6 were grouping themselves with 'mercers, woollen drapers and milliners' to protest at the 'grieving for foreign princes' which robbed them of their livelihood: lace was not permitted to be worn during the period of mourning. By 1767, lace merchants might carry with them as much as £1,000 of stock. They are said to have been unscrupulous with cottagers, handing back any lace that was even one inch short of the amount asked for, and practising a monopoly system whereby if the maker sold any of her lace to a rival buyer, no more work would be given to her. There were lace shops in Paternoster Row, London, by the second half of the seventeenth century, and in Covent Garden by 1725.

Lace schools. These can be considered in three categories: commercial, charitable and revival.

(a) Commercial: needlework was always a favourite pastime of aristocratic ladies, and in the eighteenth century apprenticeships in lacemaking were much in vogue for their daughters, who were sent to France for 'finishing'. Workhouse children produced lace by which their cost to the parish could be defrayed. In spite of remarks on 'the sallow complexion, the weakly frame, and the general appearance of languour and debility of the operatives', they probably were better off than the children in textile factories, whose working hours were not cut down to seventy-two a week until 1819. In the village schools, groups of fourteen to twenty children, aged from five years upwards, worked twelve hours a day, five and a half days a week, and were paid 6d a day by the lace dealers. Neither exercise nor any other subjects were included in the curriculum, and the children were penalised if they lagged behind a certain speed. By 1860 machine laces were making even this cheap labour unprofitable; in 1870 general schooling was made compulsory; and by 1880 most of the lace schools of this kind had closed.

(b) Charitable lace schools were set up in distressed areas, e.g. at Burano (1874), in Ireland (crochet, tatting and Youghal, c 1847), and also in Naples, Sardinia and St Helena. Though at first dependent on subsidies and 'conscience orders', they eventually became commercially productive.

(c) Revival schools, e.g. at Le Puy (1859) and Bayeux (c 1860), were encouraged by the Empress Eugenie. In 1890 the Imperial Central School of Lacemaking was founded in Vienna, and the Vienna Workshop in 1903. In Bologna the Aemilia Ars Society flourished from 1898 into the 1920s. Though the laces made were for sale, the prime aim was to restore good quality and maintain as high a standard as possible. The present-day lace schools at Alençon, Le Puy and Bruges are similar, though less ambitious, and some of the traditional laces which they make are sold as souvenirs. School and evening classes, as part of a broader curriculum, were started in the early twentieth century by Mrs Fowler of Honiton and others.

Lace tells. Rhythmical chants used by groups of lacemakers to keep their work going at a steady pace, to relieve the monotony, and to distract their minds from the physical discomfort of sitting for long hours bent over a pillow. Details of the songs are given in Thomas Wright's *Romance of the Lace Pillow.*

Lace tokens. Coins bearing a value of a halfpenny or a farthing, minted by private tradesmen. They appear to have started when there was a general scarcity of small copper coinage and to have served as credit notes, since they bore the name of the person issuing them – 'payable at' – and could only be exchanged with him, i.e. they did not pass into general circulation. The earliest lace token dates from 1648. For the lacemaker the token could be almost as bad as the truck system, since it restricted the exchange value of the lace they had made.

Lacis (French, network, from the twelfth-century 'lacer', to lace). While 'network' is applicable to this type of lace it is hardly definitive, being a word of many meanings and including not only buratto and filet but also reseaux, machine nets, sprang and hand-made net stitch. There is thus a strong argument for using the French term, but even that is not unambiguous. Head, Thomas Wright, Nevill Jackson, Palliser and Powys regard 'lacis' and 'filet' as interchangeable terms, while Dillmont and Caplin distinguish filet as having a knotted ground and lacis a woven one, i.e. they equate lacis and buratto. Hungerford Pollen's distinction into filet lacis (knotted) and buratto lacis (woven) is probably the most lucid; and Lefebure, quoting from a dictionary of 1684, defines lacis as 'a thread (i.e. flax) or silk formed into a tissue of net or réseuil, the threads of which were knotted *or* interlaced the one with the other'. By this definition, lacis is a generic term including both the knotted-ground filet and the woven-ground buratto, i.e. lacis includes filet, but filet does not include lacis.

The two main types of stitch used to decorate both forms of lacis are described under *Filet.* The designs used from the fifteenth to early seventeenth centuries were geometric or religious or scenes of classical mythology, with basilisks, playful or vengeful cupids, unicorns, winged lions and other fabulous beasts (Fig. 17a). Lacis is known to have been made in Italy, Germany and the islands of Sicily, Sardinia and Crete. Here, coming perhaps under Middle Eastern influence, coloured silk threads – of rust, gold or green – were used, with very beautiful results.

An Exeter Cathedral inventory of 1327 lists three pieces of filatorium (network) used for throwing over the altar; an effigy in the cathedral, of Bishop Stafford (died 1398), wears a network collar. A fourteenth-century inventory of St Paul's, London, refers to knotted net (filo nodato). Jourdain quotes a painting of 1488, in Bologna, where the square openings of the dresses of the three ladies are filled with a border of lacis (see *Bavaro*). The poet Skelton (1460-1529) makes the earliest known reference to both samplers and lacis in one line, referring to a noble lady's pastime: 'The saumpler to sew on, the lacis to embraid'. These early dates help to confirm the priority of embroidered laces over any other form. A sampler of netting occurs in an inventory of the Spanish Joanna the Mad in 1509 (see *Samplers* (a)). The early pattern books (Schönsperger 1523, Quentell 1527, Vavassore 1530, and others), although explicitly for drawnwork, could be adapted for lacis, using the counted mesh technique. The popularity of Vinciolo's book – for cutwork, counted threadwork and darned netting – in the French court is shown by its being reprinted many times between 1587 and 1612; and his second work had six editions between 1594 and 1613.

Lama lace. A woollen machine lace whimsically named after the south American quadruped, which had soft lustrous 12-inch (305 mm) long hair. Peruvian alpaca had been introduced into England in 1836 and woven into cloth. 'Lama' lace, using mohair was produced c 1850 by R. Birkin, an inventive Nottingham manufacturer; and in the 1850s and 1860s convincing copies of Chantilly shawls and capes in white and black 'lama' were being made on the Pusher machine. The outlining thread was run in and the picot attached by hand after the fabric had left the loom.

Lappets, streamers, pinners, tabs, barbes. (a) Paired streamers of lace attached to the back of the head, and obligatory for court wear from c 1660 to well into the nineteenth century. They could be looped up and fixed with a diamond pin for informal occasions, but they had to be hanging for court, as the permitted length was determined by protocol (see *Veils*). Some 6 foot (1.8 m) long lappets of Argentan (Fig. 15b) are puzzling: it is possible that such extreme lengths were always pinned up, or perhaps that they depended from an immensely high plume of ostrich feathers, as shown in an engraving by Heideloff in his *Gallery of Fashion*, 1798. In the late seventeenth and early eighteenth centuries, the lappets were associated with a head-sute comprising a semicircular cap-crown and a huge fontange inset with jewellery and flowers, which became as grotesquely exaggerated as the ruffs called millstones, the piled-up mountains of hair called têtes de mouton (sheep's heads) or the later tunnelled-out poke bonnets and parachute-like crinolines.

Lappets, and the quantities of matching lace which accompanied them, were very expensive. In 1760 a head-sute might cost £200. See *Head* and *Irish lace*. They were so highly prized that ladies wore them to the grave: Ann Oldfield, actress, in 1730 lay in her coffin in 'a fine

Brussels head, a Holland (linen) shift with a tucker and double ruffles, and a pair of new kid gloves'. See *Burial in lace.*
(b) In the nineteenth century 'lappet' also referred to a long tie, made in one piece, but otherwise the same shape as the eighteenth-century ones.
(c) 'Lappet' was also used for the short ear pieces attached to a fall cap. (Fig. 44c.)

Lappet lace. See *Loom.*

Lea. See *Count.*

Leader, worker, weaver, runner (French = voyageur). The bobbins which are actively moved during the lacemaking and carry the threads in and out of the passives or downrights. These latter act as the warp threads of a loom, while the leaders act as wefts.

Leadworks, spots, dots, plaits, tallies (Bucks), **cutwork** (Devon), **point d'esprit** (French). As well as being synonyms, most of these words have a double meaning: (a) 'plaits' also refers to ordinary plaiting as in Genoese, Valenciennes, Mechlin ground and others; (b) 'cutwork' is also an early form of embroidered lace; (c) 'leadwork' is easily confused with 'leafwork', a rare alternative for 'leaf' or 'wheatear'; (d) 'leadwork' is also easily confused with 'lerdwork', a Devon name for fillings.
    Leadworks are small square-shaped decorations of closely worked basket stitch often regularly arranged through the reseau of bobbin laces, for example in Lille. See *Plait* (b).

Leavers, Levers. (Fig. 32a, 33a.) This lacemaking machine is regarded as the invention of John Levers, a frame smith of Sutton-in-Ashfield, who moved to Nottingham and produced in 1813 a single-tier bobbin-net machine which has ever since, with all its later modifications, been known as the Levers. Some factions prefer 'Leavers', now generally used as the commercial name. The first model was only 18 inches (457 mm) wide, but before long a 54-inch (1,372 mm) width was produced, and ultimately 230 inches (5,842 mm). The essential difference between Levers's machine and Heathcoat's was that the thread-holding bobbins were so thin that up to thirty per inch could be fitted in across the width, and only one row of bobbins was necessary instead of two, hence 'single tier'. This meant that patterned laces could be made more easily, and also that the net was not traversed. In 1828 the machine was adapted to power, and in 1834 the Jacquard was applied to it.
    The enormous Levers of the twentieth century can handle vast quanti-

ties of thread, and, loaded to capacity, its 12,000 miles (19,000 km) of warps and wefts could stretch half way round the equatorial circumference of the earth. It can produce 'webs' consisting of many widths of edging made side by side, linked only by a joining thread which can be drawn out when the lace has been removed from the loom and washed, bleached and starched (see also *Flounce*). Hand finishing is still required to clip back the floats of thread passing between one repeat of the design and the next (see *Cordonnet* (f, iii)).

The bobbins which hold the weft threads are like wafer-thin cotton reels, mounted in equally thin carriages. The carriages run in grooves, or combs, and swing backwards and forwards between the vertically stretched warps, which are able to move to right or left for varying distances according to the pattern. The movements are controlled by a continuous band of Jacquard cards so that identical repeats of the design can be produced over and over again. The movement in three planes (right and left for the warps, backwards and forwards for the bobbins) enables the threads to be twisted around each other, while for the more solid clothwork of the design the warps are held steady, producing, as on an ordinary loom, a woven effect. Additional beam threads are involved for the outlining cordonnet.

The machine can be adjusted to make three different textures: bobbin finings, where the solid parts have the appearance of miniature zigzags; gimping, in which the solid parts have a woven appearance; and *Ciré*, which uses two layers of thread, silk and rayon, to produce a polished sheen.

Today, the high running costs of the Levers put it at a disadvantage against the descendants of the Stocking and Warp Frames, which can make looped nets with incredible speed, using synthetic fibres. In the preparation to produce a lace, there has first to be the artist to evolve the pattern which, even at this stage, must be properly related to numbers of bobbin and warp threads, as well as to the speed at which the lace passes over the roller; then there must be a draughtsman to number the threads and translate every movement of each into a series of figures on squared paper; finally, using those figures, the Jacquard cards which control the selection of the warp for patterning must be punched out. Hooks, which are arrested by the solid parts of the cards, slip through these open holes to engage momentarily each with its own warp thread. The completed cards are assembled in sequence on an endless moving band driven by a chain. When this is set in motion, the whole thing works rather like a pianola, the threads being harmoniously manipulated to create the design. See *Jacquard*. The yarns have to be specially prepared and are often more highly twisted than for hand-made laces. See also *Machine lace* (e).

Lefebure, Auguste. In 1829 he took over the lace manufactory at Bayeux in northern France from Mme Charpentier and succeeded in building up a flourishing trade in 'blondes mates', which were exported to Spain and South America (see *Caen*). In 1857 his son Ernest was taken into the business, and in 1864 Ernest's brother Anatole. The brothers Lefebure produced fine exhibition pieces of the French needlepoints Alençon (1860s) and Argentan (1874), which were specially designed by Feuillette. Two dress flounces of Alençon exhibited in Paris in 1867 had taken forty women seven years to complete and cost £3,400 (see *Alençon*). Their work was undoubtedly expensive but also coveted: the number of workers increased from 400 in the early nineteenth century to more than 10,000 by 1860.

Legs. See *Brides* and *Guipure* (d).

Leopard. A type of East Midlands bobbin in which the bone or wood shank is studded with circular pewter spots.

Le Puy. A lacemaking area of central France producing bobbin laces which, in the eighteenth century, were widely exported to all parts of Europe, as well as to Mexico and Peru. In the mid nineteenth-century revival of 1859, a lace school was opened and, of the 240,000 lacemakers in France, 130,000 were from that area. They made Cluny lace and also a definitive form, usually of black silk, and characterised by straight rows of wheatears like the pinnate veining of a leaf, inset reseau medallions often enclosing a small flower, and a ground of picoted brides (Figs. 2b and 3c). This lace was used for large shawls and deep flouncing.

The East Midlands of England copied Le Puy lace, as well as Cluny. Some English products of the second half of the nineteenth century are indistinguishable from the French. The school was reopened in 1974 under the directorship of Mme Mick Fouriscot.

Lester, Thomas (1835-1909). A lace designer who, in his earlier days, worked in his father's shop in Bedford making up sample books of the Bucks 'point ground' designs which they could supply. With the slump of the 1840s and competition from patterned machine laces, the slow-to-make Bucks became uneconomic, and Lester turned his attention to an imitation of the newly introduced, and popular, lace of Malta. His innovations, called Beds Maltese, were of flax thread, not silk, but like Maltese itself they were continuous in the sense that ground and pattern were made in one. They could nevertheless be constructed of irregular-shaped sections, made by several different workers and then invisibly joined, so that the completion of the work was greatly accelerated.

Lester's designs were both fine and complex, every part of the pricking being carefully detailed, from the gimp veining of the heart-shaped leaves to the many tiny raised plaits and the neatly filigreed nine-pin border. His handkerchief edgings, collars and fall pieces show a fanciful imagination combined with an eye for realistic detail: here giraffes, emus and eagles with separately feathered wings stretch their necks in a forest of jungle trees, strut through deserts of asphodel or turn their heads as they perch on lofty branches. Such pieces were inordinately expensive, made only by professionals, for commission or exhibition purposes. His bread-and-butter money came from the yardages of lace worked for his shop by the villagers. He is said to have been a good employer, giving presents of incised bobbins ('A gift from Lester's') to makers whose work was particularly good. See also *Design* (vi).

Levers. See *Leavers.*

Liège. A town associated with lace production in the late seventeenth and eighteenth centuries. According to some authorities, point de Sedan was made there. Liège was annexed to Belgium in 1830 and was formerly strongly under French influence.

Lierre (Belgium). A centre for embroidered nets in the nineteenth and twentieth centuries.

Lignin. Chemically, a complex aromatic substance deposited in the cellulose walls of the supporting and water-conducting cells of plants, forming the so-called 'wood'. It is lignin which gives the distinctive qualities of resilience, coolness, strength and weight to flax as opposed to cotton fibres, which are pure cellulose. See *Fibres, Flax.*

Liguria. Another name for the republic of Genoa, sometimes applied to early Genoese bobbin lace.

Lille. A Flemish town annexed to France in 1667, recaptured by Flanders in 1708 (Siege of Lille) and returned to France again in 1713. It produced a lightweight lace popular in the eighteenth century in both black and white, but lacking any of the rich designs of, for example, the Valenciennes lace of this period. Its quality declined with the Revolution, and by 1800 it was worn only by 'the most ordinary women'. In the first half of the nineteenth century the sketch-line designs, made only of gimp, were enclosed in a cloudy fond simple, relieved by a scattering of tiny point d'esprit. After the revolution of 1845, preceding the empire of Napoleon III, little was made commercially.

Limerick lace. An embroidered net, made in Ireland. It was started in 1829 by Charles Walker, who had learnt net embroidering at Coggeshall in Essex. He made some splendid stoles and veils, caps and dresses, which were quite expensive, costing up to 30 guineas for a 4 yard (3.7 m) flounce. In 1842, having sold his very flourishing business, he died, and Limerick embroidery of that superlative quality was never made again, though the industry was revived with some success in the late 1880s. (See Fig. 19a.)

Both tambour and needlerun techniques were used, and the lace was noted for its variety of delicate fillings, as many as 47 different ones being found in one collar. Often needlerun fillings were combined with tamboured outlines. Two thicknesses of thread were sometimes used, giving a greater softness and delicacy. In the early twentieth century, Limerick was the most expensive of the Irish laces.

Small amounts of 'Carrickmacross' were produced there, and some net-on-net appliqué, though this is more usually associated with Brussels.

Linen stitch. See *Toilé*.

Lingerie (French, linge = linen). (a) Originally a term for underlinen, i.e. underwear made of fine lawn or cambric. In the twentieth century the term was extended to women's underwear of any fabric – silk, art silk or synthetics. See *Underwear*. (b) 'Lingerie' was also used of work with woven linen or with linen thread. Thus Vinciolo's second pattern book, 1606 edition, is 'pour toutes sortes d'ouvrages de Lingerie' (all kinds of linen work).

Loom. A mechanical frame of wood or iron used for weaving. Though the power loom was invented by Cartwright in 1780, even-weave linens for drawnwork, cutwork and reticella continued to be hand-woven into the twentieth century.

Sometimes the laying down of a heavier thread, e.g. along the border of the material, gave it a look of needlerun embroidery, and this decoration was referred to as *lappet lace*.

More openwork patternings (Fig. 39d) could be produced by hand manipulation of warps and weft so that the weft was sometimes turned back on itself, creating solid and open areas, in a geometric or representational design. The product was *loom lace*, known from 1698, when it, along with 'foreign Bone lace, Needlework Point, and Cutwork', was prohibited from importation into Britain. Loom laces are known from Spain, in the eighteenth century and later. More mechanically produced forms involved the carrying forward of long threads or floats from one part of the design to the next.

Luddites. A militant group of textile journeymen and machine hands who, feeling themselves threatened with poverty and unemployment, blamed the machines and set out to destroy as many as possible. Initially these were Stocking Frames, but in the renewed outbursts of violence in 1811-18 Heathcoat's bobbinet machine and others, newly invented, suffered, especially in the Nottingham area. Altogether nearly a thousand machines were destroyed. According to Felkin, although the actual name of the participants derived from an idiot boy, Ned Ludd, who smashed up Frames in 1779, similar destructive attacks had occurred as early as 1710, in London, when the very large number of apprentices taken on by the Stocking Frame manufacturers, at extremely low wages, was putting adult framework knitters out of a job.

Lunéville. See *Cordonnet* (d, i).

Lyons. An important French centre for silk machine laces. As early as 1774, Louis XVI sent industrial spies to Nottingham to study the Stocking Frame, which, a few years earlier, had begun the manufacture of 'point net'. Lyons soon surpassed Nottingham in the 'finish' of its silk tulles, and a fierce competition developed between France and Britain: the English inventions – the Warp Frame (1775), the organ barrel for automatic patterning (1780) and Dawson wheels, also for patterning (1807) – were quickly copied in France, while the English were equally quick to apply the French Jacquard. In 1815 an Old Loughborough was smuggled across the Channel. In England, Heathcoat had used these machines for cotton nets. In France, because of import restrictions on cotton, silk was used, with great success, and nets such as Meklin, tulle illusion and black Grenadine were soon being made.

Machine lace. The types of lacemaking machines and their modifications are many, varied and complex, and only a few of the main forms and dates are listed. Three types of production are distinguishable:
(1) Laces made by looping. The machines work with numerous needles, producing a delicate fabric which looks like fine openwork knitting.
(2) Laces made by twisting on a kind of modified loom where there are stretched warp threads, held vertically, and where instead of one weft thread passing across the warps there are hundreds of separate wefts on separate bobbins which swing back and forth between the warps, which themselves instead of being stationary are shunted to right or left between each swing. The final result is not crossed threads as in woven fabrics, but threads twisted around each other to make a mesh.
(3) Laces made by embroidery machines. This, like (1), is dependent on needles.

(a) Stocking Frame. (Figs. 30a and b, 31a and b.) This was first invented by Lee in about 1589, was spurned by Elizabeth I, and worked for a time at the French court, under the patronage of Henri IV. In the seventeenth and much of the eighteenth century it was the main producer of machine hosiery, its only competitor being the Warp Frame (1775). Among the fashion effects created for stockings in the second half of the eighteenth century were eyelet holes. The adaptation of the Stocking Frame to produce these stimulated the idea of making an entirely lacy fabric, and this was achieved with the silk 'point net' of 1769, an invention attributed to Robert Frost. It was named from the technique of manufacture: the selection and transfer of the loops to make the pattern was by the points of wire hooks, or ticklers. The net was very fine, and the gauge was measured by the number of needles working to the inch. It was some-times patterned with run or tambour embroidery but was extremely fragile, and any snag would cause extensive laddering. The early Stocking Frames were 20 inches (508 mm) wide and worked by hand, as a cottage industry. Some 1,800 of them were in existence by 1810, mostly in the Nottingham area.

(b) Warp Frame. (Figs. 30c, 31c and d.) This first went into production in 1775. Its loops were arranged vertically instead of horizontally, i.e. along the warp line instead of the weft line. This gave a greater stability of texture, and the width of material produced could be cut up into hosiery instead of having to be shaped on the machine. By 1795 it was producing silk looped nets as fine as gossamer, and in 1816 Warp Frame net, decorated with silver strip, was used for Princess Charlotte's wedding gown. By the 1850s it had succumbed to the competition of the bobbinets, but the technique was revived in the twentieth century by Raschel machines using synthetic fibres.

(c) Bobbin Net, Bobbinet, Twist Net Machine. (Fig. 33b.) It was John Heathcoat in 1808 who first successfully produced a net made by the twisting of threads in such a way that they were locked secure. It was a net which so closely resembled the hand-made bobbin ground 'fond simple', both in the structure of the mesh and in the diagonal (traversed) course of the weft (or bobbin) threads, that the two could scarcely be told apart. In this invention he rose triumphant above a host of others, since the mechanical inventiveness of the late eighteenth century was so prolific that very similar ideas occurred to numerous people at the same time. The set-up and procedure of Heathcoat's machine is described under *Bobbin net*. The gauge or fineness of the mesh is calculated by the number of bobbins working per inch of the machine's width: if there are ten, it is called 10-point. The coarsest is 4-point, the finest 16-point (compare 30 for *Leavers*). Vertically, according to the tension of the machine setting, between ten and thirty holes per inch could be fitted in.

See *Hole count*. With the subsequent stretching of the net in finishing, the meshes could be made isodiametric.

(d) Pusher Bobbin Net Machine. This was invented in 1812 and took its name from the long metal prods which pushed the bobbins between the warp threads. Like Heathcoat's bobbinet prototype, it was set up with two rows of bobbins, one in front and one behind the curtain of warps, which swung together, but the pushers, and some other modifications, made it substantially different. Both solid design and ground convincingly imitated blonde and Chantilly laces. The outlining thread or cordonnet was always run in by hand. As many as five thousand Jacquard cards might be needed to produce the large floral pattern of a shawl or veil. The Pusher ceased extensive production in the 1870s but continued to make shiny black silk or rayon scarves and stoles into the twentieth century.

(e) Leavers, Levers. (Fig. 32a, 33a.) The details of this extremely important machine are described under *Leavers*. Basically, yet again, it was a modified Old Loughborough, but after the first few years its lace was not traversed. It has been credited with having the strength and intelligence of an elephant, combined with the delicacy, patience and artistry of a spider. It is also cumbersome, expensive and takes a great deal of time to set up. The dates of the birth and death of the inventor, John Levers, are not known. Having produced this machine of seemingly limitless possibilities, he dissociated himself from the firm and so failed to make his fortune, though the turnover amounted to £3,000,000 a year in the mid nineteenth century. He emigrated to France in 1821 and is thought to have spent the rest of his days there.

(f) Lace Curtain Machine. This derived in principle from the Bobbinet machine but had distinctive differences. Like the Levers, it used only one row of bobbins but had two sets of Jacquard cards, one acting on each side, so that denser or more open effects could be achieved. Also, each bobbin thread, instead of traversing all the warps, twisted with only two of them, producing the characteristic square mesh. Designs were floral or geometric, chunky rather than graceful. A pair of cotton curtains, 4 yards (3.7 m) long, could be produced in two hours and, during the many years of their popularity, tons of them left Nottingham every week. In the 1860s they were thought very beautiful as they hung suspended at the windows, intercepting the light. There has recently been a revival in their popularity, after some two decades during which Raschel curtains of synthetic fibre were preferred.

(g) Barmen, Patented Circular Machine. Barmen is a town-amalgamation of West Germany, which lies near the border with the Netherlands, and which was renamed Wuppertal in 1930. The Barmen, or Circular, was adapted from a braid-making machine and imitated bobbin rather than needlepoint laces, the threads being manipulated and traversed in the same way as by the handworkers. In particular, it copied with great accuracy the braid-like edgings and insertions of torchon, Cluny and filet, as well as point de Paris, Binche, Antwerp and Valenciennes (of the nineteenth century variety). It was developed in the early twentieth century and is still used. Its disadvantage is that it can only make one or two widths at a time and is therefore expensive compared with a Levers machine, which can produce fifty 3-inch (76 mm) edgings side by side along the width of the machine.

(h) Embroidery machines: Schiffli, Bonnaz, Cornely. The Cornely was used mainly in the first half of the twentieth century as a hand-operated sewing machine to fix a thick thread (cordonnet) around the outlines in patterned machine laces. It applied the cordonnet to one surface only of the lace, so that it appeared raised. The cordonnet it made was continuous, unlike that worked on the Levers machine, where the clipped floats show cut ends at the beginning and end of each motif.

The Bonnaz was a chain-stitch machine used to embroider patterns on net in imitation of tambour work. See *Bonnaz*.

The Schiffli is an enormous machine, often now 20 yards (18 m) or more long, with the ability to reproduce the same design many times over at once. It can be used to imitate the patterns, though not the technique, of needlerun laces such as those of Limerick and Brittany. To prevent distortion of the net during this embroidery process, it is backed with a specially prepared cotton, previously treated with a mixture of starch and sulphuric acid. When the embroidery is finished, the background is singed away. In this way both 'shaped pieces', such as collars, and 'all-overs', i.e. dress lengths, can be made. The design was originally controlled by a pantograph: as the course of the threads was traced stitch by stitch on a master design, the net itself was moved and the hundreds of needles embroidered simultaneously along the whole width of the machine. Many variations of this embroidery on net are possible, for example imitations of Carrickmacross, Margot – an embroidery in thick cotton on a tulle ground, and the brilliantly coloured chrysanthemums and peonies worked on black Heathcoat net in Japan and America today.

When the embroidery is worked directly on to the backing material without any intervening net, the result is 'chemical lace', originally called 'machine embroidered guipure', but soon abbreviated to 'guipure' (qv). The name 'chemical lace' derived from the use of chemicals (chlorine or caustic soda) to remove the backing. Less violent processes, such as blasting with hot air or dissolving in water, are now possible, enabling the embroideries to be worked in silk or other delicate fibres. In the early years, many old designs were copied, including Irish crochet, Brussels duchesse, and sixteenth-century reticellas. Schiffli broderie anglaise is recognisable, like its other products, by the fuzzy appearance of the stitches, resulting from the very large number of needles working so closely together. See also *Swiss embroidery.*

Macramé (Spanish = morisco, Moorish). A knotted lace of ancient origin, thought to have developed from the knotting of the warp fringes of woven materials, to make them secure from unravelling, and to provide additional decoration. Two thousand year old Assyrian wall carvings appear to show decorative macramé work on tunics; and the sixteenth-century painting by Veronese of the *Marriage in Cana* shows a cloth with macramé fringing. See also *Genoa* and *Groppo.*

Madeira. A Portuguese island off the west coast of Morocco. Madeira work – whether in the form of eyelet holes or of the more holey broderie anglaise – demonstrates a transition from purely surface embroidery to something sufficiently like cutwork to be called a lace. See also *Broderie anglaise.*

Maglia de Spagna, Spanish ground. See *Reseau.*

Maiden, lady, pillow horse. A wooden stand used to support the bobbin lacemaking pillow, especially when it was either heavy or rounded underneath so that it would roll about unless prevented. It also helped to raise the pillow to the most convenient height for working. Maidens were constructed in a variety of forms but were mostly three-legged. Far simpler stands could be made from boxes with the sides cut away in the form of an arc, to secure the curve of the pillow, but these needed in addition a table to put them on. See also *Pillow.*

Maille carrée (French, square mesh). A term sometimes used for Valenciennes diamond-meshed ground, in contradistinction to the maille ronde or round Valenciennes ground. (Fig. 28b.) See *Reseau.*

Maille à cinq trous (French, five-hole mesh or ground). See *Reseau.*

Malines. See *Mechlin.*

Maltese. A nineteenth-century silk lace, made in black and in a colour like ripe corn. It is known from 1833, when Lady Hamilton Chichester brought in lacemakers from Genoa. Maltese and Genoese laces are thus of the same genre: both have podgy wheatears, plaited strands and a basically geometric design. Since the main market was to be a tourist one, the four scimitars of the Maltese cross were introduced. The thick soft silk made the lace production both quick and inexpensive, and its lustrous flamboyance was well suited to the bombastic styles of the 1850s. With these unassailable qualifications, it flooded the English market. England's response was Beds Maltese, an innovation disapproved of by the traditionalists, who regarded Bucks point as the only lace. During the twentieth century Maltese lace steadily deteriorated until that of the 1970s bore almost no resemblance to the popular productions of a hundred years before. See also *Bedfordshire* and *Lester*.

Manila. See *Swiss embroidery and lace* (c, ii).

Manilla. See *Philippines*.

Mantilla. A Spanish shawl made in white lace for weddings and in black for other occasions. It often took the form of a large oval, about 3 feet (914 mm) across, bounded by a deep gathered flounce, except along one side where an ungathered rectangle could be raised to cover the tall comb, while the flouncing was brought forward below the chin and fastened across the breast. More recent shapes were like large triangles or overgrown fall caps. The lace could be Spanish bobbin or, in the later nineteenth century, needlerun or machine.

Margot. An embroidery in thickish cotton on a tulle ground, worked by the Schiffli machine.

Marli. A Lille-type lace of the eighteenth century, with a simple 'point ground' decorated with needlerun or with point d'esprit. See *Tulle* (d).

Mat, math, mate. A Belgian name for clothwork, equivalent to the French toilé, but sometimes including both whole stitch and half stitch. See *Toilé*.

Mechlin, Malines (Flemish = Mechelen). (a) 'Malines' was used in France and England for all Flemish bobbin laces from the seventeenth century to about 1720. Anne of Austria (see *English lace* (b)), mother of Louis XIV, had a 'frizette' of Malines; and a pair of Mechlin ruffles is recorded in 1657. Its importation into England was prohibited between 1660 and 1669, but it was then purchased in immense quantities. It was made at the béguinages from about 1681 until 1756, when it was largely displaced by blonde.
(b) From the late seventeenth century, Mechlin also referred to a specific Flemish continuous lace, with a silky gimp thread and a ground of minute hexagonal meshes, each with two sides plaited three times,

parallel to the long axis of the lace, and four sides crossed. This ground required eight pairs of bobbins and was worked without a pricking. The older forms sometimes had an oeil de perdrix ground but were distinguishable from Binche by the presence of the gimp (Fig. 7a). A cinq trous ground also occurred, and a fond d'armure, though both were rare. The design of these early forms had a fluid beauty, but as the eighteenth century wore on the units of design became smaller and more closely repeated, with meanly regular flowers and ribbon scrolls. Though still filmy, the laces became more and more tightly gathered and more and more profusely worn until the pattern became so unimportant that gauze would have been an adequate substitute. By the end of the century, the lace was reduced to repetitive roseheads, and the wide expanse of reseau was relieved only by an orderly arrangement of spots or drifting leaves.

(c) Machine copies of Mechlin were made towards the end of the nineteenth century, so faithful in design and technique that only the cordonnet clipped on both sides of each motif gave them away. Even the ground looked plaited. The Levers machine made less proficient copies in the 1930s. Caplin, illustrating Levers Mechlin, says: 'Lace like this is sometimes called Alençon Val.'

(d) At least three other kinds of so-called Mechlin were made by machine: (i) A net made on the Warp Frame from 1810 to 1819. (ii) From 1816 to 1824 identical copies of the typical Mechlin ground were made on the Horizontal Lace Platting machine. This also produced a few veils of machine droschel. However, they were much too expensive to be competitive and were eventually sold at a loss. (iii) In 1829 a 'fender' net, sometimes called warp lace, was made on the Levers machine. It consisted only of single warps twisted around each other in the manner of a wire fireguard or fender. The original three twists were reduced to two, and finally to one, making it so light as to be almost invisible. It was, however, very unstable, having no locking bobbin threads to hold it, and was useless unless held stiff by gum. (iv) A Meklin net made on Heathcoat's machine was a fully traversed twist net but with a low gauge and hole count so that it used little thread and was inexpensive. It was used to line coffins.

Medici collar. See *Ruff*.

Mercerised cotton. A forerunner of the artificial fibres and synthetics. It was invented about 1850 and first produced commercially in the 1890s as Sylko. Its prime aim was to act as a substitute for silk. Natural cotton fibres were dipped briefly in strong caustic soda and then held stretched while they were washed and dried. This treatment increased the lustre and softness of the cotton but also weakened it a little. Mercerised cotton is sometimes used for bobbin and for machine laces.

Merletti a piombini (Italian, bobbin lace). 'Piombini' refers to small lead weights used in place of ordinary bobbins. 'Merletti' is a diminutive of merli, meaning battlements, and so refers to a castellated or dentate border; in other words it is equivalent to the early usage of 'dentelle'. The patterns in *Le Pompe*, 1557 (see *Bobbin lace*) are for merletti, and the sixteenth- and early seventeenth-century Genoese and Venetian laces are examples. See also *Trine*.

Mesh. (a) The single unit of a reseau or net, i.e. each hole encircled by threads. (b) The entire network or reseau ground. This usage in lace is ambiguous and also unnecessary since other very adequate terms such as 'net' or 'network' for machine and 'reseau' or 'ground' for bobbin laces are available.

Messages in lace. (Fig. 43b.) English needlepoint laces of the seventeenth-century point plat or eighteenth-century hollie point types were quite frequently dated, as were cutwork samplers (e.g. 1648) and commemorative Honiton (e.g. Queen Victoria's jubilee, 1897). Religious valedictions such as 'Liberta' (long may you remain free, in health, in mind and in person), which occurs in Vavassore's pattern book of 1530; memento mori such as 'A bon fino' (to a good end), also a Vavassore pattern, shown as drawnwork in Holbein's painting of Anne of Cleves, 1538; and a souvenir message in hair lace 'Though far apart, Yet neere in heart' are examples of the type of messages that may be found. 'Brabant' occurs on a sixteenth-century Flemish coverlet (Cinquantenaire); and a band of needlepoint depicting the theme of Judith and Holofernes bears a legend in ancient Portuguese (St Gallen).

Mezzo mandolina. First mentioned in the *Specchio della Virtuose Donne* of Isabetta Catanea Parasole, 1595, which contained patterns for punto a maglia, mezzo mandolina, bobbin and needle laces. Abegg regards it as a type of filet. Johnstone translates it 'stitch of half an almond shape', a fair description of the simplest form of buttonhole stitch loop. (Fig. 14(1).)

Mezzo punto (Italian, half or middle stitches = mixed stitches). A mixed lace composed partly of bobbin or woven work and partly of buttonhole stitches. Several varieties can be distinguished:
(a) A bobbin tape, shaped to the design, is made on the pillow. The needlepoint fillings and brides – or, rarely, reseau – are then added.
(b) A straight tape is made with bobbins or woven on a loom. It is then

folded and puckered to fit a design drawn or printed on a backing cloth. The fillings and ground are worked as in (a).

Both (a) and (b) were made in Genoa and Naples in the sixteenth and seventeenth centuries.

(c) The technique was reborn in the second half of the nineteenth century under the name renaissance lace. Branscombe and Battenburg used straight tapes, but a whole range of fancy tapes was available.

(d) Point de Milan was a commercial Belgian lace of the early twentieth century using straight tapes, Milanese designs and needlemade fillings and reseau. See also *Milanese lace* (b).

(e) 'Mixed lace' is more commonly used than 'mezzo punto' for Brussels duchesse, in which needlepoint medallions nestle among the bobbin blooms; for the late nineteenth-century point d'Angleterre made of bobbin flowers in a point de gaze ground; and for the eighteenth-century Brussels needlepoint sprays bedded in a droschel ground.

Michael Angelo lace. A rare name for Italian rosaline.

Mignon. A filling stitch found in needlepoint laces such as Alençon.

Mignonette. (a) A narrow Lille-type lace used for caps and head-dresses in the eighteenth century. (b) A ·flax lace popular for engageants and dress trimmings in the 1750s and 1760s, with a delicate pattern and a light ground of Spanish, or of point de Paris, reseau. It was made mostly at Bayeux.

Milanese lace. (a) A bobbin lace named from the city of Milan, in the plain of Lombardy, in north-west Italy. It is first mentioned in 1606 as 'silk Milan lace' in the wardrobe accounts of James I. In 1613 Louis XIII prohibited the wearing of 'Milan passement' in France. It was obviously a luxury item, or prohibitions would have been pointless, but whether of braid or lace, precious metal or flax, we have no way of telling.

In the seventeenth century, Milanese was a lace of baroque grandeur, with formalised lilies spreading their petals outwards to meet and touch until almost no open space remained. (Fig. 25a and b.)

By 1700 the smaller designs were of elaborate floral sprays curving their way through a round Valenciennes ground. The fillings were immensely varied, and the whole was worked with immaculate precision. Milan was part of the Holy Roman Empire from 1535 to 1714, and the better lace of this period flaunted the two-headed eagle.

During the first half of the eighteenth century, Milanese laces were outmoded by the airy laces of Flanders. Their quality declined and became coarsely non-continuous, with the reseau threads carried quite obviously across the back of the solid parts. In the nineteenth century, the flabby cotton version had almost no market value.

(b) Point de Milan. A commercial Belgian lace of the first half of the twentieth century, which was sold in the stores. It was a tape lace with needlepoint fillings and a ground after the manner of Alençon brides tortillées.

(c) Machine copies of (b) were made as edgings.

Millward, John. A lace manufacturer and designer of Olney, Buckinghamshire, c 1800-60, best known for the roundels of Bucks point which he made for baby caps. They were exported to America until the outbreak of the Civil War in 1860.

Mittens. Fingerless gloves made on the Stocking and Warp Frames, or in a variety of hand-made laces, and fashionable from c 1750 to 1840, and again from the 1880s. Gloves of point d'Angleterre appear in late seventeenth-century fashion engravings (Fig. 21c).

Mixed laces. Those made of mixed techniques, such as bobbin and needlepoint. See *Mezzo punto.*

Modano, Tuscan filet. An Italian name for square-meshed knotted laces. Vavassore's pattern book of 1532 (second edition), *Corona di Racammi* ('Crown of Embroidery'), contains designs for 'Modano ricamato' or embroidered network. The 'point Modena' made on the Levers machine in the early twentieth century was probably a copy of the hand-made Modano.

Modes. See *Fillings* and *Jours.*

Mosaique (French, mosaic). A filling stitch – small diamonds within a picoted frame – used in needlepoint laces such as Alençon.

Motif. A unit of the lace design. See *Toilé.*

Muslin. A hand-woven cotton material first imported from India c 1670. Its popularity grew during the eighteenth century: it was used for aprons, fichus and engageants, decorated either with Dresden work or with tambour embroidery. It was a favourite of Marie Antoinette's when she played at being pastoral. The muslin material was translucent and very light, an entire neo-classical dress would weigh only a few ounces, and therefore the only possible laces to be worn with it were modestly plain silk tulles or spotted marlis.

Naming of laces. In naming a lace we say three things about it: its technique, its country of origin and its age: for example, bobbin lace – Milanese – eighteenth century. Naming it is in a sense the same as identifying it, for the naming of the lace fits it into an accepted key. For this to be possible, there must be agreement that bobbin lace, Milanese lace and eighteenth-century lace are all capable of recognition because they have generally agreed characteristics. Recognising the technique is fairly straightforward: buttonhole stitches indicate a needlepoint lace; a solid portion formed of crossed and twisted threads indicates a woven lace, which could be drawnwork, bobbin or machine. But recognising when and where a lace was made presents many problems.

Basically, both geographical and temporal origin are assessed by reference to design, to the type of fibre, and to the ground i.e. the way in which the motifs of the lace are held together. The difficulties arise from: (a) Geographical origin: the names are retained, though the laces are made elsewhere. Not only did workers migrate, or were forced to migrate, to different areas, but individual areas made or imitated many different kinds of lace. The Lefebure manufactory centred at Bayeux copied Argentan, black and white Spanish laces, blonde and Chantilly. The suffix -type is useful here, for example Chantilly-type made at Bayeux, Valenciennes-type made at Ghent. See *Geography*.
(b) Temporal origin: laces were copied at a later date, so that we may have to say for example 'nineteenth-century imitation of eighteenth-century Argentan', 'twentieth-century imitation of sixteenth-century punto in aria'. See *Dating*.
(c) Different names are used in different countries: for example what is called 'Brussels appliqué' in Britain is called 'application anglaise' in France; the lace known in Britain as 'point de neige' is called 'roselline' in Italy, and so on.
(d) Rare laces where there are insufficient known examples or documentation for the lace to be named by reference to a key. Examples are Argentella, reseau Venise, punto a groppo and Ragusa: in none of these are we precisely sure when, where or how they were made.

Embroidered laces are often not placed geographically since they were made identically in many different places. We do usually try to date them, though repeated copying over the centuries makes this also very difficult.

Machine laces are usually named from the machine which produced them, sometimes with additional description to make them distinctive, e.g. 'Heathcoat's tulle illusion'. Sometimes they take over the names of hand-made laces which they do not in any way resemble, e.g. Binche and

Alençon. See also *Foreign terms.*

Nanduti. See *South American lace:* Paraguay.

Needle. (a) For needlepoints and for knotted laces of the punto a groppo and puncetto types, a long fine needle, slightly rounded at one end and with an eye at the other, was used. (b) For filet lace, a meshing needle or shuttle was used to make the knotted ground. (c) For taking sewings in non-continuous bobbin laces a needle-pin is used.

Needlepoint. (a) A general term for laces made of buttonhole stitches. They developed as a form of embroidery, and the recognised sequence is: simple cutwork; reticellas made of squares cut out of linen and filled in again with needlepoint patterns; reticellas made of laid-down squares, not associated with any woven linen; the square framework was completely discarded, and the pattern drawn freely on a parchment from which, when the lace was finished, it could be neatly snipped away. The various geographical types of needlepoint laces proliferated from this last. See also *Buttonhole stitch, Punto in aria, Reticella.*
(b) Needlepoint is also used of a canvas embroidery which has no relation at all to lace.

Needlerun. An *Embroidered net* made with a running stitch. See also *Filet.*

Neo-classicism. A trend in fashion which began in the 1780s. Gowns began to imitate the simplicity of classical Greek and Roman draperies and to be made of soft muslins instead of richly damasked and brocaded silks. From the lace point of view it was a revolution as real and as disastrous as the bloody political one, and the two were closely linked not only in the general levelling trend of the time but also by the very real fear in France of appearing noble. Many French lacemaking centres closed for ever. England, though she followed French fashions less slavishly than before, still assumed the low-necked and high-waisted gowns of the First Empire. So hand-made laces were already fading with neglect before the onslaught of the machines put an end to their commercial viability.

Net. A mesh ground, made by machine rather than by hand. A number of different nets have been produced between 1769 and the late twentieth century:
(a) Point net: a fine knitted net first made on the Stocking Frame in 1769

(see *Machine lace* (a)). Some patterns were called 'spider net'.
(b) Fast-point net: invented in 1786. It incorporated a locking stitch which made point net less likely to unravel.
(c) Warp Frame net: invented in 1795. It was similar to (a) but with the loops running vertically instead of horizontally (see *Machine lace* (b)).
(d) Two-twist bobbinet (Fig. 19): invented by Heathcoat in 1808, and still made today by the same firm. The threads which made the mesh are not looped but twisted and traversed as in hand-made fond simple. It was far more successful than either (a) or (c). The wide demand and the immense profits to be made caused many people to give up their jobs and invest in impractical inventions and worthless machines in a 'twist net fever' induced by the expiry of the original patent in 1823. After only two years, overproduction, inferior quality goods and numerous infringements of patents resulted in bankruptcies and a lowering of wages, a trade depression which lasted into the 1840s. See also *Heathcoat*.
(e) Three-twist Brussels net, diamond net: invented in 1831 on a modified bobbinet machine. Instead of two twists on four sides of each mesh it had three, resulting in a diamond shape instead of a hexagonal one. There was no hand-made equivalent, and the net was much used for the application of Brussels bobbin or needlepoint motifs for wedding veils. A four-twist net in fine thread produced some superb appliqués, in which fragile motifs seemed to float in the air, the anchoring net being almost invisible. Production ceased c 1970.
(f) Nets imitating droschel or hand-made Mechlin grounds. See *Mechlin* (c).
(g) Mechlin net: made on the Levers machine from 1828 to recent times, though never in large quantities. It was also known as fender net or straight-down net. See also *Mechlin* (c).
(h) Tulle: a silk net, such as 'tulle illusion', a two-twist bobbinet made on the Heathcoat machine (Fig. 33b). In France, tulle is a general term for all machine nets and also for some hand-made grounds, such as Alençon. See *Tulle*.
(i) Novelty net: a trade term for the outlandish hat and motoring veils – spotted, fretted and banded with velvet – which were especially popular in the first quarter of the twentieth century (see *Chenille lace*).
(j) The grounds of patterned machine laces: technically, these are also nets, aiming to imitate the general appearance of a hand-made mesh.
(k) Raschel: a looped net made by warp knitting and using synthetic fibres to produce modern hosiery, curtains and garments known in the trade as 'intimate apparel'.
(l) Net-stitch: a reseau ground used in Honiton lace, sometimes made with a needle, but more commonly with bobbins by taking sewings and working without the guidance of pins. The meshes follow the shape of

the design, rather than working in regular lines, and are often variable in size.

(m) Net ground: another name for the fond simple of Bucks bobbin lace, which was the inspiration for Heathcoat's bobbinet. 'Point ground' is more frequently used.

(n) Net stitch or netting stitch: the knotting stitch used to make the ground of filet. See *Lacis*.

(o) Net or network: used in England of several different techniques, e.g. filet (French, net), lacis (French, network), reseau (French, network), reticella (Italian, rete, a net), and a form of netting known as sprang. See also *Reseuil*.

Net-on-net. See *Appliqué*.

Netherlands, Holland. The north-east part of the Low Countries, important for its exceptionally fine flax, and reputedly for the production of a bobbin and a needlepoint lace in the seventeenth century, though some authorities question that any lace was ever made there and say that the term 'dentelles hollandaises' refers to a lace made in Flanders for export to Holland. See *Dutch lace*.

Netting. The knotted *Filet* ground, made of net stitch.

New Pitsligo. A town in Aberdeenshire where a small bobbin lace industry was started in 1850, using designs similar to those of the East Midlands. See *Scottish lace*.

Nine pin border. The plaited border of Beds Maltese lace, which bears nine pinhole picots.

Non-continuous laces, fil coupé, fil attaché, free, à pièces raportées. Laces in which the threads used for the motifs (closed parts) are not the same as those which make the fillings and ground (open parts), i.e. the threads are not in continuity right across the lace from heading to footing (see *Continuous laces*). These two opposing techniques form the basis of a major distinction among bobbin laces. The advantage of non-continuity is that a team of well matched lacemakers can work on the same length of lace at the same time, their separate pieces being subsequently joined, so that orders can be executed far more quickly.

There are three types of assemblage:

(a) The threads linking motif to motif are separate ones but put in as the work proceeds. This is found in the maze-trail laces, such as Russian, where the brides are short and few.

(b) The distinct motifs – flowers, butterflies, birds – are brought together in a design, tacked in position and then linked by a reseau or by brides. (Fig. 5b.)

(c) The separate motifs are applied to machine nets or to hand-made grounds, forming an appliqué. This is not possible in continuous laces.

In spite of the benefits of speed and freedom of arrangement, there are fewer non-continuous than continuous bobbin laces. They are: Honiton, Brussels and Brabant including point d'Angleterre, East European, Milanese and an eighteenth-century form of Flemish which resembles it. All needlepoint laces, except hollie point, are non-continuous.

No pin. A Honiton lace filling consisting of a series of square leadworks arranged in a chequered manner.

Normandy lace. Normandy was an important lacemaking area of the eighteenth and nineteenth centuries, including the needlepoint centres of Alençon and Argentan and the bobbin centres of Bayeux and Caen, which produced a great variety of silk, flax and cotton laces in both black and white. The lace known merely as 'Normandy' was a light country lace with a simple design of lumpish shapes embalmed in a cinq trous ground, and sometimes known as dentelle à la Vierge. Dieppe lace was of a Valenciennes type, with a plaited ground and designs of spotted shapes known as poussin (chicken) or Ave Maria. They were used to trim peasant caps and were greatly treasured.

North Bucks Lace Association. Founded in 1897 in an attempt to stimulate improvements in design and workmanship among the cottage lacemakers, many of whom had given up even attempting to make Bucks point and were producing only the simplest torchons and Clunys. Harry Armstrong was instrumental in establishing a mail order business – the Bucks Lace-making Industry – which supplied the London stores, especially Peter Robinson. At that time point-ground lace sold for 2s 6d to 40s a yard, torchon for 10d a yard, and lace-bordered handkerchieves for 2s 6d to 50s each. (Fig. 47a.)

Northampton lace. See *East Midlands*.

Norwegian lace. See *Hardanger*.

Nottingham. This city, notorious for its machine-lace making, was even in the late seventeenth century associated with the Stocking Frame: 'the Manufacture of the town mostly consists in weaving of Stockings' wrote Celia Fiennes in 1697.

The Warp Frame, the Bobbinet machine and most of the modifications following from it were all invented in or around Nottingham. Until 1811 it was the only extensive centre of machine lace in the world, and the 'twist trade' made it enormously rich. But the Warp Frame was copied in France, and the Old Loughborough was imported to Calais and to Lyons, so that French machine laces, especially silk nets and blondes, soon offered keen competition. By 1851, Nottingham had a total of three thousand lace machines. The population increased by a great influx of people from 47,000 in 1810 to 79,000 in 1830 and, by 1866, to almost twice that.

Nottingham lace was sufficiently highly regarded for Queen Adelaide to wear a ball gown of warp net in 1831, and for Queen Victoria's daughters to appear dressed in Nottingham lace at the recurrent family christenings. Nottingham lace curtains were immensely popular for nearly a hundred years, from the 1860s to the 1950s.

Novelty veiling. See *Net* (i).

Oeil de perdrix, partridge eye, fond de neige, snow ground. A bobbin lace stitch, giving the appearance of perforated spots or eyes, and used as a ground in late seventeenth-century Binche. This ground distinguishes it from the early Valenciennes, which had a minute cinq trous ground, though the designs and techniques of these two laces were otherwise identical. The *Revolte des Passemens* (1661) described fond de neige as 'squadrons of snow', and it has indeed the appearance of a small blizzard. (Figs. 7c, 17b.) See also *Reseau*.

Old Loughborough. Heathcoat's Improved Bobbinet Machine, 1809.

Opaque lace. Lace made for a short period in the seventeenth century with almost no ground at all, that is with almost no holes, i.e. almost not a lace. Examples are found in point d'Angleterre and Mechlin, which were in fact translucent rather than literally opaque, in early Milanese, and early gros point. See *Design* (b, iii).

Open braids, dots and fibres. Stitches in Honiton lace: 'open dots' is another name for 'portes', the little pores in the toilé occurring either singly or in groups. Fibres are the bars stretched across the central cavity of a leaf.

Organ barrel. A form of patterning in machine lace, superseded by the Jacquard. See *Lyons*.

Origin of lace. (a) Time. Embroidered and knotted laces of a simple kind probably date from before Christ but were not important as fashion before the late fifteenth century. Bobbin and needlepoint laces are verified as important in dress from portraits and pattern books from c 1540. See *Dating, Bobbin lace, Flemish lace.*
(b) Place. Lace undoubtedly began, and mainly continued, within Europe. The most important commercial centres were in Italy, Flanders and France. See *Geography.*
(c) Technique. Opinions differ as to whether lace originated in embroidery, weaving, fishernet knotting or the manipulation of fringes. No doubt all played their part: embroidery developing into embroidered laces and needlepoints; weaving into bobbin and machine laces; knotting and looping into a whole variety of forms such as punto a groppo, puncetto, macramé, crochet, knitting and tatting.

Outworkers. Lacemakers, embroiderers on net, framework knitters or twist hands to whom work was farmed out, i.e. they worked in their own homes, not in a workshop or factory.

Pagano. A sixteenth-century Venetian, a cutter of wood blocks for printing and a creator of lace designs. He published pattern books:
1542. Cutwork and 'punto gropposo' (see *Groppo* (i)).
1543. Drawnwork.
1543. Cut linen (punto tagliato), some as intricate as the most complex reticellas, sporting two-headed eagles, a mermaid and a vase of flowers.
1550. *Punti Tagliati e Fogliami* (Cutwork with foliage). The illustrations indicate elaborate reticellas, the surfaces of the design being projected into little spikes of Venetian picots, while the wavy mane of the lion and the curled fleece of the sheep are realistically three-dimensional. A Florentine poem c 1520 refers to a hand-made lace (merli da man) sculptured in bas-relief (scolpi de basso rilevar), the lovely foliage like an acanthus (quel bel fogliame, ch'un acanto) – a very apt description, in fact, of gros point de Venise, which is also sometimes referred to by that name, though usually dated not earlier than 1620. The double application of this term is confusing: Palliser refers to a col rabat in gros point as sixteenth-century, when it is well known that that form of collar originated in the second quarter of the seventeenth century. See *Venetian lace* and *Reticella* (ii).
1554. *Ponti Tagliati Ponti in Aere* (Cutwork and punto in aria). Here, the title page shows the lace being made, on a parchment with a needle; and contemporary portraits, for example one of Catherine of Medici, 1550, depict ruffs and Medici collars edged with the fine needle-made toothing.

1559. *Il Burato.* Since buratto is basically a needlerun embroidery on a square woven mesh, any earlier pattern for filet or drawnwork could be adapted to it.

1557. *Le Pompe,* a pattern book for bobbin laces, attributed to the Sessa brothers. It is probable that some of the blocks were cut by Pagano, and some of the designs may also have been his. See *Bobbin lace.*

Paletot. Basically a tailored coat, but also used of a lace jacket falling to hip length, shaped at the waist and with pagoda sleeves, which was fashionable in the second half of the nineteenth century.

Palliser, Mrs Bury (1805-78). Mrs Palliser's researches into the literature and documentation of antique laces throughout Europe, and through all the ages, were as tireless as they were painstaking. It is astonishing that she could have matched up so closely the immense amount of verbal information which she garnered with the visual aspect of the laces which she saw and collected, so that over a hundred years later there is, in the majority of cases, no basic cause for disagreement.

She was a sister of Captain Marryat, author of *Midshipman Easy.* She lived at Sidmouth for a number of years and did much to foster interest in, and enthusiasm for, the Devon laces. Her collection of lace samples is at the Royal Albert Memorial Museum, Exeter. See also *Branscombe.*

Palm, palmette. See *Shell* pattern.

Pantograph. See *Machine lace* (h).

Papillon. Part of the head-sute of the eighteenth century. A yard or two of edging, matching the lappets in design, was frilled flatly around the curved border of the cap crown, over the forehead, as a vestige of the fontange so popular in the last decades of the seventeenth century.

Paraguay. See *Spider lace, South American lace.*

Parchment. (a) The working pattern pricked for bobbin lace from a designer's draft which was made on squared paper. Traditionally, the translucent goatskin was placed over the draft, and the holes, which would later receive the pins, were made with a needle pricker. Old parchments were jealously guarded and treated as heirlooms, but with the failure of the lace market in the late nineteenth century many were boiled down for glue. In modern times, a stiffish card is used instead of parchment, the design being pricked through from a sketch or an old pricking placed above. The card is less durable, and the holes are more

likely to be distorted by the pull of the threads and pins. See also *Bobbin lace, Pattern.*
(b) A parchment pattern was also used in making needlepoint laces.

Parchment lace. See *Cartisane, Gimp* (b).

Passemens, La Revolte des. A near-epic poem by 'divers authors' published in Paris in 1661, and dedicated to a cousin of Mme de Sévigné. It related, in a warlike manner, the rebellion of laces against a sumptuary edict of Louis XIV in November 1660. Each lace, wherever worn, or by whom, has its own protest to make. We are thus provided not only with a list of many names but also with their opinions of themselves and of each other. It would be a good deal more instructive, however, if we knew for certain just what each name referred to.

Passement. (a) Apparently a general name for both braids and laces, as applied flat to clothes or as borders, from the fifteenth to the early seventeenth century. As lace became freer of the material of the clothes and became more of a decoration in its own right, 'passement' was replaced by 'dentelle'. The *Revolte des Passemens* shows that it was still at that time understood in a comprehensive sense; and in 1663 there are references to a Corporation of Passementiers, who had a monopoly for making all kinds of lace.
(b) The pattern, used for both bobbin and needlepoint work, is sometimes called a 'passement', for example by Goubaud.

Passementerie. This represents a revival of a moribund term, in the nineteenth century, which was an age of resurrections. It was used for all kinds of fringes, ribbons and gimps (braids), but not of lace. Nevill Jackson says it is an old name for lacemakers, perhaps in mistake for 'passementiers' or 'passementières'.

Passives, downrights. A term used in lacemaking for those bobbins, and the threads attached to them, which remain straight, while the worker, runner, leader or weaver bobbins and threads twist around and across them.

Patent net. Sometimes applied to Urling's Patent Net (see *Gassed cotton*). However the term 'patent net' antedates this invention, being recorded in 1806 and 1813, and so was probably applied to each new lace-machine modification, prior to machine patterning.

Pattern (French = le patron). (a) See *Parchment* for the pattern used in bobbin laces. (b) Patterns for needlepoint laces, apart from the reticella forms, were also on parchment, the design drawn in ink or printed from copper plate, and the lace worked by attaching outlining threads to the parchment, filling in the solid parts with buttonhole stitches, and the open parts with bars or a needle-made reseau. For some designs samplers were copied, or pictorial pattern books. (c) For nineteenth-century knitting and crochet there were verbal instructions. (d) For tape (point, renaissance) laces a pattern was printed on soft leather or glazed cotton, the machine tape was tacked on, and then the gathers or folds were pleated together; one tape was linked to another, and the enclosed spaces were decoratively completed. (e) Counted thread techniques, such as filet and drawnwork, could be followed from block patterns printed on a square grid.

Patterns in lace. These are the typical designs which help to identify various laces. In continuous laces they are repetitive – one can speak of a long repeat, or a short repeat – for example in Bucks, where pastoral names for patterns abound, such as acorn and thistle, beehive, cat's face and hog's nose. In the non-continuous laces such as Honiton it is the individual motifs which are distinctively named, since they are separately made and not arranged in a repeat. Examples are the Honiton and Devon rose, shamrock and turkey tail. Fillings can also form a very distinctive part of the pattern, for example: in Honiton again, diamond, blossom, brick, toad in the hole, swing and a pin, and pearl; and in Alençon, enchainettes, mignons, couronnes and étoile. See also *Design*.

Pattern books. In the sixteenth century almost four hundred editions of 156 pattern books for embroidery and lace were printed, mainly in Germany and Venice. The earliest to show lace was by Schönsperger, c 1523. These books were used as practical guides, in much the same way as the DMC stitching books of the nineteenth and twentieth centuries. They were usually in pictorial form, with no verbal instructions. See also *Venetian lace, Pagano* and *Bobbin lace*.

Pearl, purl, picot (more rarely, knot, thorn, turnpin).
(a) A short loop used to enrich the outline of a motif, a border or a bar. (i) In continuous bobbin laces, picots along the heading are made by threads continued outwards from the body of the lace. (ii) In embroidered nets, separate picot edgings are stitched on by hand. These edgings were at first made with bobbins. Later, machine picot edgings could be bought by the yard. (iii) In 1828 an improvement of the Levers machine by Birkin (see *Lama lace*) enabled the picots to be made in one with the rest of the lace width, so reducing the amount of hand finishing

required. In the 1840s another adaptation of his enabled the picot edge to be incorporated even on scalloped 'webs' (see *Leavers*). (iv) In the raised needlepoints, picots on brides and on cordonnets were of marvellous complexity and formed an important part of the lace design (see *Couronnes*).

(b) Palliser's glossary gives 'Pearls, or purls = bars', which is possibly a confusion with 'purl bars' meaning bars with picots. Goubaud is equally ambiguous: 'Purl pin or purling is used for connecting parts of the design and for joining sprigs' could mean the bars themselves, or it could mean the picots or pinholes around the motifs through which sewings are taken in order to attach the bobbin threads to make the bars.

(c) 'Pearlin' or 'pearling' is a Scottish word used in the seventeenth century for lace. To encourage home manufacture, James I forbade the importation of all 'foraine pearlin'. The word was perhaps derived from 'pirl' meaning 'to twist'. In expressions such as 'pearled ruff' it is difficult to know whether pearling is intended in this sense or whether it refers to oyster pearls, with which the refulgent dresses of Elizabethan times were often encrusted.

(d) Purled lace or pearling. In the sixteenth century these terms could refer to a narrow needlepoint border in the form of thin loops overlapping like fish scales, and worn on coifs, for example by Mary Queen of Scots.

Peasant lace. A general name for heavy linen laces, which were practical, durable, solidly worked and of simple design. They are characteristic of Eastern Europe, north Italy and Sicily.

Pelerine, palatine. A small shoulder cape, first worn in the late seventeenth century.

Pelisse. Basically a long overdress or cloak, sometimes made entirely of lace, for example Beds Maltese or Le Puy.

Petit reseau. The reseau ordinaire of Alençon, but worked on a more minute scale and used as a filling.

Petticoat-breeches, rhinegraves. Wide-legged shorts, rather like a divided skirt. The legs, frilled with lace, were just visible beneath the hem of a gentleman's tunic. They were in fashion from about 1630 to 1670. An engraving by Gagnières of Louis XIV, c 1670, shows him garbed in this manner (Fig. 21a); and Charles II wore petticoat-breeches at his marriage to Catherine of Braganza in 1662. Puffed-out overtrousers, trimmed with some 250 yards (229 m) of ribbon bows, were often worn with them. They were decried by the dramatist Wycherley (1640-1716): 'They make thee waddle', he says, 'with all those gew-gaw ribbons, like a great old fat slovenly waterdog.'

Philippines. A group of islands in the Pacific. The capital city is Manilla. In the second half of the nineteenth century they were associated with: (a) very fine drawnwork on pina cloth, a stiff translucent material of a pale yellowish colour; (b) circlets of simple crochet made of Manilla grass, which is possibly the same as Manilla hemp (*Musa textilis*), also used for drawnwork; (c) lace made of aloe fibre (*Aloe socotrina*), which becomes mucilaginous on contact with water.

Picot. See *Pearl.*

Pillow (French = coussin). The hard structure, covered with cloth and padded traditionally with straw, which has pins stuck into it during the making of pillow (bobbin) lace. Thus it supports the pattern, which is held in position by the pins; the threads, also held by the pins; and the bobbins, held by the threads. Pillow shapes vary, but there are four main types:
(a) Round, lobster or bolster. This type has to be supported to stop it rolling around. See *Maiden.* It was used in the past for torchon, Cluny, Beds Maltese, Bucks point and occasionally for Devon laces.
(b) Narrow pillows some 3 feet (914 mm) tall are used for quickly made silk laces, for example of Spain and Malta.
(c) French pillows are flat-based, with revolving cylinders. They are used for narrow widths of lace. The cylinder has the pattern, pins and thread fixed to it, and as it revolves endless lengths of lace can be made without the pricking having to be set up again.
(d) Mushroom or flat pillows consist of a large circular piece of wood evenly padded so that it is higher in the centre and slopes gradually to the edge. It is used most commonly for sprig laces such as Honiton and Brussels, but it is also admirable for continuous laces such as point de fée. In Belgium the pillows are often mounted on tables which can be rotated to bring one side or another of the lace to a convenient position for working.

Pillow lace. See *Bobbin lace.*

Pillow horse. See *Maiden.*

Pins. A necessary part of the making of bobbin lace. In the sixteenth century pins were very expensive, costing 6s 8d per thousand in 1543, and the country folk are said to have used fish bones or splintered chicken bones as a substitute. When brass pins became cheaper they were used in varying degrees of fineness according to the gauge of the lace thread, for example LL for finest Honiton, LLL for coarser Honiton, LW for Bucks point, and DLW for torchon and Beds Maltese.

Pina cloth. A crisp corn-coloured lightweight material woven from the woody fibres of the pineapple plant. See *Philippines*. (Fig. 18d.)

Pinhole, porte (French, door). Tiny pores, like the prick of a pin, left in a bobbin lace where the threads were in fact crossed around a pin during the making. They may occur regularly along one side or both sides of a braid or trail, or appear like miniature portholes enlightening a closed surface. The word 'porte' is used in needlepoint laces where gaps are left between adjacent buttonhole stitches.

Pinners. (a) See *Lappets*. (b) A bib apron, pinned to the bodice of a dress. Pinner = pinafore (pin + afore).

Pita. A fibre obtained from the century plant and used for both bobbin and knitted lace in the Azores. See *Aloe*. In Madeira, in the twentieth century, the texture was copied using starched cotton.

Pizzo (Italian, lace). A term used in Genoa for Genoese lace. See also *Merletti*.

Plain weave, gimping. See *Leavers*.

Plait (French = tresse). This term has two quite different meanings, both relating to bobbin laces:
(a) The plaiting of four threads together to form a strand. It may form:
(i) the entire lace, with the strands articulating like thin bones, as in the sixteenth-century Genoese plaited lace which imitates a skeletal punto in aria; (ii) the free border or heading of the lace, e.g. in Maltese and Cluny; (iii) the bars or brides of a guipure lace, e.g. Beds Maltese (continuous) or Honiton (non-continuous); (iv) reseaux. Examples are the diamond-shaped meshes of Valenciennes; the heavier round Valenciennes of Milanese and some Flemish lace; and the upper and lower sides of each mesh in Mechlin and droschel, the first being plaited three times, and the second four.
(b) The tiny square-ended plaits, sometimes known as point d'esprit. Again four threads are used, but the technique is basket stitch, not plaiting. (See also *Wheatears*.) They are found: (i) diapered in the ground

of Lille and some patterns of Bucks and Mechlin, or forming little embellishments within the closed work of East Midlands laces; (ii) as fillings in Honiton laces (here they are known as leadworks or cutworks – which, out of context, can be confused with cutwork embroidery); (iii) occasionally forming the entire ground of the lace, as in some Honiton and in Beds so-called 'plaited' laces (Fig. 3a): verbally this form could easily be confused with (a, i), visually the difference is very obvious; (iv) raised plaits decorating the surface of Beds Maltese first appeared about 1856 and were used in designs by Thomas Lester. See also *Raised work* and *Florentine knots*.

(c) Maidment uses 'plaits' as an abbreviation for 'plaited bars' (a, iii), but this is confusing.

(d) Nevill Jackson admirably demonstrates the difficulties of interpretation resulting from deficient terminology. She uses 'plait' in all the following senses: for the gimp thread of Mechlin lace; for any lace which has strand plaiting anywhere in it; for whole stitch, for example in her illustration on page 88 of her *History*, where the clothwork is labelled 'plait'. She continues: 'The gimp or toilé ... looked at through a strong magnifying glass ... is plaited.' Here the three quite different terms – gimp, toilé and plait – are all equated.

(e) Plaiting machines – such as the Horizontal Lace Platting Machine (1810), the Circular Comb (patented 1824) and the Dentellière (1860) – all imitated reseaux of the (a, iv) type, but since their products were even more expensive than the hand-made forms their inventions did not survive.

Plaited lace. See *Plait* (a, i) and (b, iii).

Plastron (French, breastplate). These prettily shaped pieces were made c 1890-1910 of a wide variety of laces such as Honiton, Beds Maltese, Bohemian and Irish crochet. They curved round the base of the throat and descended in a narrowing line from shoulder to abdomen, giving a waspish look to the waist, and forming a screen across the front opening of the bodice.

Plat (French, flat). (a) A Belgian term referring to the denser patterned part of the lace as distinct from the ground. See *Toilé*. (b) Point plat – i.e. flat, as opposed to raised, work – is a term used in needlepoint laces. See *Venetian lace*. (c) More rarely, since they seldom have raised work, 'point plat' indicates a bobbin lace, and 'point plat appliqué' a bobbin appliqué, but this causes needless confusion.

Plauen. A town in Germany, associated with the manufacture of chemical or burnt-out laces (see *Machine laces* (h)), which are sometimes called 'Plauen laces'. These were made at Nottingham for the first time c 1908.

Point (French, stitch; Italian = punto). This word is very varied in meaning:

(a) An abbreviation of 'needlepoint', e.g. gros point de Venise, point de France, point de gaze, hollie point.

(b) As a prefix for all laces, e.g. point d'Alençon, point de Flandre, point de Milan, point d'Espagne, and point de Raguse. This has always been common usage in France.

(c) Since French was for a long time the formal language of the English upper classes who wore the lace (see *Foreign terms*), the term 'point' was also used in England as a suffix for places of origin, at least until the beginning of the twentieth century.

(d) Its retention now in 'Bucks point' may indicate the French or Flemish origin of this lace, so closely associated with the designs of later Mechlin and the ground of Lille.

(e) Bobbin lace stitches: e.g. point de raccroc (see *Raccroc*), point de fée (qv), point d'esprit (see *Plait* (b)).

(f) Bobbin reseaux: e.g. point ground (Bucks), point de Paris.

(g) Point lace: another name for the renaissance laces which imitated seventeenth-century Italian designs and used buttonhole stitches, though the greater part of their substance was a huge length of machine tape, e.g. point de Milan (see *Mezzo punto* (d) and *Milanese lace* (b)).

(h) Point net: a patterned loop net made on the Stocking Frame from 1769.

(i) Point gauge: a measure of the fineness or coarseness of a bobbinet. A 10-point gauge indicates a concentration of ten bobbins per inch width of the machine (see *Machine lace* (c)).

(j) Points: the short laces with metal tags which passed through eyelet holes to tie doublet and hose together, in the fourteenth to sixteenth centuries.

Point à l'aiguille. A French term for needlepoint.

Point Colbert. See *Bayeux, Lefebure.*

Point coupé (French, cutwork; Italian = punto tagliato). The old spelling, point couppe, appears in Vinciolo's pattern book of 1587, printed in Paris. The term is used in France for both cutwork and reticella.

Point d'Angleterre (French, English lace).

(a) A very lovely bobbin lace, occasionally with needlepoint fillings or motifs, made almost certainly in the Brussels area of Flanders, from the mid seventeenth to late eighteenth centuries. The earlier designs were like the baroque blooms and luxuriant foliage of the Venetian gros points, swelling outwards to fill the narrow lappets and extend beyond the borders into generous scallops. There was almost no open space for the ground, but the tiniest gaps were neatly filled with the minute hexagons of the droschel reseau. It was a non-continuous lace, but threads were seldom carried across the back of the work. There was no gimp or cordonnet in the usual sense, but the edges of the flowers were faintly outlined with raised work, and the tiny veins picked out with rolling. There were often beautifully varied fillings, and sometimes small enclosures of picoted brides to lighten the effect. The finest flax thread, with a 1,200 count, was used.

In spite of its name it has never been regarded in England or elsewhere as an English lace (see *English lace* (b)). The earliest references to it are in 1661:

(i) *La Revolte des Passemens*, 1661, mentions 'grande dentelle d'Angleterre', 'dentelle noire d'Angleterre', and 'dentelle façon d'Angleterre' (important English lace, black English lace, and English-type lace). The prefix 'point' is not used, and the laces from their description appear to be coarse: the black for example hires herself out as a net to catch woodcocks. They may therefore refer to something quite different.

(ii) In 1662 Charles II placed an embargo on the importation of Flemish lace, in order to encourage home production. His idea of home production was to import Flemish workers to make Flemish lace on English soil, using English thread. A lace similar to point d'Angleterre may therefore have been made in England by these workers, and Celia Fiennes's comment about the 'fine bone lace in imitation of the Antwerp and Flanders lace . . . it only will not wash so fine' may be explained by the inferior quality of English flax. The embargo was unsuccessful: the English-Flemish lace was not popular, and huge imports of Flemish lace continued under the affable pseudonym 'point d'Angleterre', which, once the lace had been successfully landed, would have been equivalent to a trade mark 'Made in England'. In 1678 a vessel was seized by the customs men and found to be carrying some 750,000 yards (685,800 m) of contraband Brussels lace, with enormous quantities of point d'Angleterre gloves, fichus, aprons, petticoats, handkerchieves and fans. (See *Smuggling*.)

(iii) In 1664 the *Mercure Galant*, a French fashion journal, speaks of 'quite a novelty . . . the skirts of "point d'Angleterre" printed on linen and mounted on silk with raised ornaments; every woman has bought some'.

(iv) In 1676 Mme de Sévigné writes of 'a gown of beautiful point d'Angleterre'. See *Chenille lace*.

(v) In 1678 the *Mercure Galant* recommends as the height of fashion corsets, vests, gloves and cravats trimmed with point d'Angleterre.

(vi) In 1695 the Venetian ambassador to England writes that, in England, Venetian lace is now outmoded by 'that called English point, which you know is not made here but in Flanders'. See *Venetian lace*.

(vii) About the same time an engraving of 'habit d'este' (summer fashion) clearly labels gloves, skirt and flounce of point d'Angleterre (Fig. 21c). In fact, French references to point d'Angleterre are so much more frequent than any others that the customs evasion is regarded as primarily French rather than English: Flemish lace was banned, English lace was allowed, so what was being imported was English lace.

(viii) About 1770 Mme du Barry's wardrobe accounts for lace list many expensive items such as 'toilette d'Angleterre' and 'garniture de peignoire d'Angleterre'. As in (i) the prefix 'point' is omitted, and the references are enigmatic: the trade name of one kind of silk taffeta was 'd'Angleterre'.

The very fine point d'Angleterre had faded, attenuated and all but died by the last quarter of the eighteenth century. The ground, like that of other laces of the period, became of increasing extent and importance to the detriment of the design until finally the frail and delicate droschel was being constructed entirely plain. To speed its production it was worked in narrow strips only ¾ inch (19 mm) wide; these were then joined by point de raccroc, which imitated the plaiting and twisting of the threads so closely that the seam was all but invisible. On this ground delicate motifs of Brussels bobbin or needlepoint were applied by stitching or by glue, the product being called 'Bruxelles à vrai reseau'. See also *Design* (v).

(b) Point d'Angleterre in the late nineteenth century referred to a Belgian lace made of fine quality bobbin sprigs linked by a point de gaze ground, and with pretty needle-made fillings.

(c) Application anglaise, or English appliqué, consisted of bobbin sprigs attached to a net ground. Though made in Belgium and called in England 'Brussels bobbin appliqué', it was nevertheless known in France and Belgium as 'English'. This anomaly is less than a hundred years old, but still inexplicable.

Point de ... (a) All French names of laces, whether bobbin or needlepoint, were at one time prefixed by 'point' (See *Point* (b)). This practice is now largely discontinued.

(b) 'Point de' is still used: (i) where the proper name is not geographical but descriptive, e.g. point de gaze, point de neige; (ii) where to omit it would alter the meaning, e.g. point Colbert; (iii) where there is no alternative sufficiently specific, e.g. point de France; (iv) where omission would only deepen the mystery and appear to substantiate a false claim, e.g. point d'Angleterre.

Point de fée, fairy stitch, witch lace. A twentieth-century version of Binche lace, with a ground similar to partridge eye, currently made at the Kantcentrum in Bruges.

Points de France. This plural form encompasses all the needlepoint and bobbin laces made under the direction of Colbert, shortly after Louis XIV's clamp-down, late in 1660, on imported laces, indeed on the wearing of costly thread laces at all, since these were invariably foreign. The aim was to imitate, in France, the laces of Venice, Genoa and Ragusa.

(a) Needlepoints. (Fig. 15.) The procedure was to invite, entice or force laceworkers from Venice to settle in France, for example around the Alençon area, where experienced needlewomen already made good cutworks and reticellas and so might be expected to have some facility for the new techniques. The workshops were established in 1664, and only four years later Louis's second son, Philippe, Duc d'Anjou (born 1668) was presented to his father in a mantle deeply bordered with a French needlepoint lace of very rich design.

Venice suffered badly from this loss of business. It was regarded as a crime against the Republic to make Venetian lace outside Venice, and the Doge threatened imprisonment of the relatives of the errant workers and that, if they themselves did not return, an emissary would be commissioned to kill them. We have no record of the effectiveness of this threat. It was in any case too late: French lacemakers had learned all that they needed to know in order to produce an ornate needlepoint which was instantly popular. Famous designers such as Bailly (1629-82), Le Brun (1619-90) and the Bérains all contributed to its success.

By the last decade of the seventeenth century the taste for heavy lace was fading: Venice was losing its importance; Flanders was producing finer and finer thread. In the lull following the exodus of lacemakers caused by Louis's revocation of the Edict of Nantes in 1685, a need for a change of style became evident. By 1717 a reseau was replacing the original ground of hexagonal brides, and by 1723 point de France in its primary pseudo-Venetian form was no more. The eighteenth-century forms are described under *Alençon, Argentan, Argentella* and *point de Sedan.*

(b) Bobbin laces. For a long time France could not even begin to compete with the superlative products of Flanders. Only a further simplification of clothes and a change in fashion from displaying lace in a way that showed its design to gathering it so that design was unimportant enabled France to break into the market with its fragile blondes, marlis and mignonettes. It was now the turn of the Flemish laces to languish.

All French laces foundered with the Revolution (1789), which was an attack not only on the nobility but on all their extravagant apparel, in which lace ranked very high indeed. Many laces were revived in the nineteenth century, in a considerably simplified form. The main nineteenth-century French bobbin laces were Bayeux, blonde, Caen, Chantilly, Dieppe, Le Puy, Lille, point de Paris, Valenciennes. They are described under those heads.

Point de gaze, point à l'aiguille gazée, gauze point, rosaline, Brussels rose point, point de Bruxelles. A needlepoint lace made in and around Brussels from the 1850s to the 1930s. Its most distinctive characteristic was the dainty gauze ground, made only of single buttonhole stitches lightly threaded through each other, which gave it its name (Fig. 5a). The designs are floral, with wild or garden flowers transformed into alien blooms by the grace and precision of their naturalistic moulding and their artistic arrangement in posies, pendants or swirling sprays. Roses are always there, often with layered petals, and an effect of sunshine is created by an interplay of densely packed and widely spaced buttonhole stitching. The fillings are like intricate mosaics, jewelled with geometric designs.

Point de gaze was imitated by the Schiffli machine, using net to represent the gauzy reseau and shaped pieces of cotton cloth for the raised rose petals.

Point de Milan. See *Mezzo punto* (d) and *Milanese lace* (b).

Point de neige, rose point, rosaline. A form of Venetian raised needle-point, with small tiered flowers and stars of elaborate picots as delicate and intricate as snow crystals. It was made from about the 1650s to 1710 as lappets and all the other costume trimmings of both men and women. It may still have been made at Burano in the later eighteenth century and is known to have been made there in the nineteenth century under the name 'rosseline'. It is not to be confused with fond de neige, a reseau.

Point de Paris. (a) A type of bobbin reseau, also called: six-point star, from its shape; fond chant, from its forming the ground of eighteenth-century Chantilly laces; fond double, because its technique of working is like a whole stitch; Kat stitch, from some fancied association with Catherine of Aragon, who resided in Bedfordshire; French ground, from being found in eighteenth-century French peasant laces; and wire ground, because the intertwining of the stretched threads looks like a wire mesh. It is also found sometimes in Bucks trolly and in Antwerp trolle kant.

(b) The reseau was copied by the bobbinet machines, from the 1820s, and used as a basis for embroidery, e.g. of fichus. It appeared again in the early twentieth century as 'Ariston double woven net curtains'. See *Honeycomb* (b).

(c) A French bobbin lace of the eighteenth century with slender trailing designs in a point de Paris ground. It was a simple lace and did not compete with those of Flanders. It was revived in the late nineteenth century for trimming lingerie and 'fancy linen'.

(d) This point de Paris lace was copied on the Barmen machine and also on the Levers, which produced simple designs of rabbits, ducks or lonely flower heads outlined with thick cordonnets.

Point de Sedan. One of the French needlepoints instigated in 1664 by Louis XIV and Colbert. Where the archetypal point de France had a precise rigid formality of small but well spaced units, point de Sedan, with all its richly varied fillings and exquisitely fine workmanship, gave the impression of a garden overgrown and gone to seed, with a riot of bursting fruits, tangled and full-blown to the point of dissipation. It attempted perhaps to emulate the floral luxuriance of the beautiful Flemish Mechlins and point d'Angleterre (Sedan was not part of France until 1642) but succeeded only in appearing vulgar and was soon replaced in fashion by the subdued Normandy laces with reseaux.

Point d'Espagne, Spanish point. A name used for laces of gold enhanced with coloured silks, which were copiously worn by the French court in the time of Louis XIV (reigned 1661-1715). Whether they came from Spain is uncertain. France in the mid seventeenth century was producing her own precious metal laces at Le Puy, Aurillac, Paris and Lyons and was even exporting to Spain and her American colonies, a state of affairs which continued into the eighteenth century even after Philip V's sumptuary edict of 1723: in 1745 a French vessel bound for Cadiz was found to be carrying illicitly £150,000 of gold and silver lace; and a further haul in 1789 amounted to £500,000, but that was the year of the Revolution and perhaps not typical.

There is no doubt that Spain produced some gold and silver laces, as evidenced by the accounts of travellers in Barcelona in 1683. She was also said to have produced at that time excellent thread (flax) laces, though these could have been the work of Flemings transported from the Spanish Netherlands, since Flanders was a Spanish dominion until 1713.

Evidence for the earlier making of bobbin lace in Spain rests on dubious literary descriptions such as those of Cervantes (1547-1616), who, in *Don Quixote*, refers to Sanchica making bone lace (this is discredited as an inaccurate translation of 'puntas de randas', probably meaning lacis); to Constanza, the best maker of randas in Toledo, who sings at her lace pillow like an angel; and to Altistidora, who 'makes her bobbins dance' (compare Heathcoat's simile, see under *Bobbin net*). However, Cervantes is known to have spent several years in Italy in the early 1570s, and he may have been describing something he had seen there. Black silk Spanish lace occurs in the wardrobe accounts of Elizabeth I in 1562.

The form of Venetian gros point commonly referred to as 'Spanish point' is certainly distinctive in design. The shape of the flowers is different, and the raised parts are not simply decorated with spines and crowns of picots but are embellished all over with elaborate bands, frills and ornamental sutures. Whether, however, this lace was made in Spain or in Venice to a Spanish specification is not known. See also *Spanish lace*.

Point d'esprit. See *Plait* (b). In the nineteenth century there were two other uses of point d'esprit: (i) an embroidered tulle or silk net; (ii) a spotted cotton machine net.

Point de Venise. See *Venetian lace* (h).

Point de Venise à reseau, reseau Venise, grounded Venetian point. A needlepoint lace, made with consummate skill, which has a reseau ground and was probably produced in Venice or its nearby islands such as Burano in the first half of the eighteenth century. Its design has some similarity to the gros points but is completely flat, like a point plat or coralline, and it has a thin filmy texture like a Flemish lace or a fine Alençon. Opinions differ, strongly, as to its geographical origin, the choice being between Venice, Brussels and France:

(i) The lace is completely flat, with no clearly visible outlining thread. Brussels needlepoint has a visible, though slight, cordonnet fixed (like that of the nineteenth-century Brussels point de gaze) by spaced buttonhole stitches. Alençon has a strong cordonnet worked over a flax core, completely covered with buttonhole stitches, and usually with small sharp picots evenly around it.

(ii) The ground in all three is an Alençon reseau ordinaire (see *Alençon* (i)). In reseau Venise it is worked lengthwise; in the other two across the narrow width.

The design, like a static baroque, has a decadent quality, as if made by a decayed city, or like a form trying to persist beyond its time. In some examples there is a marked similarity between the overall appearance of reseau Venise and of point de Sedan, though the texture is quite different. (Fig. 16.)

Cole regards reseau Venise as the parental form of both Brussels needlepoint and the French needlepoints with reseaux which began about 1717, i.e. as an unsuccessful form inspiring successful transitional forms in other countries. Head regards it as a copy of Alençon, a last attempt of the broken Venetian republic to regain some part of the market.

Whatever the truth of it may be, it is a distinctive lace needing not to be lumped with some other types but to be fitted into its own place and time.

Point ground. See *Point* and *Reseau.*

Point lace, Point net. See *Point.*

Point net hands. Workers making point net, as opposed to framework knitters, who operated very similar machines to make hosiery.

Point noué (French, knotted stitch). A knotted buttonhole stitch (qv) perhaps used in punto a groppo (see *Groppo*).

Point plat (French, flat needlepoint). Used of some English and Venetian needlepoints of the late seventeenth century, in contradistinction to raised points, in which there is a raised and padded cordonnet. See *Plat.*

Point tordu, double point grillé, twisted half stitch. A variation of the torchon ground.

Point tresse. See *Hair lace.*

Poke bonnet veil. (Fig. 34.) The poke was an early nineteenth-century bonnet developed from the helmet-shaped head-dress of the late eighteenth century by the poking forwards of the brim until the face became extremely difficult to see except straight on when it appeared, framed, as at the end of a long tunnel. By the 1820s the brims were raised and widened, almost exposing the face to view, and yard-square net veils were then attached to the crown of the bonnet to hang forwards like curtains and obscure it again. These 'curtains to bonnets', as they were called, survive in large quantities and are sometimes wrongly identified as aprons. They were made of white or black net, decorated with run or tambour embroidery or with appliqué work. The black ones were more heavily ornamented, imitating Spanish designs. The fashion went out in the late 1850s (causing a loss of tens of thousands of pounds to the lace trade), when Worth, the first couturier, opened his establishment in Paris and brought back hats to top a comprehensively planned ensemble.

Poking stick, Setting stick. An iron tool of the sixteenth century, made by blacksmiths, for setting the complex tiers and the lace trim of ruffs in their correct position.

Porte. See *Pinhole.*

Portugal was never important commercially as a manufacturer of lace, though some was made in convents, and some of aloe fibre. The Portuguese island of Madeira is known for its modern cutwork embroidery. See also *Messages in lace.*

Potten kant, Pot lace. See *Antwerp.*

Pricking. See *Parchment.*

Princess lace, Brussels princess. A type of appliqué or of guipure, made in Belgium in the late nineteenth and twentieth centuries, using fancy tapes, which were often bought in a complete kit comprising pseudo-needlepoint leaf shapes, scalloped petals for flowers, narrow strands for stems or tendrils, and even tiny medallions of machine point de gaze. It involved no handwork except their linking together by looped threads or their attachment to a length of net. See also *Point.*

Protestants. People who favoured the Reformation (1529) and so protested against the Catholic Holy Roman Empire's restrictions on further religious reform. It was the violent attacks of the Catholics upon the Protestants, in Flanders and France, in the sixteenth and seventeenth centuries, which brought a finer and more artistic lacemaking to England. See also *Refugees.*

Pulled threadwork. See *Drawnwork.*

Puncetto. See *Groppo* and *Knotted lace.*

Punto (Italian, a stitch, French = point).

Punto a festone, punto a occhiello. See *Buttonhole stitch.*

Punto a groppo. Knotted stitch. See *Groppo*.

Punto a rammendo. A darning or running stitch in *Filet* and buratto. It passes in one direction only and often covers two or more meshes at a time. (Fig. 19e.)

Punto a stuora. A matting stitch, a form of needle weaving, used to make decorative circles suspended in a space, and looking rather like the bottoms of wicker baskets where threads weave in and out of the splayed diameters.

Punto a tela. A linen stitch or cloth stitch made by darning several times in both directions in each square of filet (qv).

Punto a vermicilli. A tape lace using a very narrow braid, which is twisted into intricate curls and linked to make a lace with almost no fancy fillings, e.g. Sardinian point.

Punto avorio. See *Avorio*.

Punto contato. Counted threadwork, such as drawnwork, filet and buratto.

Punto in aria (Italian, stitches in the air). Literally a detached embroidery worked in buttonhole stitch and completely divorced from normal surface embroidery. The term was first applied to an extension of reticella, worked on parchment, in the sixteenth century (see *Pagano*). It is used, now, most particularly of the narrow dentate borders of circles and stars – made in Italy, and perhaps Flanders – which were used to trim ruffs, and which when starched stood out from the gadrooned borders like rows of barbed arrowheads.

During the seventeenth century, Venetian, French, English and Netherlands needlepoints developed their own distinctive characteristics of design and technique. Though the method of working remained the same – on a parchment pattern from which when the lace was completed it could be snipped away – the term 'punto in aria' was no longer used, and they are referred to by their geographical names.

Early punto in aria designs were copied commercially in bobbin lace (Genoa, sixteenth century) and in needlepoint as an exercise in skill (Aemilia Ars, Bologna, twentieth century). (Figs. 1a, 9, 48a.)

Punto de ajuga (Italian, needlepoint).

Punto in relievo (Italian, stitches in relief). Stitches with raised or rose work, as opposed to being completely flat.

Punto reale (Italian, royal stitch). Satin stitch, which often appears on eighteenth-century drawnworks.

Punto ricamento a maglia quadra (Italian, embroidered square-meshed net). See *Lacis*.

Punto riccio. Curved decorations, like tendrils, found especially in Tuscan filet or Modano.

Punto tagliato (Italian, cutwork, French = point coupé). See *Cutwork, Needlepoint, Reticella* and *Pagano*.

Punto tagliato a fogliami. See *Gros point, Pagano, Venetian lace.*

Punto tirato, tela tirata (Italian, drawn threadwork, French = fil tiré). See *Drawnwork*.

Purl. See *Pearl*.

Pusher. See *Machine lace* (d).

Quaker. (a) An American term for filet lace. (b) A machine lace company of Philadelphia, Pennsylvania, currently producing table cloths, on Lace Curtain machines, using old designs.

Quality. This is of extreme importance in assessing the market value of a lace. The quality can be defined in terms of the smoothness and fineness of the thread; the closeness and evenness of the texture; the complexity and competence of the varied stitches and fillings; and the harmony and unity of the design.

Regularity of appearance and harshness of feel are often quoted as tests to distinguish a machine-made lace. However, the highest quality of hand-made laces will show almost perfect regularity of workmanship. Also, if they are late nineteenth-century pieces of large size, they are likely to have been stiffened with gum to make them stand out smoothly, a process which gives them the texture of a machine finish. Crisp, sharply patterned Chantilly shawls and point de gaze trains are especially objects of error.

Quarter. A quarter-yard, or 9 inches (229 mm), used as a measure of width in machine laces.

Quatréfoil fillings (French, four leaf). Four-lobed shapes clustered together in late seventeenth- and early eighteenth-century Flemish bobbin laces such as Mechlin and point d'Angleterre.

Quesnoy, Le. A town in French Flanders once important for the bobbin lace Valenciennes and the needlepoint Points de France. It lost its importance after 1715.

Quills, quillings. (a) Quill. A small bobbin with a long neck made to hold the gimp thread, from a skein, ready for it to be wound on to a trolly bobbin for use on the pillow.
(b) Quillings. Cotton machine net made in narrow widths. They were named from being sharply folded, like the quill feathers on the wing of a bird, and were worn around the mob cap and neckline of the bodice in the time of William IV. In 1834 there were 1,100 quilling machines in the Nottingham area. The fashion was revived in the late nineteenth century.
(c) Quilles. Trimmings of hand-made lace, worn gathered or pleated, and attached vertically to the right and left sides of the skirt of a dress to hang in fluted folds. Late seventeenth and eighteenth centuries.

Rabat. See *Col rabat.*

Raccroc, Point de (French, from the verb 'raccrocher', to hook up again).
(a) Made as a triple linking seam, only 1/10 inch (2.5 mm) wide, used to join narrow (¼ inch to 1 inch; 6 mm to 25 mm) strips of droschel so neatly that it is seen only as a faint shadow. The central row is plaited, like the droschel itself, but the two outer rows are looped through the already completed bobbin meshes.
(b) Less commonly, a stitch used to join strips of fond simple. The reseau here is on a much larger scale than droschel and is twisted not plaited, so that only a single almost straight thread twining in and out of alternate right and left side loops is required. It is found in long Bucks stoles in which the 2 foot (610 mm) width is made by joining three 8 inch (203 mm) wide pieces. Similar joins occur in Spanish bobbin mantillas. In Maltese, point de gaze and Chantilly, where the pattern assemblies are larger, the joined pieces are irregularly shaped to fit the design, like a simple jigsaw, and sometimes two linking threads are used, twisting through the meshes on either side, and then crossing each other. A matching thread is used and the joins, unless they begin to split apart, are

almost impossible to find.

Rack. A measurement of bobbinet length used because the stretchability of the product made cheating on yardage too easy. It was equivalent to 240 meshes and was measured as the net was made.

Ragusa, Dubrovnik. A town on the Dalmatian coast, formerly a small republic, facing on to the Adriatic. It was founded in the seventh century AD and was at various times under the influence of Venice, Byzantium and the Ottoman empire. In the sixteenth century it was a great mercantile power, trading with America and India, and having treaty obligations with Spain. It was destroyed by an earthquake in 1667, and so its laces, which are well enough recorded not to be completely apocryphal, have taken on a legendary quality. They cannot with certainty be matched up with any lace now known. Some information about them is recorded between 1654 and 1667:

1654. Louis XIV claimed a 25 per cent tax on imported laces of Ragusa, Genoa and Venice.

1661. In *La Révolte des Passemens*, 'poincte de Raguse' is described as being so resplendent that it brings everyone to financial ruin. It is linked again, in this respect, with Venice and Genoa, and also with Aurillac, where gold and silver lace was made.

1661. In a poetic metaphor of preparation for battle, in *La Révolte*, Colonel Ragusa is put in charge of the right wing of the voluntary 'Cravates', taking command of 'dentelle d'Angleterre' and 'Moresse'. What information this gives us is uncertain. 'Cravate' could refer to the linen scarf or cravat, the ends of which were characteristically decorated with squares of lace. But 'Cravate' was also a nickname for Croatian soldiers and so could be taken as a reference to the Croatian (Dalmatian) origin of the lace. 'Dentelle d'Angleterre' probably does not mean point d'Angleterre (qv); and 'Moresse' (Moorish-Iberian) could refer to a knotted lace, characteristic of North Africa (see *Groppo* (iv)) or to a Spanish lace of some kind, even perhaps to a Spanish raised needlepoint similar to a Venetian gros point, or, again to the flowing Islamic designs (arabesques or moresques) which appeared in Spanish drawnworks of the sixteenth century (see below).

1661. Passages in *La Révolte* indicate a jealous rivalry between Ragusa and Venice. The two republics were closely connected, Ragusa being a trading post for Venice, so that Venetian laces might pass through Ragusa, and Ragusa laces through Venice, without the two being sharply distinguished by their names. Lefebure suggests that Ragusa was an ancestral form of Venetian lace characterised by formal Islamic scrolls and arabesque blossoms, and that the influence of Venetian Christianity transformed its designs into representational forms.

1664. Ragusa was named by Louis XIV as one of the laces worthy of imitation when he was setting up his own lace manufacture (see *Points de France*). Venice and Genoa were also named.

1667. Ragusa, allied to the Habsburgs, sided with Austria against Louis when he invaded the Spanish Netherlands. His revenge was to prohibit the importation of Ragusa lace into France. In the same year the ancient city was destroyed.

So much for contemporary references. Even in these there is room for guesswork. The rest is theorising, on premises of varying validity. It has been suggested that Ragusa lace was:

(a) A gold lace (Mincoff and Marriage). This is a generally held view, and the association of Ragusa and Aurillac supports it.

(b) A form of Venetian raised point. Its postulated link with Spanish lace (see above) and its recurrent linkage with Venice in the French writings are evidence in favour.

(c) A flat needlepoint using a double buttonhole stitch. Gertrude Whiting in *La Révolte* illustrates it with a compact lace similar to that usually attributed to the Netherlands, but inset with a crowned Byzantine lady encompassed by children. See *Dutch lace* (b).

(d) A knotted lace. Powys describes it as a Byzantine punto avorio made by knotting and illustrates it with an exquisite cartouche of Leda and the swan enclosed in a gros point flower. Nevill Jackson describes it as a 'knotted guipure . . . formed of threads knotted together like the fringes of Genoese macramé'. Pfannschmidt describes it as three-dimensional, with a knotted stitch, drawing on Phoenician/Mycenean ornamentation, and known variously as punto avorio, punto dei greci and punto sarazeno (ivory, Greek and Saracen stitch). The reference to Moresse may indicate a knotted lace; and Ragusa's geographical and political association with Turkey would have made her familiar with the knotted work of that country (see *Knotted lace*). See also *Tatting*.

(e) Cutwork. Head makes this suggestion, without elucidation. Reticella has also been put forward as a possibility (Risselin) because of the similarity of the Croatian word 'radizena'. However, this has a different root from reticella, meaning not 'net', but 'woman's work' (Lewis) – which could be equated with nun's work, and so round again to cutwork and reticella; but the derivation is tortuous and unprovable. It seems likely also that an expensive lace, exported to the august court of France, would be known by its Italian not its Croatian name, since in this Venetian outpost the richer portion of the population would almost certainly have been Venetians.

(f) Embroidered lace. Lefebure, arguing from nineteenth-century Croatian products and the fact that old trading routes visited the Greek islands, suggests that Ragusa lace was a drawnwork made by the Greek peasants. But the high esteem in which it appears to have been held, and its costliness, make this hypothesis unlikely. Similarly, the suggestion that 'Ragusa' referred to the drawnworks of the Sicilian town, rather than to the Dalmatian city, is untenable and would overlook the undeniably close association of Venice and Ragusa.

(g) Gimp. Palliser, referring like Lefebure to nineteenth-century products — which, considering that Ragusa had only recently been rebuilt after nearly two hundred years as a ruin, was not very logical — illustrates a simple gimp lace with picots as possibly 'the old, long-lost point de Raguse'. However, she does point out a similarity between this work and a pattern in *Le Pompe*, 1557 (see *Bobbin lace* and *Pagano*); and if the gimp were made of gold thread instead of silk, it would indeed be inordinately expensive. Caulfield and Saward also suggest a gimp.

(h) Lacis. According to Hungerford Pollen, buratto is sometimes called 'punto di Ragusa'.

Raised work. Literally, work which is raised above the general surface of the lace.

(a) In Honiton, Brussels duchesse and eighteenth-century point d'Angleterre, the outline to be raised is made separately as a minute braid with pinholes along one edge only. This braid, known as ten-stick or gimp, is then placed face down on the pillow, and the rest of the leaf or flower worked over it. Penderel Moody calls this 'gimp-raised' as opposed to the plainer 'rolled-raised'. See *Ribbing*.

(b) Raised plaits are a characteristic of nineteenth-century Beds Maltese, of Le Puy and of some late seventeenth-century Milanese bobbin laces (see *Florentine knots*).

(c) Raised wheatears. These are not entirely synonymous with plaits, being pointed instead of square-ended, and also rather longer. Used for decoration, they appear not as flat little strips but as rounded knobs or buttons. (Fig. 3b.)

(d) 'Rose' is sometimes used to express 'raised', so that any needlepoint lace with any raised work could then be called 'rose point'. Thus Venetian gros point, point de neige and Brussels point de gaze are all lumped together under this name. This is not desirable since it confuses rather than clarifies the subject. See *Rosaline*.

Randas. See *Spanish lace*.

Raschel. This machine is basically the same as the old Warp Frame, which ceased production in the 1850s. It has enormous numbers of needles, which make vertical (warp-directional) rows of loops with cross-connections for stability. In the early twentieth century it made gas mantles. Since the 1960s, with the development of synthetic fibres, it has been able to make braids, curtains, tights and elasticated underwear, though its net is not sufficiently firm for Schiffli embroidery (see *Machine lace* (h)). Production is extremely rapid: between 14 and 24 needles work to every inch (25 mm) of the 75 to 130 inch (1,905 to 3,302 mm) widths of the machine, and it can 'knit' a length of nearly 12 inches (305 mm) per minute, or up to 2,280 square inches (14,711 sq cm). (Fig. 30c.)

Rayon, artificial silk, art silk. A filament fibre first invented and patented in 1883 in an attempt to find a substitute for silk – hence the name 'artificial silk'. The first commercial art silk machine was launched at Courtauld's in 1905. The name 'rayon' was first used in 1927. The basic idea was to copy the silk moth caterpillar and extrude a liquid under pressure through fine pores so that it firmed on contact with air to produce continuous threads of almost infinite length.

The raw material is not animal protein as in natural silk, but the plant carbohydrate, cellulose. This is obtained either from wood pulp steeped initially in caustic soda or from the compacted fibre waste from the cotton boll. Rayon was used very extensively for machine laces in the first half of the twentieth century, but less so since the invention of nylon. See also *Artificial fibres*.

Real lace. A term used in contrast to 'artificial' or 'machine-made', intending to distinguish the 'real' bobbin and needlepoint laces from the embroidered, craft or machine laces. But the term is unsatisfactory: it is emotive, suggesting that the real laces are vastly superior, whereas in some cases they are only a great deal more expensive. Also, commercially minded vendors, aware of the social distinction, tended to call any lace with any vestige of handwork – such as Limerick or Brussels princess – 'real', in order to attract buyers. 'Real' had apparently in those days the same allure and duplicity as the modern 'new'.

Refugees. Five major waves of refugees, mainly Protestants fleeing from Catholic persecution, can be distinguished between the sixteenth century and the present time.
(a) 1568. From the Spanish Netherlands to England after the Duke of Alva's persecutions.
(b) 1572. From France, after the Massacre of St Bartholomew's. It is said that Queen Elizabeth I refused them permission to land. She had, only four months earlier, signed a treaty of friendship with France and desperately needed to keep that country's support against her cousin,

Mary Queen of Scots, whom she felt as a continual threat not only to her crown but to her life. The Catholic-directed massacre had been approved by the Pope; Charles IX, who instigated it, was Mary's brother-in-law; and one of the side effects of the slaughter had been to magnify the power of the Duc de Guise, Mary's mother's brother. The balance of power was so finely adjusted that even to give sanctuary to the escaping Huguenots might have seemed to France a hostile gesture and have brought about Elizabeth's destruction.

(c) The Edict of Nantes giving religious freedom, in 1598, was never very effective, but with its revocation by Louis XIV in 1685 hatred of the Protestants reached new heights of violence. Since the western boundaries of Flanders were now French, there was an exodus of both French and Flemish lacemakers, with their distinctive techniques.

(d) At the time of the Revolution of 1789-92, the necks of lacemakers were equally at risk with those of their clientèle, and any who could fled the country.

(e) During the First World War of 1914-18, the lacemaking towns and villages of south and west Belgium were converted into a battlefield. Immigrants again sought refuge in England.

English lacemaking therefore, if not entirely derivative, was at least very strongly influenced by ideas and techniques from abroad. The most noticeably adopted features are: the Lille ground in Bucks; Mechlin or Lille designs, also in Bucks; the non-continuous Brussels method of lacemaking used in Honiton; the droschel ground of the late eighteenth to early nineteenth centuries; the technique of applying motifs to a plain ground; and the raised and rolled work.

Regency. (a) In France, the period of Louis XV's minority, following the death of Louis XIV, when his uncle Philippe, Duc d'Orleans, was Regent (1715-23). (b) In Great Britain, the long period towards the close of George III's reign when his son, the Prince Regent (later George IV), acted as ruler during his father's recurrent bouts of insanity (1800-20).

Regrounding. The replacement of the original background of bars or reseau, in whole or in part, with either a similar ground, a different hand-made ground or a machine net. In the last case the net was cut away behind the motifs. When the net was continuous across the lace, with the motifs stitched on to it, it was not regrounding, but appliqué work.

Regrounding was common practice in the nineteenth century in order that antique laces could be made fit to wear or, rather like fur coats, remodelled for the latest fashion. For a collector, regrounding greatly reduces the value. For example, in seventeenth-century Venetian needlepoints the original brides were starred and picoted, strung across the open spaces like small constellations. They often broke under the pull of the heavy flowers, and replacement brides, however neatly made, were usually quite plain. See also *Ground*.

Renaissance lace. (Fig. 44c.) Lace in which the outline of the design is made of bought tape. The inspirational name refers to the rebirth of antique Italian forms. These were copied on to glazed cloth or suede; the tape was tacked to this pattern and its various convolutions joined and cavities filled with buttonhole or other stitches. Several names are used for this lace, but not a single one which is completely unambiguous: (i) point lace (qv) can be confused with needlepoint; (ii) tape (qv) with trail laces; (iii) mezzo punto (qv) with a seventeenth-century form; (iv) even 'renaissance' itself sounds misleadingly like the fifteenth-century cultural revival; (v) one of the trade names for the tape was Honiton (qv), causing confusion with Honiton bobbin lace.

Varying forms of renaissance lace are known as *Branscombe, Battenburg, Princess* and *Sardinian point.*

Reseau (French, network). The ground of small meshes filling the open spaces of a lace. The precise course of the threads and the resultant shape of the mesh are an important diagnostic feature in lace identification. The threads of the reseau may be in continuity with those of the design (continuous laces) or may be quite distinct (non-continuous). In this latter case they have to be attached with a needle or, if bobbins are used, by taking 'sewings'. Historically, reseaux dominated the eighteenth century, and brides did not appear again until the mid nineteenth century, when 'guipures' were hailed as something completely new (see *Brides* and *Dating of lace* (b)).

The various reseaux are listed below:

(a) Needlepoint. (i) Alençon: reseau ordinaire, reseau tortillée, reseau mouché; (ii) Argentan; (iii) Argentella; (iv) Burano; (v) point de gaze, rose point, nineteenth-century point d'Angleterre ground.

(b) Bobbin. (i) fond simple, simple ground, fond clair, Lille, point, or net ground, tulle mesh: found in Bucks, Lille, Chantilly, Spanish bobbin, blonde; (ii) fond double, double ground, point de Paris, Kat stitch, wire, French, six-point star, star, star-pointed ground, hairpin stitch, fond chant: found in French point de Paris lace, and in some Bucks, Chantilly and Antwerp; (iii) cinq trous, five hole, fond à la vierge, virgin ground, rose stitch (Beds): found in Antwerp, some early Valenciennes, some torchon and yak; (iv) Valenciennes, square, diamond mesh; (v) round Valenciennes, round mesh: found in some Milanese, and eighteenth-century Flemish laces; (vi) Spanish, maglia de spagna, twisted hole

ground, twisted half stitch: found in silk laces, often from France and Italy, as well as Spain. (vii) Mechlin, Malines. (viii) droschel, vrai reseau, Brussels bobbin mesh, Flemish ground: found in eighteenth-century point d'Angleterre, and Devon laces; (ix) honeycomb, fond de mariage: found in some Bucks, often used as a filling; (x) partridge eye, oeil de perdrix, fond de neige, snowflake ground: the characteristic reseau of Binche, sometimes found in Mechlin; (xi) torchon.
(c) Embroidered laces. These are not said to have a reseau as such, but: (i) a structure remarkably like a fine network is often formed by drawn or pulled threadwork; (ii) filet has a square mesh, knotted at each corner; (iii) buratto has a square woven mesh.
(d) Machine. The grounds are called *Nets* rather than reseaux. Of the twist nets, the following types can be distinguished: (i) two-twist; (ii) three-twist; (iii) point de Paris; (iv) square - lace curtain; (v) imitation Valenciennes; (vi) imitation Mechlin; (vii) imitation droschel.

Reseau Venise. See *Point de Venise à reseau.*

Reseauil. See *Rezel, Knitted lace* and *Lacis.*

Reticella (Italian, a little net). A form of cutwork involving large-scale removal of squares of woven linen, the resulting appearance being like a giant mesh or network (Fig. 48a). As a technique for constructing a framework within and around which embroidered designs could be displayed it was slightly less tedious than drawnwork, but a good deal more so than the knotted squares of the filet ground, or the woven buratto. Reticella is distinctive in the large size of its meshes (¼ to ½ inch; 6 to 13 mm), and in using buttonhole stitch, instead of a running or darning stitch.
Historically, it arose later than the *Embroidered laces.* The earliest record which could possibly refer to it is in the Sforza inventory (1493) where it is called 'redexela' (a local variant of 'reticella'). In 1530 Tagliente's pattern book lists 'rete', and Pensieri (1548) 'punto in rede'. In 1560 Queen Elizabeth's wardrobe accounts list partlets (small ruffs) 'de opera rete' and 'de opera Rhet' (i.e. of net work). It is uncertain whether at this time 'rete' could have meant any other kind of network, such as filet, but it seems unlikely: filet is hardly suitable for a partlet, and portraits of this period show the linen of the ruff (as opposed to its outer border) chequered with delicate squares crossed and starred with minute geometric forms, which cannot be anything but reticella. Vecellio's patterns of 1591 and Parasole's of 1598 are clearly stated to be for 'lavoro a ponto reticello' (reticella work).
Reticella is generally regarded as a forerunner of punto in aria, and

some intermediate forms show its struggle to free itself from the constraint of the linen ground:

(i) By replacing the technique of cutting out the network with the technique of laying it down in the form of strands crossed at right angles. This process would require a parchment for support and so could lead on to a form which was not restricted by geometric considerations (imposed initially by the warp and weft of the linen) but could be free-flowing.

(ii) By extending the decoration upwards in a three-dimensional manner, i.e. by creating raised work, sometimes known as 'punto tagliato a fogliami' (see *Pagano*), a trend which developed in the early seventeenth century into the fabulous Venetian gros points.

The word 'reticella' is less commonly used, in archives, than the broader term 'cutwork', but that 'cutwork' included reticella forms is clearly shown for example in the designs of Vinciolo's *Ouvrages de Point Couppe* of 1587 (Fig. 6a); and the cost of cutwork – nearly £3 a yard in the same year – shows that it must have been both skilful and elaborate. Also reticella is technically distinct: in simple cutwork the pattern, as the name suggests, is formed by cutting, i.e. holes make the design, and the woven material where uncut forms the background. In reticella the situation is completely reversed: the open network (by whatever means it is formed) makes the background, and the solid buttonholed portions form the design.

See also *Needlepoint, Pagano, Punto in aria* and *Venetian lace* (b)).

Revivals in lace. For an industry to need revival it has to be ailing, and soon after 1800, by a combination of the industrial revolution, the French Revolution, and a change to extreme simplicity of fashion, lacemaking was almost dead. Revivals during the nineteenth century were by patronage (Napoleon I, Alençon and Chantilly; Queen Adelaide and Queen Victoria, Honiton); by charitable societies seeking to provide a livelihood for the distressed (Irish crochet, 1840; Burano needlepoint, c 1870; North Bucks Lace Association, 1897); art and craft movements (*Old Point Lace and How to Copy It* Daisy Waterhouse Hawkins; *The New Lace Embroidery, Punto Tagliato* Tebbs; Ruskin work); and very successful commercial revivals (in Malta, Bayeux, the East Midlands, and most especially in Belgium, where children and nuns worked for almost nothing so that the merchants were able to undercut English prices and still have plenty of profit for themselves). See also *Lace schools* (c).

Rezel, réseuil. A sixteenth- and seventeenth-century word meaning a network: c 1600 Marguerite de Valois, sister of Henri III, and first wife of Henri IV, possessed a rezeuil d'or. It antedated reseaux by nearly a hundred years and was probably a lacis with a knotted ground, perhaps similar to Cervantes' randas, c 1614 (see *Point d'Espagne* and *Spanish lace*).

Ribbing, rolled work, rolled-raised. A form of raised work found in Honiton lace and in Brussels duchesse. It is used for the inner detail of the veins of leaves, or the separation of the flower petals, rather than for the emphasis of outlines as in raised work. The ribbed part is made as an extension of the size needed, then rolled and tied, i.e. curled over and fixed in position with thread from the bobbins.

Richelieu. (a) A French cardinal and statesman (1585-1642). He was succeeded by Mazarin (died 1661), and then by Colbert. (b) A form of openwork embroidery used for household linen c 1890-1950. Transfer patterns were ironed on to the material. The outline was indicated by a double line, and close regular buttonhole stitches were worked between the two lines, round the outside of the pattern, which was usually of formalised flower and leaf arrangements. Linking bars, with picots, were stretched above the surface of the material to join the flowers together. Then the material was cut away from below the bars to leave open spaces. It was thus the reverse of broderie anglaise, in which holes form the design and the embroidery outlines the holes. In Richelieu work the holes do no more than add contrast and relief, and it is therefore only dubiously a lace.

Robing. The lace trimming of a lady's dress in the eighteenth century, consisting of a straight, later U-shaped, band at the back, rising over the shoulders, and passing down either side of the bodice rather like revers. From c 1760, the robing continued down the skirt. The lace matched in type and design that of the cap crown, lappets and engageants.

Rococo. See *Design.*

Rolled work. See *Ribbing.*

Rosaline, rose point. There is at present no conformity of usage in these terms.

'Rose point' can mean: (a) all raised needlepoints, i.e. all Venetian raised points would be rose points. They are, however, more commonly distinguished into three forms – gros, rose and point de neige – since they form a series both of decreasing size and of increasing freedom and liveliness of design, the flowers and brides becoming more numerous and decorated with greater frivolity. They also form a time sequence. (b)

Venetian gros and rose only, with point de neige being called 'fine rose point' (Jourdain). (c) Venetian rose and point de neige, with gros point being kept distinct (Palliser). (d) Venetian point de neige only, with gros and rose both being called gros (Lefebure). (e) Brussels point de gaze (Caplin, Powys, Risselin). Point de gaze ground is then called rose point ground.

'Rose ground' can mean, in addition: (a) cinq trous, also called rose stitch (Maidment): see *Reseau*; (b) reseau rosaceae (French, rose ground), the reseau of the rare French needlepoint, Argentella.

'Rosaline' can mean: (a) point de neige (Italian = roselline) used perhaps more for the nineteenth-century copies made at Burano than for the seventeenth-century Venetian forms (Ricci, Powys, Hungerford Pollen); (b) Venetian rose point (i.e. the middle of the series: gros – rose – point de neige); (c) Brussels point de gaze; (d) a late nineteenth-century Brussels bobbin lace with crinkly edges to the toilé and a suggestion of button roses in the design: when these have raised work in their centres the lace is called rosaline perlée; (e) a late nineteenth- or twentieth-century Italian bobbin lace with boldly curling stems terminating in half-stitch buds, and associated today with *Cantu*.

Ruff, band, fraise. A form of collar worn throughout Europe from the mid sixteenth to the late seventeenth century.
(a) The millstone. A circular ruff, which began as a small partlet c 1550 and grew until it formed a rigid encumbrance encircling the neck and spreading to such a width that eating became extremely difficult. Etiquette required that its tiered and goffered linen, its purled or punto in aria edging, should appear incessantly immaculate. The extravagance of its decoration – elaborately embroidered, sparked with jewels, glinting with gold lace, the agony of its wearing and its ridiculous appearance, seeming to impose a dismemberment of body from head, aroused alike the fury of reformers and the spite of lampoonists. Philip Stubbes (*Anatomie of Abuses*, 1583) speaks of the effects of inclement weather: 'if Aeolus with his blasts, or Neptune with his storms, chance to hit upon the crazie barke of their brused ruffes, then they go flip-flap in the wind like ragges that flew abroad, lying upon their shoulders like the dishcloute of a slut.' But they were important articles: Catherine of Medici (1519-89) brought the Venetian ruff designer Vinciolo to live at the French court; and Elizabeth I in 1580 passed a sumptuary law restricting the diameter of ruffs permitted to each social class.
(b) The open ruff, Medici collar. Introduced by Marie d' Medici, second wife of Henri IV, c 1580. It formed a curved screen behind the head, its frail reticella decoration displayed by underproppers of wire wound round with gold or silver thread.

(c) The falling ruff. Like the millstone, it consisted of layered circles of plain or embroidered lawn, edged with sharply dentate lace, but instead of being held stiff by starch it was allowed to fall softly from the throat to rest against the shoulders. (See *Col rabat*.)

By the 1620s the ruff was completely out of fashion. It reappeared again, near the end of the eighteenth century, as gathered frills of gauze or tulle worn high round the neck, leaving the decolletage untrammelled. In 1837, at a drawing room held by William IV, a gown trimmed with blonde 'and a little blonde ruff à la Queen Elizabeth' was worn. On muslin gowns of the period the pelerine collar sometimes rose up the neck and turned outwards to end in a circlet of teeth, stiffened with Ayrshire work.

Ruffles. A decoration of the sleeve ends. See *Cuffs* and *Engageants*.

Runners. (a) Laceworkers who embroidered machine nets, using running or darning stitches. Also those who ran in the cordonnet thread on patterned machine laces. The work employed thousands of women and children in the nineteenth century. See also *Embroidered nets.* (b) In Devon, the worker bobbins. See *Leader.* (c) Strips of decorated net or of linen with openwork embroidery, intended to run down a table centre. Those of net are sometimes mistaken for stoles.

Ruskin lace. (Fig. 47b.) A form of embroidered lace – drawnwork and cutwork – revived by John Ruskin (1819-1900) in the 1870s, using linen hand-spun and hand-woven by the cottagers around Coniston.

Russian lace. (a) Drawnwork embroideries of the late fifteenth century, using coloured silks. (b) Bobbin laces of abstract form. The narrow trails, often threaded with red and blue, follow a maze-like path through deep scallops to emerge again and wander into the next. The repeat is short and vermiculate. Short brides are sewn into the trails as the work proceeds. (Figs. 26, 27d) (c) Bruges-Russian and Beds-Russian have the same trail-like form but are less meandering and a good deal more neatly organised.

Samplers (Old French = essemplaire, an example).
(a) Samples of stitches, often arranged in bands, and intended as something which a needlewoman could copy. She might use it to analyse the technique of a stitch or to choose a combination of stitches, to decorate a coif or a handkerchief border. The whole thing might be copied, and perhaps even new stitches added. The inventory of Joanna

the Mad, daughter of Ferdinand and Isabella, and sister of Catherine of Aragon, lists fifty samplers, in 1509, probably the earliest record of them. See also *Lacis*.

(b) Such reference samplers were worked by adults. In the eighteenth and nineteenth centuries innumerable practice samplers were worked by young children, but these are of embroidery stitches, not lace.

(c) The printed pattern books of the sixteenth and early seventeenth centuries were also collections of samples, or samplers. They showed not stitches but designs which the embroiderer or lacemaker could copy, sometimes by counting the threads, but as often as not she would have to work out her own technique.

Sardinian point. A lace made with a very narrow machine braid, looped, and linked by fine thread, with the minimum of decoration. It is said to have been named from the visit of the King of Sardinia to England in 1855. See also *Punto a vermicilli*.

Saxony. An area of central Europe to the north of Bohemia, from which it is separated by the Erzegebirge Mountains. It was an independent kingdom until 1813.

(a) A kind of lace is known to have been made there in the sixteenth century, though its identity is obscure. Our knowledge of it centres around Barbara Uttmann (1514-75), whose epitaph refers to her 'invention of lace in 1561'. 'Invention' may well be used here in the sense of the introduction, into Saxony, of a technique known elsewhere. Reputedly, Uttmann herself was taught by a refugee lacemaker from Brabant. It is known that Swiss bobbin lace was established at this time, having originally been taken there from Venice in 1536 (see *Swiss*). The first textile pattern book, for embroidered lace, had been published by Schönsperger in 1523 at Augsburg, some 180 miles south-west of Annaberg, where Barbara Uttmann lived. The first portrait to show bobbin lace had been painted in 1549 by Lucas Cranach (1472-1553), appointed court painter to Frederick the Wise, Elector of Saxony, in 1495 (or possibly by his son, Lucas Cranach the Younger, 1515-86). Among all the legends which surround this period it is not easy to separate fact from wishful thinking. Uttmann's lace is variously described as a knotted tricot, a plain thread net, and bobbin work; and she is said to have built up an industry which employed 30,000 people. On the factual side, inventories of Eléonore d'Autriche, sister of the Emperor Charles V and second wife of François I, list 'treillis d'Allemagne' (German latticework or network) in 1543. A similar entry, for Henri II in 1557, specifies black, for a black damask robe, with bisette (qv) as an alternative. This suggests the two might be similar.

(b) Saxony did not at any time produce any very good bobbin laces. In the 1850s, however, she did make copies of Chantilly and old Brussels proficient enough to be exported to Paris and sold as antique.

(c) Dresden work (point de Saxe) was, on the other hand, superb: these superlative mid eighteenth-century drawnworks were quite without equal. (Fig. 18c.)

(d) Schiffli machines were set up in Saxony in 1881 and began to embroider nets in imitation of the needlerun Breton laces. These nets were exported in huge quantities to England, threatening to swamp the Levers patterned machine laces.

Scandinavian laces. Laces from Denmark, Norway, Sweden and Iceland. None were made for export. Drawnworks go back to the seventeenth century, torchon laces are known from the nineteenth and twentieth centuries. See also *Danish, Hardanger, Hedebo* and *Swedish.* (Figs 10, 12, 13.)

Schiffli machine. See *Machine lace* (h), and *Swiss embroidery* (c).

Schönsperger, Johann, the Younger. The author of the first textile pattern book, printed at Augsburg c 1523. It was a collection of woodcut designs for weaving and for embroidery in double running stitch, but also adaptable for counted threadwork, though the first book which was undisguisedly for drawnwork was by Vavassore, in 1530. See *Pattern books.*

Scottish lace. There were no commercial centres for lacemaking in Scotland, and lace does not even appear to have been worn in any quantity. There are references in the sixteenth century only to pearling, to 'cuttit out work' and to lacis as made by Mary Queen of Scots during her long imprisonment.

(a) In the eighteenth century a charitable school was organised by the Duchess of Hamilton. About 1850 a home industry was started by the local rector at New Pitsligo (Aberdeenshire). Both produced torchon-type laces.

(b) The cobwebby knitted laces of the Shetland marriage shawls (see *Knitted lace*) can be traced back to the 1840s. In 1854 they were copied on the Stocking Frame using a grey wool; in 1862 the 'newly brought out bright colours' (synthetic dyes, notably vivid magenta and emerald, developed in 1858) were used, with great success.

(c) Scotland was noted for its beautiful Ayrshire work, especially during the first half of the nineteenth century. (Fig. 38c.)

(d) In the nineteenth century, it also produced fine quality cotton thread.

Sedan. See *Point de Sedan.*

Semé (French, sown). Used of a scattering of spots, sprigs, leaves or tears through the reseau. It was especially characteristic of late eighteenth- and nineteenth-century laces such as Alençon, Mechlin and Lille. (See also *Tulle* (b, vi).

Setting up. The preparation of a bobbin lace pillow so that it is ready for working. See *Dressed pillow.*

Sewings, crochetage. A term used in non-continuous bobbin laces. It is a way of joining the reseau or bride threads to the units of the design. In Honiton lace a needle pin – traditionally a long needle fixed into a dead Lucifer matchstick – is used to draw a length of thread through the pinholes along the edges of the motif in the form of a loop. A bobbin is then passed through this loop, and the thread is tied, ready for use. To make the sewing easier, the shaft of the Honiton bobbin is smoothly tapered at the tip, and it has no spangles. (Fig. 24c.)

Some of the sixteenth-century bobbin lace patterns (*Le Pompe*, 1557) are said to require sewings (Paulis).

Sewing machines. A mechanical means of sewing which minimised the amount of handwork required. The first chain-stitch machine was patented in 1804, but it was another twenty-six years before a Frenchman, Thrimonnier, developed one which would work reliably. Singer patented the first sewing machine in America in 1850; in 1851 a Judkins lock-stitch machine, capable of five hundred stitches per minute, was shown at the Great Exhibition; and in 1855 the Willcox and Gibbs chain-stitch machine came on the market.

From the lace point of view the evolution of the sewing machine had a twofold significance. Firstly, it was now possible for clothes to be ready-made in large quantities, and at relatively low cost. 'Fashion' was therefore brought within the reach of the multitude; and the demand for lace – already democratised by the Warp Frame and Bobbinet machines – was reinforced, to the benefit of all lacemakers. Secondly, chain-stitch embroidery on net could now be done by machine, as well as by hand tambouring. The designs, however, were necessarily simpler and used thicker thread, and their crudity harmed the market for the fine Limerick work. See also *Tambour.*

Sfilatura. Italian for drawn threadwork, where the threads are drawn out individually rather than a number at a time to make an open space. The remaining threads are decorated with needle weaving.

Sforza inventory. A very detailed inventory drawn up in 1493 in order that fair division of an estate could be made between two sisters, Angela and Ippolita Sforza Visconti, of the family of the Duke of Milan. It is sometimes quoted as evidence of the existence of bobbin lace (qv) in the fifteenth century. See also *Bavaro, Reticella.*

Shaped lace, shaped pieces. The technical term for machine laces made not as an all-over yardage, but literally as shaped pieces: collars, berthas, plastrons and so on.

Shawls. Square, triangular or oblong coverings of varied material, worn around the shoulders and upper part of the torso mainly for warmth, but also for decoration. They were very fashionable in the late eighteenth century when the almost topless translucent muslin dresses of the neo-classical era made them a necessity; and from then to the 1830s, when the fashion for swollen skirts and bulbous sleeves made any kind of overcoat impossible; to the 1850s, when fashion decreed that no lady should be seen abroad without one; to the 1860s, when they, in company with the crinolines, reached their greatest size (12 feet by 6 feet or 3.7 m by 1.8 m, for Paisleys); and so to the 1870s, when gradually shawls became relegated to objects of utility. While many of the shawls were of wool, the summer ones, from the 1820s, were of drawnwork muslins, and later of appliqués on droschel or net. Later still they were of hand-made laces such as Le Puy, Chantilly, duchesse and point de gaze: large and boldly designed enough to be dramatically eye-catching, they were equally popular in black and white. Shawls of embroidered nets and of patterned laces made by the Pusher and Levers machines were also popular, and much cheaper.

Shawl collar. See *Fichu.*

Shell pattern. (Fig 42c.) A shallow scallop repeated along the heading of a torchon lace. The scallop is sometimes rayed to look like an opened *fan,* sometimes extended downwards like the pinnate leaf of a *palm.*

Shetland. See *Scottish lace* and *Knitted lace.*

Shift, smock. The female equivalent of the male shirt: a straight linen tunic with a wide neck opening and straight sleeves. It was worn under a dress in such a way that the fine laces attached to it appeared around the bodice and at the sleeve ends. The earlier ones sometimes had extensive cutwork decoration, e.g. one given to Queen Elizabeth I by Sir Philip Sidney in 1557. See *Underwear.*

Shoe roses. Rosettes of closely circled gold or silver lace or of thread lace stiffened with starch, worn mainly on men's shoes c 1600, when the fashion changed from flat heels to 2 inch (51 mm) high ones. The roses were often beribboned, spangled with jewels and sequins, and so large that they necessitated a straddled kind of walking. James I complained that they made him look like a 'ruff-footed dove'.

Sicilian laces. (a) Drawnwork and filet were made in Sicily from the sixteenth century and used for ecclesiastical purposes or for household linen. Some were embroidered with brightly coloured silks – bluish green, rose pink and canary yellow. (Fig. 18a.)
(b) A closely textured bobbin lace was made in heavy flax thread in the eighteenth and nineteenth centuries to an indeterminate design, something like a disorganised and overgrown Binche.
(c) A simplified form of Irish crochet was made at Messina in 1912.

Silk. (Fig. 23d.) An animal fibre, of a protein nature (fibroin), used for hand and machine laces. It has always been highly regarded for its lustre, warmth and softness combined with both lightness and strength. It is the only natural fibre which occurs as a filament, or continuous thread, as opposed to short – 1 to 8 inches (25-203 mm) – 'staples', which have to be persuaded to cling together by spinning before a continuous thread can be produced. A silk filament 2,000 yards (1.8 km) long can be unwound from each chrysalis. The winding or reeling process is followed either immediately, or after weaving, by degumming, in which the gum cementing the threads together in the cocoon is removed, together with up to one third of the total weight. This loss can be made up again by an artificial weighting process which gives the silk body and makes it crisp but also eventually causes it to rot and shred.
(a) Reeled silk, from the continuous filament, is the finest. The care required in its preparation, to prevent breakages, makes it very expensive.
(b) Spun silk is made from smaller fragments obtained from damaged cocoons and spun together. It is less smooth and even, but cheaper.
    Silk originated in China about 2,500 BC and reached Europe by the sixth century AD. It was used for all the 'blonde' laces of the eighteenth and nineteenth centuries, and for black lace throughout the ages. England's attempts to cultivate silk moths, including *Bombyx mori* (literally, 'silk of the mulberry tree') were unsuccessful, as had been Henri IV's planting of fifteen thousand mulberry trees in the Bois de

Boulogne in 1598. In the twentieth century, silk thread for Heathcoat's tulle illusion comes mostly from Japan; but enough was collected at Lullingstone, England's only silk farm, to weave the material for the wedding dress of the Princess of Wales in 1981.

Six-point star ground. See *Reseau.*

Slavic laces. See *East European laces.*

Slider, cover cloth. In bobbin lacemaking, a sliding cover – of horn, isinglass (gelatin) or cloth – placed over the lower part of the pricking to prevent friction between thread and parchment.

Slip. See *Count.*

Slugs. See *Snails.*

Smock. See *Shift.*

Smuggling. The various sumptuary edicts, importation duties and restrictions issued in particular by the governments of England and France had as their object firstly the curtailment of expenditure on costly laces, which was ruining country and private individuals alike; and secondly the encouragement and support of home industry. The idea was that the money no longer squandered abroad would be redirected towards native talent. Instead, it was redirected, with the most amazing resourcefulness and ingenuity, to the illicit acquisition of the prohibited goods.

In the sixteenth century, the target of the edicts was the gold and silver laces of Genoa and the cutworks of Italy and Flanders. The quantities involved were enormous, and the cost well worth the smugglers' skill. The methods, in that and the following two centuries, were robust and picturesque: sacks of lace, over 100 pounds (45 kg) in weight, and £6,000 or more in value, were substituted for bodies in coffins nominally of relatives who had died abroad. Loaves of bread were hollowed out and filled with lace; turbans concealed a small mountain of lace above the head; babies were swaddled in it; the covers of books enclosed not literature but lappets, cap crowns, and endless yardages of point and pearling. See also *Point d'Angleterre.* It was not only the merchants who smuggled: occasionally gentlemen were caught, such as an attaché to the Spanish embassy in 1764 who was 'unloaded' by customs officials of over four hundred shirts with fine Dresden-work jabots and ruffles. Dogs also were trained to smuggle: starved, wrapped with 26 pounds (12 kg) of lace, squeezed into the peeled-off skin of a larger dog, they were sent trotting over the Belgian border into France. But they were not always successful: forty thousand smuggler dogs were destroyed between 1820 and 1836. See also *Point d'Espagne*.

In the nineteenth century even machines were taken under the smuggler's wing, for example an Old Loughborough, dismantled and concealed in luggage, arrived at Douay (France), where it was reassembled, in 1815, during Napoleon's final Hundred Days.

One of George III's last acts, in 1806, was to increase the duty on foreign laces for the benefit of English makers. By 1835 they were again in distress, and they blamed the ease of smuggling for their troubles: in England only some five to seven per cent of contraband was seized, while France had a magnificent fifty per cent record.

Snails, slugs. The little shapeless space fillers which occur so frequently in Honiton guipures, possibly made by children.

Snatch pin, winkie pin. In Honiton lace: (a) the making of loops along one border of a leaf. See *Stem stitch*. (b) bars or brides with little loops or picots which were made by the yard and used for joining the Honiton sprigs either by being sewn in as the work proceeded or by the whole assemblage being joined together later. Goubaud also calls these 'purls'.

Snatchpin. A very narrow braid worked with bobbins to a considerable length and used for joining the individual sprigs in Honiton lace. A similar braid is sometimes used in Bruges.

Sol lace, sun lace. A Spanish or Spanish-influenced lace typically designed with a repeat of a fiery sun with radiating beams. See *South American lace, Spanish lace.*

South American lace. Peru: a drawnwork, said to antedate the Spanish conquest by Pizarro (1478-1541). It was still being made in the earlier twentieth century. Paraguay: a form of sol lace, called nanduti, known from the eighteenth and nineteenth centuries. The pattern, often very complex, was drawn in charcoal on a cloth stretched over a frame. Circles and diameters were transfixed over the surface of the cloth, and then the thread was woven in and out of them, using a needle, to form intricate webs. The silk used, with its dull gold glow, created an impression of evening sunlight. Larger pieces, such as collars, sometimes incorporated twelve variations of the sol theme and took weeks to complete.

As part of the Spanish and Portuguese empire, South America had many European settlers. The richer brought trunkloads of lace with them and continued to import it – the finest Flemish being particularly favoured – until Philip V's sumptuary edict of 1723 (see *Point d'Espagne*) had to be applied more stringently to South America than to the homeland. Even the native ladies wore deep lace on their petticoats, and lace trimmed the long cotton drawers of the gauchos.

Torchon lace, from Spain and Portugal, was also imported in large quantities in the nineteenth and twentieth centuries. See also *Spanish lace, Spider lace.*

Spangles. A set of seven or nine beads hung on a circlet of wire from the lower end of each bobbin. They are found only in the East Midlands of England, and even there not on South Bucks bobbins. Typically there is one fancy and three square-cut beads on each side, and a special bottom bead referred to as Pompadour, Kitty Fisher or Venetian. This bottom bead could be made of semi-precious jade, amber, coral or cornelian, or of a button, seashell or souvenir. More rarely it was enclosed in a tiny cage of beaded wire, and known as a bird-cage spangle. The square-cuts were cut from a square stick of pink, white or blue glass and pressed with a file while still warm enough to take the imprint. There is no reliable evidence of spangled bobbins before the nineteenth century, and it is conceivable that they were an attempt to counter the annoyance caused by the machine-spun thread, the over-tight twisting of which made the bobbins roll about on the pillow. Spangled bobbins are difficult to use in non-continuous laces since they have to be passed through a loop of thread when a sewing is taken. See also *Bobbins.*

Spanish ground. See *Reseau.*

Spanish lace (and see *Point d'Espagne*). The source of all laces is to some extent in doubt: in portraits and on effigies we see a lace but do not know its origin; in inventories we read the name of a lace and the country that it came from, but we cannot tell what it looked like. In Spain, this problem appears magnified: the names used are unfamiliar; evidence of their ever having been made in Spain is slender; and the power of Spain over Italy and Flanders in the sixteenth and seventeenth centuries was so great that she could have imported, and claimed as her own, laces and lacemakers from any part of the known world. That much lace was being imported is evidenced by the tenfold increase in import duty in 1667: its main effect, as ever, was to encourage smuggling, the lace being landed at Cadiz as bales of mosquito netting (see also *Point d'Espagne*). Certainly with Napoleon's invasion of Spain in 1808 and the Disestablishment Act of 1830, the opening up of the convents revealed

laces of many varied kinds, all of which poured on to the market as
Spanish point, giving rise to many misconceptions.

(a) Randas, said to have been recorded from the fourteenth century, was
probably a lacis, equivalent to rezel, and made sometimes of coloured
silks or of precious metal thread.

(b) Cadenetas: chain-stitch laces worked with a small hook using silk or
gold, and possibly the cheyne lace referred to in Elizabeth I's sumptuary
edict of 1568. They are reported by the evidence of travellers to have
been very tedious to make, and a strain on the eyes.

(c) Caireles and rapacejus: silk or metal fringings, similar to macramé,
known from the fifteenth century.

(d) Deshilado: fifteenth-century drawnworks of Arabic octagons and
stars, i.e. with a Moorish influence, again using gold and silver thread.
The wearing of them was forbidden by sumptuary edicts of Philip II and
III (reigned 1555-98, and 1598-1621), grandson and great-grandson of
Juana la Loca (Joanna the Mad, qv).

(e) Ruedas (wheel) and sol (sun): derivatives of drawnwork made on,
rather than in, a backing cloth, having made this transition in much the
same way as reticella converting from cutwork into punto in aria. Both
ruedas and sol took the form of circles or octagons, crossed with
diameters, and then woven around with silk threads to look like a very
complex spider's web. They were made in Spain, in South America
(nanduti), in the Canary Islands (Tenerife work) and in Mexico
(sometimes called Tucuman).

(f) Redecillas: knotted nets, from the fourteenth century, used for coifs
(see *Chain stitch* (a, i)) or to cover the face. The plain ground was
sometimes hand-embroidered. They had no similarity to the laces known
as reticellas, a word with no Spanish equivalent.

(g) Bocadillo: an early simple form of cutwork, rather like the latter-day
broderie anglaise, though richer.

(h) Spanish needlepoints of seventeenth-century Venetian gros point type
may have been worked in Spanish convents or imported from Venice (see
Point d'Espagne and *Venetian lace* (c)). They do not appear to have been
exported from Spain.

(i) Gold and silver laces: all kinds were worn as copiously and as
disastrously, from the economic point of view, in Spain as in other
European countries in the sixteenth and seventeenth centuries.
Prodigally rich yardages, marketed as point d'Espagne, are generally
regarded as being products of France, though certainly some were made
in Spain, for example at Seville.

(j) Spanish bobbin lace, Spanish blonde: a continuous lace, using two
thicknesses of thread, a heavier for the solid part, and a finer for the
fond simple ground. Their soft lustrous silk and dense design made them

ideal for the softly draped white or black mantillas and flounces of the late eighteenth and nineteenth centuries. The lace was worked in 4 inch (102 mm) wide strips, on tall pillows, and invisibly joined. Copies of these bobbin laces were made at Bayeux and exported to Spain. Simpler bobbin laces, of flax, were produced for household use.

(k) Machine net with needlerun embroidery: a floral repeat design was worked in a heavy silk thread along the border, with smaller sprigs scattered through the ground. Both black and white were worked throughout the nineteenth century.

(l) Machine 'Spanish lace': very varying qualities were made on the Levers and other machines, always heavily patterned with flowers.

Spider lace. (Fig. 42.) (a) Nanduti (Guarani or South American Indian, web): usually made of silk, sometimes of aloe fibre. See *South American.*

(b) Darned filet (opus araneum, Nevill Jackson): used especially where the design takes the form of circles in matting stitch (punto a stuora), around which the threads of the diameters are caught together by tress stitch (punto treccia), as by a hair clip.

(c) Spider lace: (a) and (b) relate to some real or fancied resemblance to a cobweb. The spider lace of Madagascar (recorded in 1890) is said to be made actually from gossamer. To stimulate the spider to exude its silk, other than in forming a web, it is plied with intoxicating juices until it begins to whirl round and round, with a thick thread reeling out from its abdominal spinnerets. The sticky threads are collected and worked into a bobbin lace. It must be kept from contact with water but can be cleaned by soaking in pure alcohol, then stiffened with a little gum arabic and pressed between two cloths with a cool iron. One feels some gnostic significance would be needed to make this amount of effort worth while, on a large island where certainly other fibres must have been available – unless it was simply that they could get no other silk.

(d) Spider net: a delicate lace first made on the Stocking Frame about 1770, as a variant of point net. It looked like an exceptionally fine openwork hand knitting.

(e) Spider pattern: in bobbin laces (especially torchons), the little woven blobs hung in a space by the paired threads, up to twenty, from which they are made. They look very like a spider with legs stretched waiting to pounce.

Spinning, spindle, spinning jenny, spinning wheel. Basically, spinning is the conversion of the tiny fibres obtained from a plant or animal into long threads or yarn which can be used to make a lace or other textiles. All the fibres – except silk and the synthetics (see *Artificial fibres*) – are short and therefore, to make a usable yarn, they have to be made to cling together, and this is done by spinning.

The sheaf of fibres to be spun is, primitively, held in the hand or attached to a distaff (simply a stick used for this purpose) at one end, and at the other end the fibres are passed through a hook or notch on to a *spindle*. The principle is to set the spindle rotating, which gives a twist to the sheaf of fibres. The spinner all the time gently feeds the spindle from the distaff, and the fibres are gradually transformed by smoothing, easing and twisting into a theoretically endless length of yarn.

The invention of the *spinning wheel* gave, in effect, an extra hand by providing a foot treadle to turn the spindle. A fifteenth-century improvement enabled the thread to be carried from the spindle by a flyer to a bobbin where it was wound ready for use.

The skill of the spinner lay in producing a smooth yarn of even diameter throughout. Peasant forms are marked by irregular lumps. The seventeenth- and eighteenth-century professional spinners spun a flax thread so fine it could not be felt between their fingers. They had to proceed gently all the time, or the almost invisible thread would break; they had to work in humid conditions, and in dim light where the thread was picked out by a single beam against a dark background so that any irregularity in it could be removed. So, for twelve hours or more on end they had to concentrate unremittingly and discipline themselves to make no sudden movements. If the thread too often snapped or tangled or drifted away like a cobweb in the still air, they would be penalised for wastage: the flax was weighed before and after spinning, and the spinner would be blamed for any discrepancy. The best Antwerp thread of the eighteenth century cost as much as £240 per pound (0.45 kg). Such a pound would contain up to 360,000 yards (329 km). The fineness of the thread was measured in 'counts' or 'leas', i.e. the number of 300 yard (274 m) hanks to the pound; and the finest count of the eighteenth century was 1,200.

The industrial revolution overturned the art of hand spinning much as it did the whole field of textiles. Spinning, from being a highly skilled occupation, became within the space of a few years a near automatic and very rapid process. Hargreaves's *spinning jenny* of 1766 was not unlike sixteen spinning wheels stripped down, compressed into one frame and operated all at the same time by one worker. Arkwright's machine, patented in 1769, was more automated and could be driven by water or steam instead of by human power. The spinning jenny, like the Stocking Frame, was operated by cottagers in their own homes, but machines were now becoming too cumbersome, too noisy and too huge to be worked anywhere except on a specially constructed factory floor. Crompton's mule of c 1774 and the electrically driven ring spinner of the twentieth century completed the downfall of hand spinning, and this in turn contributed to the outmoding of hand laces.

The machine-spun thread was very tightly twisted, it was thicker, and it favoured cotton instead of the far more expensive flax. The machines were too brash to handle the 1/20 mm gossamers for which the eighteenth-century hand-spinners had lost their sight. The whole texture of the lace was therefore changed. John Heathcoat told Felkin in 1844: 'I consider that my first bobbin net patent machine (1808) did for the making of lace in relation to the pillow what the jenny did for the spinning of yarn in relation to the old wheel.' He is referring to the spinning of sixteen threads at once and to the making of many meshes of net at once, instead of in each case only one; but he might just as well have been talking of the destruction of an art.

Spliced. Bobbins made by the riveting together of two different materials, e.g. wood and bone, or of two different colours, e.g. dark and light woods, by overlapping tapering ends, like the long slanting cuts used in the splice-grafting of fruit trees or roses. Splicing is found mainly in East Midlands bobbins.

Spots. (a) Point d'esprit. See *Plaits* (b).
(b) A ground powdered with spots is typical of late nineteenth-century Brussels laces, especially the large flounces or wedding veils, where they look like sprinklings of confetti. In appliqué veils, the hundreds of spots were made individually by bobbins and then stitched on. In tambour-embroidered veils each tiny spot was made in chain stitch with a hook.
(c) Spotted net. In 1834 a spotting apparatus was patented in France. In 1824 spotted net had been made in England on the traverse warp; in 1832 it was made without clipping threads, i.e. without floats; and in 1835 it was applied to the Pusher. Around that time many people on many machines were working at spotted nets, which were replacing the hand-sprigged muslins of the earlier nineteenth century. These nets were also sometimes known as 'point d'esprit' from their similarity to the hand-made reseau of for example Lille.

Sprang, Egyptian plaiting. (a) A form of plaited work made by the twisting of threads. The threads are not free-hanging as in normal plaiting: in fact there is just one very long continuous thread, which is passed backwards and forwards around opposite ends of a long wooden frame forming a series of 'warps'. The warps are then twisted centrally in such a way that the movement is conveyed both upwards and downwards. Thus the work continues from both ends at once towards the middle, sometimes with quite complex patterns. No implement is used for the twisting but bars are stretched across to hold the work already done, since it is obvious that if the central threads were released the tension resulting from the twisting would cause all of them immediately to spin undone again and return to their original straight position.

The antiquity of the craft is shown by relics from the tombs of Upper Egypt, dated by some as early as 2,000 BC, while others believe that sprang did not originate in Egypt until the Coptic period of the first century AD. The relation, if any, of this technique to lace is obscure: its utilitarian, rather than decorative, function perhaps disqualifies it; and it lacks the essential areas of varying density which distinguish design from ground.
(b) Some Icelandic drawnwork and lacis is known as sprang.

Sprig. The individual motifs or design fragments of, for example, Honiton lace. The sprigs were often made by many different people and then assembled to form the lace, either by being fixed on to a machine net (appliqué), or by being linked together by a reseau or brides. Laces made of such sprigs are called 'sprig laces'. See *Non-continuous*.

Square mesh. Valenciennes *Reseau*. Not a good name, since drawnworks and lacis also have a square-shaped mesh.

Staples. See *Fibres*.

Steinkirk. See *Cravat*.

Stem stitch. (a) Honiton: another name for ten-stick, a narrow braid made with five pairs of bobbins. It has pinholes along one side only and is used for curly stems and tiny circles. The raised work sometimes bordering the rims of flowers is made with this. See also *Raised work*.
(b) In embroidery, slanting overlapping stitches arranged in a single line, often used as surface embroidery in combination with drawnwork.

Stitches. In lace these comprise: the repeated movements of a needle and thread, as used in embroidered and needlepoint laces; the loops made with a hook as in crochet, or with unsharp needles as in knitting; the crossing and twisting of threads characteristic of bobbin laces; the stitches of tatting and macramé, which are called knots, though in this context the difference is a hair-splitting one. Thousands of such stitches exist in all, and only a very few examples can be given here:
(a) In filet and buratto, linen stitch is so called because it produces a closely woven look by a movement, as in ordinary darning, of the needle

across the ground in one direction, and then evenly over and under in the other direction until the meshes are filled. Running stitch is longer, crossing two or three meshes at a time in one direction only (see *Filet* (a)).
(b) In drawnworks such as Dresden and in the needlemade fillings of embroidered net such as Limerick, some fifty-two varieties of counted thread stitches occur. One example is described here, just to show how very long a description of all such lace stitches would be: 'Chessboard filling stitch – a drawn fabric stitch consisting of rectangular blocks of satin stitch alternating first vertically and then horizontally in "chessboard" fashion. Each stitch is taken over three threads, and each block is composed of ten satin stitches' (Thomas).
(c) In knitting, the stitch names apply to the small repeat units of the pattern rather than to individual movements of the needles. Even stocking stitch, garter stitch and cable stitch are only established by the working of several rows and a number of horizontal loops. Examples of the many other 'stitches' available are: ribbon ladder, Turkish stitch, rose leaf and daisy pattern.
(d) In crochet the situation is similar. Openwork stitches which can be built up into lacy patterns include Russian, knotted, double or triple open, connected trebles and pineapple.
(e) In needlepoint laces: (i) some eighty possible variations of the basic buttonhole stitch can be used for decorative fillings; (ii) eighteenth- and nineteenth-century needlepoints have in addition enclosures of tiny gem-studded forms which are prescribed groupings of stitches rather than strictly individual movements of needle and thread, as the buttonhole stitches themselves are. The original French names of these forms are often retained, e.g. gaze quadrillée (lozenge-shaped stitch), St Esprit avec rangs claires (an eight-point star within a circle), mosaique, mignon, enchainettes, point à trou and couronnes.
(f) In bobbin laces, 'stitch' refers not to something made with a needle or hook but to a process of twisting and crossing a certain number of threads in a certain manner producing for example whole stitch or half stitch (see *Whole stitch*), which can occur in any type of bobbin lace (Fig. 24a). Decorative groupings of whole stitch or half stitch produce little blocks of fancy work which are also called stitches, e.g. brick, honeycomb, mayflower, quatrefoil and diamond cutwork, which, being characteristic of particular areas, can help to identify a lace.
(g) Reseaux can also be regarded as a form of stitch.
(h) Point de raccroc is a joining stitch, important in linking strips of continuous bobbin laces, which are restricted by their method of making to widths of not more than about 4 inches (102 mm). See *Raccroc*.
(i) In macramé, the designs are built up by varying combinations of half-hitch and flat knots. In tatting, they are formed by varying arrangements

of the lark's head, otherwise known as double reverse half-hitch.

Stocking Frame. See *Machine lace* (a).

Stole. A long wide scarf, about 2 feet by 9 feet (610 mm by 2,743 mm), fashionable from the late eighteenth century to the 1940s, and worn variously over the head, looped round the neck, swathed across one or two shoulders, or falling straight down the front to the floor.

Straight down. Machine nets or patterned laces which are not traversed, i.e. the bobbin threads proceed not diagonally but horizontally.

Straight lace. See *Continuous laces*.

Straps. See *Brides*.

Suffolk lace. A commercial lace school was established at Malmesbury, Wiltshire, in 1838, training and employing children of five years and upwards. In 1907 lacemaking was revived under the patronage of the Countess of Suffolk, and traditional designs such as cat's eye, turkey's tail, spectacles, gin bottle and button were made. Though made in Wiltshire, they are thus sometimes known as 'Suffolk' laces. They resemble strongly not only some of the East Midlands laces but also those of Downton (Wiltshire), some 50 miles to the south. Illustrations of Suffolk laces in Palliser and of Downton in the Salisbury Museum handbook are almost identical.

Sumptuary edicts. These were laws which served a triple purpose: to restrict imports of foreign goods for the sake of the country's economy; by imposing a tax on imported and on home-manufactured luxuries, to increase the revenue; to restrict the wearing of the finest clothes to the aristocracy so that they would not be aped by the lower classes.

   None of these purposes succeeded: the kings made exceptions of themselves and their families, and the court followed suit; the newly rich merchants, especially those connected with the wool trade, could, even in the time of the Tudors, well afford the enormously expensive materials and saw no reason to acknowledge the supremacy of birth over wealth; and smugglers made nonsense of the customs regulations.

   Edicts were issued in every country of Europe, and almost yearly, so ineffective were they. Examples of them are:

In *England*, c 1555. Mary I: 'wreath lace or passement of gold or silver ... or white works, alias cut-works, made beyond the sea' were forbidden to anyone below the rank of a knight's wife.

1568. The cost of imports for Queen Elizabeth's wardrobe – 'parsement, cap rebone [ribbon?], bone lace, cheyne lace [chain-stitch lace?]' – amounted to £10,000. Five Acts to restrict such importations were passed between 1562 and 1579, but for her own use Elizabeth brought laces from Venice, Spain and Genoa, and tailors to make her clothes after the French or Italian manner.

1616. James I banned 'all lace from Millan', as well as embroideries, and all gold and silver decoration 'fine or counterfeit' (i.e. pure, or adulterated with base metals).

In *France*, 1611. Richelieu, under the Regency of Marie d' Medici, restricted imports from Milan, and gold and silver lace and fringes.

1660. Louis XIV's statesman Mazarin, as one of the last acts of his life, brought out an edict 'Contre le Luxe', i.e. against all luxurious dressing. The acute concern he aroused among the socialites stimulated their elegant lampoon *La Révolte des Passemens* (see *Passemens*). The charming engravings of Abraham Bosse (1602-76) throw a revealing light on their obsession with finery – the noble ladies and gentlemen discard their lace as if part of their own flesh was being torn away. With the death of Mazarin in March 1661, Louis XIV, with his passion for extravagant living, allowed the sumptuary laws to lapse.

In *Venice*, 1542. After disastrous wars, Venice forbade the wearing of gold, silver and coloured silk embroideries as a genuine economy measure – the goods and money were needed to maintain her commerce abroad. In the seventeenth century, the French edicts preceding and following the establishment of the Points de France in 1665 did great harm to Venice's lace trade, France having been one of her biggest customers. The English prohibitions must also have hurt. In spite of harsh punishments involving the destruction of huge quantities of immensely valuable lace, the sumptuary edicts scarcely achieved their purpose. They had, on the contrary, a very undesirable effect, the encouragement of smuggling. See also *Cost, Import restrictions*.

Sun lace. See *Sol* and *Spanish lace* (e).

Surface. A French or Belgian word referring to *Motif, Plat, Toilé*.

Swedish lace. (Figs. 12, 13.) (a) Torchon (bobbin) lace of geometric design, including a form called Dalecarlian.

(b) Cutworks and drawnworks, also geometric, and sometimes coloured with pink, red or blue. They were made from a heavy linen and sometimes called 'birch bark embroidery' because they could be stretched over a frame of bark for support and carried by the peasant girls to the fields.

(a) and (b) are utilitarian laces, made for church and household linen, bridegroom's shirts and bier bands. (c) and (d) are ornamental laces.
(c) Gold lace appears in the wardrobe accounts of King Gustavus Vasa (reigned 1523-60). His young grand-daughter was buried in a dress and shoes covered with gold and silver lace. Coifs netted with gold are recorded from the fourteenth century as having been made by nuns.
(d) Splendid imitations of Spanish raised needlepoints were made by nuns, before the suppression of the monasteries (Palliser). However, this event took place during the reign of the Calvinistic Charles IX (reigned 1600-11), and the Venetian gros points, generally regarded as contemporary – or even synonymous – with the Spanish, are usually dated not earlier than 1620. See *Pagano*.

Swing filling. A stitch used in Honiton lace: a square leadwork suspended by its four paired threads in the centre of a flower. See also *Cutworks, Leadworks*.

Swiss embroidery and lace. (Figs. 35, 36.)
(a) Bobbin lace is not generally regarded as an important Swiss product. However, it is mentioned in the sixteenth century in a pattern book printed in Zurich by Froschauer (c 1561). The author, RM, says that lace was brought to Switzerland from Venice in 1536, and the woodcut on her title page shows two lacemakers at work at their pillows. In the seventeenth century French refugees from the persecutions which Louis XIV tolerated, even if he did not initiate them, are said to have settled there and to have exported the lace they made to France, to the intense annoyance of the King. In the eighteenth century, gold, silver and flax laces were all made; Neufchatel made lace which rivalled that of Flanders; and in 1762 Rousseau, settling at Motiers, confessed: 'That I might not live like a savage, I took it into my head to learn to make lace. Like the women, I carried my cushion with me when I went to make my visits, or sat down to work at my door and chatted with the passers-by.' During the nineteenth century the number of lacemakers diminished dramatically, from 5,500 in Neufchatel in 1814 to ten in 1844.
(b) Swiss embroidery is associated with St Gallen from the mid eighteenth century. In the nineteenth century, a hand embroidery of edelweiss and other Alpine flowers, with padded petals and leaves filled with tiny knots, was worked in pale grey silk on a thin, slightly stiffened batiste.
(c) Switzerland is probably most famous for its nineteenth-century machine embroidery.
(i) The so-called 'hand machine' was invented in 1828 by Josua Heilmann, using pincers to take the place of the guiding fingers of the embroiderer's hand, and needles pointed at both ends and threaded

through an eye in the middle. The thread was knotted at the eye to hold it firm and was of limited length, about 42 inches (1,067 mm). When the thread ran out, new sets of needles, threaded by hand by two constantly busy people, were supplied. The movements of the needles were similar to hand embroidery, and a wide variety of stitches could be produced. Initially twenty needles were used, all operating at once, and shortly afterwards 130. A later machine, 9 feet (2.74 m) wide, was controlled by a pantograph which was worked by hand, though power was sometimes used to drive the carriage. Eventually 15 foot (4.57 m) wide machines with pincers for 312 needles were produced. The needles moved only up and down: the fabric was moved in its frame so that the design could be embroidered. By 1860 delicate fillings (similar to those of Ayrshire) could be worked by machine for hand-made holes. In 1868 modification by Otto Rittmeyer made it possible for the holes to be pierced by machine. Thus, from 1873, a kind of Madeira work could be made. Chemical lace was first produced in the early 1880s on the hand machines, but after about five years the work was transferred to the Schifflis.

(ii) The Schiffli machine works on quite a different principle, using a continuous thread and a boat-shaped shuttle, from which it derived its name (Swiss-German, schiffli = boat). It was invented in 1863 by Jsaak Gröbli. By the late 1870s, although white embroidery on cotton was no longer so fashionable, all kinds of embroidery on net were being produced in large quantities. 'Manila' work was solid embroidery on silk, muslin or fine wool, in which small open spaces were filled with net. In 1878, the machines were 4½ yards (4.1 m) long and had shuttles pointed at both ends which could work thirty-five stitches a minute. By 1887, the machine had grown to 6 yards (5.5 m), with eighty-six stitches per minute. By 1915 it was 15 yards (13.7 m) wide and had 1,026 needles. It worked six times faster than the hand machine, but because of its delicate constitution it was costly to maintain, and its chemical guipure laces, for which it was justly famous, were relatively expensive (38s a dozen). Its stitch was basically the lock stitch, as in the domestic sewing machine, and the presence of the two threads which make this stitch, at the back of the work, reveal its origin. The Jacquard attachment for the Schiffli was perfected between 1897 and 1911. Embroidered silk nets, first made in Switzerland in 1879, were by 1881 being made also in Saxony. Within a short time, Saxony became the main producer of all kinds of embroidered net, while the chemical laces remained the speciality of Switzerland.

See also *Machine lace* (h), *Bonnaz*.

Synthetic fibres. See *Artificial fibres, Rayon.*

Tallies. A Bucks name for point d'esprit. See *Plait* (b).

Tambour (French, a drum). A form of chain-stitch embroidery worked with a thin steel hook. The name is derived from the circular frame on which the material is stretched during the working, looking rather like the skin stretched across the top of a drum. The thread is held beneath the silk or other material, then drawn through with each movement of the hook so that it forms a series of loops, giving in effect a continuous line of chain stitch (Fig. 31a and b). It was extensively used in the Orient – Persia, India and China – many centuries ago but is thought not to have come to Europe until the seventeenth century. Little is heard of it until the 1760s when translucent muslins from India, perhaps already tamboured with sprigs, were coming into fashion for aprons, caps and dresses.

In the second half of the eighteenth century and the early nineteenth, tambouring was a fashionable pastime for ladies of the French and English courts, as needlepoint had been earlier and filet before that. Periodicals such as the *Lady's Magazine* (1770-1832) were now spreading designs and instructions to a far wider field. Records of the Dublin Society of 1760 refer to the teaching of tambour work in Ireland. From the 1790s it provided a flourishing occupation in the West of Scotland and in Belfast, laying the foundation for later Ayrshire work.

Though tambour is often a surface embroidery, it is also found: (i) in Dresden work where the tiny chain stitches may outline the drawnwork designs; (ii) in tamboured nets from Limerick (Ireland), Coggeshall (Essex) and Brussels, between approximately 1829 and 1910; (iii) in the outlining and attachment of the muslin-on-net and net-on-net appliqués of the Victorian and Edwardian era; (iv) in chain-stitch embroidered nets which were made by the Bonnaz machine, c 1890 and later. These were on the whole a lot coarser and of poor design. Maria Edgeworth, the novelist (1767-1849), makes a strange allusion, reputedly in 1810, to 'a worked muslin cap that cost 6d, done in tambour-stitch by a steam-engine'. Both the chain-stitching machine and the steam by which it is driven seem a little premature for that date. See also *Chain stitch, Embroidered nets.*

Tape lace, tape guipure. Any lace where the main design is formed by a tape-like structure:
(a) Mezzo punto (qv).
(b) Renaissance (qv). See also *Mezzo punto* (c).
(c) Crochet braid laces. Machine tapes – called 'plain', 'point lace', 'medallion' or 'mignardise' (French, daintiness, affectation) – were bought by the yard, arranged in a simple manner and then linked by

crochet, the thread being hooked through the loops placed by the manufacturers along the sides.

(d) Trail laces. The clothwork, or toilé, of a bobbin lace sometimes takes the form of a sinuous tape coiling on itself with varying degrees of complexity: it is then called a trail. In the plainer forms – which include Russian and other East European laces, as well as occasional Old Flemish and central Italian (Abruzzi) – the trail is no more than a straight tape, shaped only at the U-bends of its undulations, with the nearest parts fixed to each other by sewings. In eighteenth-century Milanese and Flemish trail laces the width of the tape varies, and there are decorative 'portes' to alleviate the solidity, for example in the snail's head (Fig. 25b). The general impression remains, however, one of a disciplined writhing of snakes. See also *Russian, Trail.*

Tatting, tatting shuttle. A form of knotted lace which may be said to have originated in the eighteenth century from the knotting of embroidery threads, in preparation for couched work, by which ladies passed the time on tedious coach journeys, sometimes using a shuttle for ease of manipulation. This knotted thread could be converted into a lace by curling it into loops, which could then be caught together using a needle and thread, thus building up patterns of small circles arranged as squares, triangles, diamonds and so forth. The basic knot was the lark's head. In the 1870s there were two important innovations: the introduction of picots, which added interest and daintiness to the work; and the use of a second shuttle with a second thread, by which the loops could be knotted together, without the need for additional sewing.

Thomas Wright and Caulfield regard tatting as a copy of the sixteenth-century Ragusa gimp, and knotted, laces, but there is no foundation for this assumption – except that such laces were made in Dalmatia in the nineteenth century.

The *shuttle* has a short central column on which the thread is wound, covered by two elliptical shells, pointed and curved towards each other at the ends. This enables the shuttle to pass smoothly through the loops of thread without catching. It is often made of polished bone or tortoise-shell, occasionally of steel, more recently of plastic.

Tela (Italian, cloth or linen). Tela tagliata = cutwork; tela tirata = drawnwork. The prefix 'punto' is more commonly used.

Ten-stick. See *Stem stitch.*

Tenerife lace. (Fig. 42b.) A form of Spanish ruedas, made in the Canary Islands, usually of cotton. A circular or four-sided frame is used, with some fifty-two pins stuck around the rim to hold the threads of the diameters. Varied designs of concentric circles are then worked around them. As many as twelve rosettes may be made, one on top of the other. Eventually the pins are removed, the rosettes separated, and the whole thing set up again. Similar work was done in the Azores. See also *Spanish lace* (c), and *South American*.

Thread lace. Lace made from flax, or linen, thread, as opposed to gold, silver or silk. The nature of 'thread' was not specified until the early nineteenth century, when cotton thread strong enough for hand-made lace was first produced.

Time taken to make lace. See *Hours of work*.

Tippet. (a) In the eighteenth century a little scarf; in the mid nineteenth a small shoulder cape. Mrs Delany, a literary lady (1700-88), criticises in her correspondence a lady for wearing her tippet too provocatively: 'no more of a tippet than serves to make her bosom conspicuous rather than to hide it'. In the nineteenth century it might be made of cotton with broderie anglaise decoration or be trimmed with lace. Queen Victoria's children wore tippets of Isle of Wight lace. Similar garments were occasionally worn by men and made then of cloth or fur.
(b) In the fifteenth century the tippet was a long streamer attached to the sleeves of the outer robe. From the fourteenth to the late seventeenth centuries, a streamer attached to the hood was worn at state funerals, its length being determined by protocol. It was, conceivably, the forerunner of the lappet.

Toilé (French, linen or cloth). (a) Defined by technique: the whole stitch only of bobbin lace, which looks exactly like a woven linen. Synonyms are clothwork, clothing, cloth stitch, linen stitch.
(b) Defined by appearance: the motifs or solid parts of the design may be (i) an actual woven linen (drawnwork); (ii) darned to look like warp and weft (filet and buratto); (iii) a woven muslin or batiste, appliquéd to net (Carrickmacross, and similar); (iv) even needlepoint motifs may be so closely textured that they look like cloth.
(c) More general usage: indicating all the denser, patterned parts of the lace including motifs, trails and fillings, as distinct from the ground. Lace can then be said to consist of: toilé + reseau/brides. Synonymous terms would be: close (closed) work + openwork; or, motif/design + ground; or, dense part + lighter part.

   Toilé, in this sense, could also be rendered by the French or Belgian terms 'mat' (flat), 'plat' (indicating a smooth expanse to which raised work may or may not be added) or 'surface' (referring to the broad landmasses of design linked to each other in all directions by narrow bridges, or floating in a sea of reseau).

Tönder. See *Danish lace.*

Torchon (French, duster, rag). A strong bobbin lace made of flax thread, most commonly as narrow edgings or insertions 1 to 2 inches (25 to 50 mm) wide. The design is a simple geometric one, using a small number of bobbins, but variations in the ground and filling stitches – basically torchon, twisted half stitch and rose – can give it a dainty prettiness (see *Reseau*). Lozenges and crossed trails have their sides set at 45 degree angles to the footing; spiders and tallies may hang in the ground; and the heading is often a scalloped fan (Fig. 42c). An outlining thread (gimp) was at first known only in the Swedish variety but is now copied elsewhere; and coloured threads may be used to enhance the effect as in Joseph Foddy's samples at Northampton Museum and in Czechoslovakian forms. Caulfield (1882) describes torchon as 'largely used on the Continent for common purposes'. Its strength and inexpensiveness made it ideal at that time for the trimming of linen or cotton underwear. It was made commercially in Belgium, France, north and south Italy, Saxony, Sweden and Spain, but not in England until the end of the nineteenth century (East Midlands), and Palliser does not include it in her account of English laces. Historically, torchon may be equated with the beggar's lace (Gueuse) recorded in the seventeenth-century *Révolte des Passemens* (1660-1) as coming from the country around Paris. Certainly both laces were denigrated by their names, but Gueuse is described as having simple flowers, while torchon is never representational.

From the early twentieth century, near-perfect copies of torchon were made on the Barmen machine. This considerably reduced the market for the hand-made form, even of the cotton type imported from China.

Trail, path, ribbon work. (Figs. 3d, 26, 27.) The word 'trail' is used as in everyday language: a path, along which the eye travels, if not the feet. It may be curved smoothly or bend sharply, be of even width or fluctuate. Trails occur, for example, in East European, Beds Maltese, torchon and Cluny laces. In torchon they may be of either whole or half stitch. In Cluny the trail is 'divided', i.e. it looks less like a solid path than a curving railway track of the kind where long parallel rails are supported on sleepers. See also *Tape laces.*

Travancore. A small state in the south-western tip of India, renamed

Kerala in the 1950s. In the 1920s ornamental torchon laces were made there, for example at Nagercoil. In some the design is exactly matched by illustrations in Salisbury Museum's *Downton Lace* book.

Traverse Warp Machine. See *Blonde.*

Traversed net. See *Bobbin net* and *Machine lace* (c).

Treadwin, Mrs C. (died 1892). An important figure in Devon lacemaking in the nineteenth century. She ran an establishment in Cathedral Close, Exeter, where lace was made to order and also repaired. She herself was a skilled maker of both bobbin and needlepoint laces, and in 1848 she was appointed lacemaker to Queen Victoria, who commissioned that year a handkerchief with a border of 'roses ingeniously worked so as to appear to be growing out of the cambric'. In 1851 she won a medal at the Great Exhibition for a flounce (valued at that time at £500) which had been designed for her by C.P. Slocombe of the School of Design at Somerset House. But she found it no easy task to discipline the workers away from the shoddy 'rag' pieces, which, being quick to make, brought them in easy money. In 1874 her book *Antique Point and Honiton Lace* was published. Her versatility and proficiency are perhaps most nearly matched by the contemporary work of the brothers Lefebure in Bayeux. She was largely responsible for the Honiton revival of the 1880s. Her crisp designs, borrowed to some extent from Brussels duchesse, still bore the imprint of her own strong originality. She also provided an impetus to the Devon tape (renaissance) lace known as Branscombe, carrying on the work of teaching needlepoint stitches to the local women which had been started by Mrs Palliser some two decades before. The copy of the stone lace from Lady Doddridge's tomb in Exeter Cathedral (Fig. 9a) was her own work and indicative of her industry and love of experiment.

Mrs Treadwin's assistant, Miss Herbert, carried on the business in Exeter until she herself died in 1929, at the age of eighty-nine. She bequeathed a book of lace samples to Exeter's Royal Albert Memorial Museum.

Tresse (French, braid). (a) Plaited brides, like tresses of hair, which link one part of the design with another. They are found in continuous bobbin laces such as Maltese and Le Puy, and sometimes in the non-continuous Honiton and Bruges. See *Plait* (a, iii).
(b) Point tresse. See *Hair lace.*
(c) Metier à tresser. A braiding machine used to make a flat braid or, by a later modification, openwork laces. This is the principle on which the Circular (Barmen) machine works.

Trine (Italian, lace). A general word, sixteenth-century in origin, which covers braid and passements as well as laces in the defined sense (see *Lace* (a)). Trine ad ago = needle lace; trine a fuselli = bobbin lace. See also *Merletti.*

Trolly lace, trolle kant. (Fig. 44a and b.) A continuous bobbin lace in which the unpretentious design is outlined by a heavy gimp thread. This is a broad field, including some north European peasant laces from Antwerp and Normandy, some East Midlands laces from Downton and Northampton and, unexpectedly, some Devon laces.

It is hard to tell what other features they have in common: some, though not all, have a point de Paris ground (or Antwerp trolly net); in most the patterns have a simple and homely charm. The English trolly may have been derived from either the French or Flemish version, brought by the many refugees, and there is a convergence between Bucks and Devon: the tulip pattern illustrated by Palliser as Devon trolly is almost identical to the tulip pattern donated to the Buckinghamshire County Museum, Aylesbury, in the Burrowes Collection as Bucks point of the 1880s revival period. Both Burrowes and Palliser are sound authorities, and both lived in the areas from which the laces were said to come. But even in this relatively recent history there are discrepancies; Palliser speaks as though the production of Devon trolly ended c 1820; Thomas Wright says that thirteen-hole trolly could still be bought in Devon in 1896. Both agree that much of it was made by men. One reference to English trolly in the eighteenth century is from Mrs Delany (see *Tippet* (a)), who, in 1756, speaks of a 'trolly head', i.e. lappets and cap back of trolly lace.

Trolly bobbins. Bobbins, larger and heavier than others, which hold the gimp (or trolly) thread. In the East Midlands they often have between one and six loose rings of pewter, wood or, rarely, bone around the shank.

Trou trou (French, hole hole). A narrow insertion of Bucks point with a central row of holes for the threading of ribbon.

Truck system. A barter practice by which the cottage workers, taking their lace to the merchant, were paid not in money but in goods provided by the dealer himself, at an inflated price, and with no freedom of choice. See also *Earnings, Lace tokens.*

Tucker. A little frill, often of lace, intended to cover the lower part of the decolletage of the seventeenth-century deep-cut court gowns. Queen

Catherine of Braganza, suddenly liberated from the stuffy fashions of the Portuguese court, about 1665 shocked the English ladies by exposing 'her breast and shoulders without even ... the slightest gauze; and the tucker instead of standing up on her bosom, is with licentious boldness turned down and lies upon her stays.' Similar frills appeared spasmodically in the eighteenth and nineteenth centuries. See also *Fashion*.

Tucker family. Lace merchants of Branscombe in the mid nineteenth century, and related to the Chicks, also important lace traders of that time.

Tulle (French, net). (a) A silk net made by machine, e.g. the two-twist bobbinet 'tulle illusion' made by Heathcoat (see *Illusion*). This is the traditional English usage. (Fig. 33b.)
(b) French usage is broader and also less well defined. Thus tulle is:
(i) All machine nets, cotton as well as silk. See *Net*.
(ii) A point net made on the Stocking Frame in 1774, called 'single and double tulle'.
(iii) A Warp Frame net patented at Lyons in 1809 and called 'tulle de glace' (ice net).
(iv) Not only all machine nets, but all hand-made bobbin reseaux as well.
(v) The fond simple reseau, or Lille ground. Thus, 1765: 'Tulle - a sort of vulgar lace, but more often a plain net ground'. When slightly patterned it was known as marli. Bobbin reseaux sprigged with fly or pea motifs were known as 'entoilage à mouches' (1761) and 'entoilage de belle blonde à pois' (1773 – a good blonde net with peas).
(vi) Needlepoint grounds such as Alençon reseau ordinaire, which bears a superficial resemblance to a fond simple though made by quite a different technique. This could also be 'semé de larmes, pois ou mouches' (i.e. sown with tears, peas or flies).
(vii) A silk gauze, not a lace but filmily fine, which, worn over a flesh-coloured body stocking (in the days of the Directoire) gave an impression of nakedness beneath.
Tulle, as a silk net (see (a)), was popular from the 1820s to the 1940s. The Empress Eugenie, under the influence of the couturier Worth, ordered 60 yards (55 m) of tulle at a time for her court gowns; and tulle, along with crepe and muslin, was essential for summer dresses. The net was often dyed and then embroidered with vivid floss silks. Lately the fashion has revived, with coloured nets being embroidered on the Schiffli machine (see *Machine lace* (h)).
Two towns compete for the origin of the name 'tulle': Tulle, in south-

west France, not far from the old lace centre of Aurillac; and Toul near the eastern border, in the Nancy-Lunéville area of embroidered nets.

Turn. A Devon name for a *Bobbin winder.*

Turnhout. A Belgian town, north-east of Antwerp, producing in near-modern times a bobbin lace similar to point de Paris.

Turnpins. An East Midlands term for picots. See *Pearl.*

Turnside. See *Heading.*

Tuscan filet. See *Modano.*

Twentieth-century lace. After the failure of the late nineteenth-century revivals (qv), hand-made laces dwindled steadily, inundated by the chemical laces from Switzerland, and infiltrated by the cheap labour products of the Far East. The years between the 1920s and the late 1960s were distinguished only as a long period of apathy during which antique laces were disposed of, as of no value, and even machine laces played a very minor role in dress accessories. Then a renewal of interest began, with fashion designers buying up warehouse loads of cotton laces outmoded by easy-care synthetics, and purchasing huge quantities of unwanted nineteenth-century and earlier laces. At the same time collectors began, for the first time in many years, to hunt seriously for rare pieces. Also, a new generation of lacemakers, ablaze with enthusiasm, began to recreate the traditional patterns or invent designs of their own in traditional style. Distinct from these traditionalists were the avant-garde experimentalists using a whole new range of colours, fibres and designs, and modified traditional techniques, to produce dramatically eye-catching forms, very quickly, and at low cost. See also *Design, Lace.*

Twist. One of the basic movements of bobbin lacemaking in which the two right-hand threads are passed over the two left-hand threads in adjacent pairs. (Fig. 24a.) See also *Cross.*

Twisted half stitch, point tordu, twisted hole ground. Variations of 'Spanish' ground found in torchon laces. See *Reseau.*

Twist hands. The workers on the bobbinet machines, making a 'twist net'.

Twist net fever. See *Net* (d).

Underpropper, suportasse. A construction of wire used to support the ruff and other 'standing collars'. See *Ruff* and *Col rabat*.

Underwear. Garments for wearing beneath the top clothes to keep them fresher, and the wearer warmer. There were four basic articles: stays; shift (smock, chemise or shirt); petticoat; and drawers.

In the sixteenth century, perhaps because of the high price of linen, underwear was a luxury. Only the stays were an indispensable item of fashion. They were stiffened with wood, metal or whalebone, intended to straighten both back and front of both men and women. For women, they were covered with the stomacher, which was sometimes of white drawnwork, similar to a stout Dresden. The tight lacing of the nineteenth century could be lethal, breaking ribs which then stabbed through the lungs or liver, causing internal haemorrhage and speedy death.

The shift, worn under the corset, fell to about knee length and had square-set sleeves just long enough to present their layered frills of lace where the overclothes ended.

The petticoats of the eighteenth century were meant to be visible. They might be decked with scalloped flounces of bobbin or needlepoint lace, or be quilted and pierced with drawnwork to match the stomacher. In the nineteenth century they were concealed beneath a skirt and more plainly lace-trimmed.

Drawers were not in general use until the mid nineteenth century, when the tendency of the crinoline to become airborne or to tilt itself at embarrassing angles made a concealing nether garment essential. They took at first the form of two straight cylinders joined only at the waist. Their lower ends were tucked and frilled with lace or broderie anglaise, an innovation at that time. For men, the seventeenth-century petticoat breeches, ribboned and laced, were a mixture of overwear and underwear.

Cotton, by the later nineteenth century, was beginning to rival linen for underwear. Fine batiste, with delicate machine laces, was popular for the first two decades. Then both silk and art silk began to take over, and by 1925 garments which had been white for four hundred years began to appear in pastel shades of rose, blue or café-au-lait, with ecru medallions and godets in Levers lace. See also *Fashion*.

Urling. See *Gassed cotton*.

Uttmann, Barbara. See *Saxony*.

Valenciennes. (Figs. 7b, 28.) A lacemaking town on the French-Flemish border. It was Flemish in 1665 when Louis XIV established the Points de France. In 1678 it was ceded to him. This was a major triumph: though French needlepoints had developed successfully in those thirteen years, French bobbin laces had failed to establish themselves, and Colbert estimated that some two million livres a year (about £80,000) of French money still poured into Flanders to purchase her supernally beautiful laces. With the capture of Valenciennes, Louis actually possessed a Flemish town, with Flemish lacemakers producing Flemish designs by Flemish techniques, within his own boundaries – and he immediately dubbed the lace 'French'.

It was a continuous bobbin lace with a broad but light and ethereal design, thin and flat as a fairy-tale linen, with a minute line of holes pricked evenly around each motif, made of 1,200-count thread and produced therefore with a cosmic slowness. One pair of ruffles, costing £160, would occupy the worker's fifteen-hour day for ten complete months. Its ground was a cinq trous and provided the only feature which distinguished it from the lace of the neighbouring Binche, 20 miles away. As the eighteenth century began, the two laces diverged: Binche, stricken like other Flemish laces by the sumptuary edicts of England and France, retained its blizzard-like fond de neige, but its design weakened until it was quite obscured by the dizzying swirl of tiny snowflakes. Valenciennes, patronised by France, became more French. Its designs, from being dreamily floral, with arcadian lilies of renaissance plenitude, became more precisely delineated, with formal baskets of flowers and fruits swinging from ribbons in a fixed trelliswork of plaited meshes.

In 1780 Valenciennes had 4,000 lacemakers. The revolution of 1789 reduced that number to 250. The town failed to respond to Napoleon I's attempts to revive it, and by 1851 only two lacemakers were left. Other centres, however, in both France and Belgium, were soon producing a neat durable lace used for undergarments, by Queen Victoria, the Empress Eugenie and others. Later, the monopoly was acquired by Belgium, and the manufacture largely removed to Ghent and Ypres. It was still called Valenciennes (sometimes Valenciennes de Ghent), and the typical ground of more or less diamond-shaped meshes was retained, but the technique was modified to include extensive fil coupé and fil attaché techniques, instead of being exclusively fil continu. See *Ghent*.

A wide variety of machine imitations was made, some so exact as to be almost undetectable. The best was the Barmen form, using linen thread. Only one width at a time could be made, and so it was expensive compared with the multiple webs of the giant Levers (Fig. 32a).

Vandyke. A toothed or scalloped border of lace fashionable in the early seventeenth century to edge the falling collars. These are beautifully depicted in the portraits by Sir Anthony Van Dyck (1599-1641) of Charles I, Henrietta Maria and their children.

Vavassore. A Venetian who produced pattern books for Tuscan filet and for drawnwork, c 1530.

Veils. Coverings of translucent material worn over the head or face, and serving initially for concealment or protection.
(a) Baby veils. In the early seventeenth century a christening veil of white lawn edged with gold bone lace is recorded. Through to the nineteenth century it was customary to cover the baby's face outdoors, and from 1809 net was most frequently used.
(b) Bridal veils developed in the nineteenth century. Previously, hats were worn, and before that the hair was dressed loose or braided. Large veils were an impossibility before the invention of plain 'nets' such as the hand-made droschel in the late eighteenth century. But it was the machine nets – point, warp frame, and especially the bobbinets – which could be produced in great yardages quite cheaply, which established this custom. In 1806 a bride is recorded as wearing a 'patent net' over a satin underskirt and as having had a long veil: this would be a looped net. In 1807 'a Brussels lace veil of the most transparent fabric' could only refer to droschel. In 1815, there is a veil of white Chantilly lace; and in 1835, 'a veil of blonde lace worn from the back of the head'. In 1840, Queen Victoria wore a wreath of orange blossom 'over which, but so as not to conceal her face, a beautiful veil of Honiton lace was thrown' (Fig. 46b). The fashion filtered slowly down through the social orders and by the 1850s was reaching the remote villages. In modern times, with the cessation of commercial hand lacemaking, there has been a reversion to plain nets, of nylon or, for very special occasions, of the silk 'tulle illusion'.
(c) Court veils. For presentations at court, a tulle veil became an optional alternative to lappets in the 1830s and by the end of the century had largely replaced them.
(d) Widows' veils. Lace was forbidden during the full-mourning period, which was a disaster for the lace merchants, who, as early as 1700, were protesting against it. In the second half of the nineteenth century, black lace came to be worn in vast quantities when the first mourning period was over, especially about the face, until it was recognised that the black dye harmed the eyes and injured the complexion.
(e) Mantilla. A form of lace veil worn in Spain.
(f) Poke bonnet veils. See *Poke bonnets.*
(g) Hat and motoring veils (fascinators) were worn in the late nineteenth

and early twentieth centuries to protect the face from the sun, the wind
and the increasing dust, dirt and air pollution of urban life. They were
made of novelty nets, 18 inches (457 mm) wide and bought by the yard.
Occasionally they were of knitted lace, or of black Chantilly, Le Puy or
Honiton, of semicircular form, just long enough to extend from hat brim
to chin. See also *Net.*

Venetian lace. The Republic of Venice was at its peak in the thirteenth
century and, by 1500, before lace was even thought of as fashion, it was
in decline. The strength of Venice lay in her trading power, her position
as gateway between east and west, regulating the passage of costly silks
and golds from the Orient to all the capitals of Europe. Her vast wealth,
accumulated over several centuries, aroused the envy of neighbouring
states: she was involved in wars with Turkey and Milan; Genoa began to
encroach on her trade and trade routes; her merchants were greedy and
sometimes dishonest, so that both intermediate and receiving countries
began to impose taxes and restrictions on her transported goods; and
Diaz, in 1486, rounded the Cape of Good Hope, so opening up a free
route to the treasures of the East which Dutch, Portuguese and English
traders were not slow to make use of, depriving Venice at one blow of
both source and sink of her merchandise.

In spite of this the sixteenth century and much of the seventeenth were
a supreme period for Venetian art, with the magnificent paintings of
Titian, Tintoretto and Veronese. Venice was the pleasure city of Europe:
the cultural and fashionable élite of all the courts gathered there. She was
famous for her printing: pattern books for lace, embroidery and woven
textiles appeared in profusion. Of the 150 or so produced in Europe
between 1523 and 1596, nearly half came from Venice, beginning with
Tagliente, calligrapher to the Venetian Republic, in 1527, and ending
with Franco in 1596. In between were others such as Zoppino,
Vavassore, Pagano, Sessa, Vinciolo and Vecellio (a pupil of Titian),
illustrating the making of filet, reticella, cutwork, bobbin lace, lacis,
punto in aria and point de rebort (filet with an outlining thread to
strengthen the design). Some of the books were specified as 'for all
workers' and their patterns of counted threadwork, white against a
squared ground, could be adapted for either drawnwork, filet or buratto.
(a) Venetian bobbin laces. Those illustrated in *Le Pompe* (Sessa, 1557)
were analysed and copied by Mme L. Paulis of the Cinquantenaire,
Brussels, in the 1920s. They were of geometric design, formed of
combinations of whole stitch and plaited strands, and some of them
required the highest technical virtuosity.
(b) Venetian needlepoints were preceded by gold, silk and silver
passements. Venetian cutworks, stimulated by the ban on precious metal

in 1542, which encouraged the making of lace from flax, were soon in
immense demand. The punto in arias which developed from them gave
rise in turn to the superlative raised needlepoints, which reached a
pinnacle of perfection that has never since been challenged. A sense of
joy bursts from their sumptuous fruits and blossoms, and their
meticulous workmanship could construct six thousand buttonhole
stitches in each square inch (2.5 sq cm) of 'toilé'. The exact dating of
Venetian needlepoints is not established, but their entire span was
probably less than a hundred years. Their derivation from the 'punti
tagliati e fogliami' of Pagano (1543 and 1550) and of the Bolognese
Passarotti (1591) is clearly shown in the designs of animals and heraldic
shields, where the reticella/cutwork lifts itself, through the superimposed
decoration, away from the linen, until it breaks free in a baroque
exuberance of riotous blooms. Because of this origin, Palliser illustrates
a full-blown gros point collar as sixteenth century, but this dating is
extremely unlikely, and the form of the collar which she illustrates is
distinctly seventeenth-century. There is slightly dubious evidence that
gros points were in existence in 1619, for example the nineteenth-century
Viennese collar (Fig. 48b) is said to be based on one made for Frederick
V (1596-1632), Elector of the Rhine, when he was crowned King of
Bohemia. Frederick was the husband of Elizabeth, daughter of James I
of Great Britain, and the grandfather of George I. There is also evidence
that gros points were still being made in 1685 when Charles II, for £20,
bought a cravat as a birthday present for his brother James; and when
James himself, on the death of Charles in the same year, ordered a gros
point cravat, costing £36, to wear at his coronation. Ten years later, an
obscure communication sent by the Venetian ambassador to his native
city indicates that Venetian needlepoints were being outmoded in
England by 'punto d'Inghilterra' (English point: see *Point d'Angleterre*).
This marked a turning point in fashion, when heavy laces became
outmoded and were increasingly replaced by the airy concoctions of
Flanders. Although Venice tried to compete with its own lightweight
reseau Venise (see *Point de Venise à reseau*) it was too late. The severe
sumptuary edicts directed against Venice by Louis XIV in 1660 and by
Charles II in 1662, the establishment of the Points de France and further
wars with Turkey from 1645 to 1665 all contributed to her downfall. Her
major commerce lost, her designs stolen, her best lacemakers enticed or
kidnapped away, the lace industry of Venice could no longer survive.

All the Venetian needlepoints – gros, rose, point de neige, point plat,
coralline, and point de Venise à reseau – are referred to under those
heads. The flat needlepoints are generally thought to have followed the
raised, being a simplification and degradation of them in an effort to
salvage at least part of the market. Their designs were often so diffuse as

to appear as no more than random particles, but even then the best work was of such exquisite fineness that it still appears sublime. The name 'coralline', says the fable, comes from an articulated coral called Mermaid Lace brought from the South Seas by a sailor and copied by his betrothed in flax thread and buttonhole stitches. The name usually includes any Venetian flat point made up of very tiny pieces assembled in a ground of brides.

(c) The influence of Venice on French needlepoints is well documented (see *Points de France*). Less clear is her influence on Spain. Though Venice was never a part of the Holy Roman Empire, her political association with Spain was a close, even a menacing one, with the Emperor Charles V being crowned King of Lombardy in 1529, and so advancing the Spanish Empire to the very doorstep of the small republic. In this situation samplers, pattern books, laces, perhaps even lace-makers, must have been transported for some 150 years from Venice to Spain. Gros points would certainly have appeared in Spain, whether or not any were actually made there, and may well have been specifically commissioned in that ornately bejewelled and intricately contorted design often referred to as Spanish raised point (see *Point d'Espagne* and *Spanish Lace* (h)).

(d) The relationship between Venetian lace and that of Ragusa is also far from clear. Ragusa in the sixteenth century was, like Venice, an independent republic, but the two were closely associated: Ragusa was a trading post for Venice; Venice owned the coastal islands to the north of Ragusa; and that part of the Dalmatian coast was a stronghold of the pirates who plundered costly merchandise from the vessels of the Venetian fleet. It has been suggested that some of the Venetian needlepoints were made in Ragusa, but this is sheer speculation: the problem of the precise nature of the costly coveted laces of Ragusa will probably never be solved.

(e) According to RM, author of a pattern book for bobbin laces in 1561, the bobbin laces of Venice were also not without influence, being the inspiration of the little-known bobbin laces of Switzerland, and perhaps from there via Augsburg of those laces of Saxony putatively associated with Barbara Uttmann.

(f) We hear very little that is definite of Venetian laces after 1700, and it is assumed that they were slowly dying. They are recorded by travellers as having failed to make the transition in design from baroque to rococo, and as being in the eighteenth century produced mainly by nuns for the church. At the marriage of the Doge's son in 1770, only Brussels, not Venetian laces were worn. In 1797 Napoleon, in his Austrian campaign, set out to destroy Venice, and Venice surrendered. In 1866 it was incorporated in the United Kingdom of Italy. 'Venice lace', wrote Mrs

Palliser in 1864, 'is no more.'
(g) Ten years later, when failure of the fishing industry brought
destitution to the island, a lace school was set up in Burano under the
patronage of Queen Margherita of Italy. By 1882 not only were the so-
called 'Burano needlepoints' being produced, but also very competent
imitations of Alençon, Argentan, punto in aria and even Venetian raised
points. The school continued to produce good lace into the 1920s and is
still active today, though for the most part the quality is not comparable.
(h) In the mid twentieth century a coarsish needlepoint, 'point de
Venise', was made in Belgium and in the Far East, mainly as large pieces
such as tablecloths and coverlets, or as ornamental medallions (Fig. 6b).
(i) Machine copies of Venetian lace, both raised and flat, were made as
chemical lace on the Schiffli machine; but because of its high running
costs and the cheapness of oriental labour the Swiss form was sometimes
more expensive than the Chinese.
    See also *Gros point.*

Venetian picot. A picot loop converted to a short stiff spike by being held
out around a pin while five or six buttonhole stitches are made along it.
See *Couronnes.*

Vestee. A net or lace front partly covered by the bodice of a dress. In the
second half of the nineteenth century it was combined with a choker
collar. A *plastron* was a similar structure, but worn over the bodice. A
modesty was a little square edged with lace along the top and worn within
the plunging V-necks of the 1920s. *Chemisettes* in the mid nineteenth
century consisted of two pieces of muslin fitting around the neck, or with
a small collar edged with lace, and then disappearing under the dress
bodice to be held in place by tapes tied about the waistline.

Victoria, Queen (1819-1901). (Fig. 46.) On 28th June 1838, Queen
Victoria wore for her coronation a supertunica of gold and silk brocade
lined with crimson silk and trimmed with gold pillow lace, and beneath
this a collobium-syndonis of very fine white cambric trimmed round the
edges and flounced at the bottom with broad Honiton lace. The accounts
kept by Harriet, Duchess of Sutherland, Mistress of Her Majesty's
Robes, record the cost of the two garments as being £410 and £80
respectively. Her wedding flounce and veil – 10th February 1840 – were
of Honiton appliqué. The flounce is illustrated on the cover of this
book. Mildred Isemonger, in an article on English lace written in 1904,
speaks of three sisters whose grandmother was one of the workers
employed to make the famous flounce of 'Acorn' (Bucks) lace for Queen
Victoria's wedding dress, 'which is now preserved at the South

Kensington Museum'. Both attribution and location are demonstrably untrue. However, large quantities of Bucks lace do appear to have been ordered for the Queen's trousseau.

The christening gown of the Princess Royal and all subsequent royal children was trimmed with Honiton, not Ayrshire as one authority claims. The dresses worn by her daughters at the christenings of newly acquired brothers and sisters were of Nottingham lace. They were also given tippets of Isle of Wight lace. In 1857 Queen Victoria patronised a machine imitation of Brussels bobbin lace with a droschel ground. Various Devon lacemakers were appointed to her, among them Treadwin, Davey, Fowler and Herbert. From Mrs Treadwin she purchased a handkerchief, a black Honiton shawl and various fine reproductions of antique lace. Her immaculately stitched undergarments were edged with narrow Valenciennes.

Vienna lace. (Figs. 27c, 48b.) A bobbin lace of the East European 'trail' type, often using earth colours of green and brown. It is known from the eighteenth century mainly as cuffs but languished in the nineteenth century until 1890, when the Imperial Central School of Lacemaking was founded in Vienna under the patronage of the Austro-Hungarian empress. Original designs were encouraged in both bobbin and needlepoint techniques, and also imitations of, for example, Milanese, Cluny and point de gaze. J. Stramnitzer made a fine copy of a seventeenth-century Venetian gros point collar said to have been worn by Frederick V at his coronation in 1619 (see *Venetian lace* (b)).

Vinciolo. See *Lacis, Ruff* (a) and Fig. 6a.

Virgin ground, fond à la vierge. See *Reseau.*

Vos, Martin de (c 1534-1603). See *Bobbin lace* and *Flemish lace* (b, ii).

Vrai reseau (French, true network, equivalent to 'real lace ground'). A hand-made ground, but usually applied to droschel. Head uses it of the point de gaze reseau.

Wages for lacemakers. See *Earnings.*

Warp, weft. On textile looms these are the longitudinally stretched threads, and the threads which work transversely across them. In machine laces the relationship is more complicated since in the bobbinet machine and its derivatives, instead of a single weft moved horizontally by a shuttle, the warps are stretched vertically and there are some five thousand separate wefts wound on bobbins, which move simultaneously backwards and forwards between them. Also the warps, instead of simply being displaced up or down to create the patterning, are moved sideways to twist with the bobbin threads. In traversed laces the bobbins are lined up in two rows facing each other and, at each twelfth swing, end bobbins are exchanged between them and gradually edged right along until after the sixty-thousandth swing they are exchanged again and slip back to their original row. See also *Bobbin net.*

Warp Frame, Warp-knitting Machine. See *Lyons, Machine lace* (b) and *Mechlin* (d, i). The looped nets produced by this machine had the advantage both of being more stable than the point nets and also quicker to make, since simultaneous needle movements were possible across the whole width of the machine, and one thousand courses, or rows, could be worked in a minute. In a weft-knitting machine such as the Stocking Frame, on the other hand, a feeder had to travel across and back, making one loop after another. The Warp Frame did not compare so favourably with the bobbinets and when, in the mid nineteenth century the twist machines produced patterned laces, it dropped out of the competition. In the mid twentieth century, as Raschels, their speed of production gives them an economic advantage over the labour-intensive Levers, while the great strength of synthetic fibres adds versatility to their productions.

Warp lace, Warp net. Obscure terms, sometimes used of the products of the Warp Frame, sometimes of twist-machine products, e.g. 'fender' net (see *Mechlin* (d, iii) and *Net* (g)). The Modern Drapery and Allied Trades report of 1914 says that Warp lace was used to line coffins.

Web. See *Leavers.*

Wheatears, leaves, fats, Maltese petals, seeds, grains, paddles. (Figs. 2b, 3b and c.) Decorations of closely worked basket stitch found in bobbin laces such as Genoese, Maltese, Beds Maltese, Cluny and Le Puy, where they form an important part of the design. They differ from point d'esprit (see *Plaits* (b)) in being much larger, elongated and pointed, since the four threads from which they are made come together in pairs at each end. See also *Barleycorn.*

Wheel design. (a) A variation of Spanish sol lace (see *Spanish lace* (e)). (b) A 'spider' in torchon laces.

Whisk, gorget. Used of several forms of lace or lace-trimmed collars and neckerchieves, and sometimes of a standing band supported by an under-propper, in the time of Charles II (see *Commonwealth*). The whisk is sometimes equated with the golilla, a Spanish form of the Medici collar, made of heavily starched linen decorated with cutwork, resting on an underpropper and edged with punto in aria. As such it is recorded in 1610. Philip IV of Spain (reigned 1621-5) decreed that the golilla should replace all other collar styles. However, it underwent its own transmuta-tion: from a standing collar to an almost flat — though still starched and resting just clear of the shoulders — semicircular collar which surrounded the nape of the neck to end in a straight line on either side of the throat, to be tied with tasselled cords. A little later it appeared as an entirely circular collar fitting closely and flatly around the lower neck.

Whitework. A general term for white embroidery on white material, it embraces various openwork forms which may, with more or less latitude, be termed lace:
(a) Cutworks, ranging from simple cut-out spaces to the complex reticellas of the sixteenth century.
(b) The nineteenth-century broderie anglaise embroidered either by hand or by the Swiss hand-embroidery machine, the stitches of which were indistinguishable.
(c) Richelieu work of the late nineteenth and twentieth centuries.
(d) Dresden work, a form not of cutwork but of drawnwork, made in Saxony in the mid eighteenth century.
(e) Ayrshire work, a complex derivation from late eighteenth-century French embroidery, from drawnwork (imitating Dresden), and from cutwork in that the centres of the flowers were sometimes cut out and then variously filled. About 1814-70.
(f) Swiss embroidery of a very elaborate form, by the hand-embroidery or Schiffli machine. The Schiffli was used for white embroidery from 1898.

Whole stitch, linen stitch, cloth stitch, plain work, cloth work, clothing. The more solid part of a bobbin lace design, giving the appearance of woven cloth, and made by the movements of a pair of worker bobbins. See *Half stitch, Toilé*.

Winding sheet, burial cloth, cerecloth, shroud. A large linen cloth some 9 feet (2.7 m) square made of widths joined by ½ inch (13 mm) bands of lace and narrowly bordered with similar edging. Most dated examples are from the seventeenth century and may have been used to drape the corpse before burial.

Wire ground. Fond double. See *Reseau.*

Wool. (Fig. 23a.) A form of animal hair, made of protein (keratin). Each fibre is covered with tiny scales, which help them to cling together in spinning but are a disadvantage in lacemaking since they cause the threads to catch on each other instead of gliding smoothly. Bobbin lace is difficult to make with wool, and needlepoint impossible.

Trade in wool was important to England's economy from early times. In the somewhat depressed period of 1678, Charles II passed the Burial in Wool Act. It was opposed on Christian grounds – 'Our Saviour was buried in linen', and on anti-Catholic grounds – 'men of the Romish religion desire to be buried in a (woollen) habit of some order . . . I fear this Bill may taste of Popery.' However, it did accelerate trade: deaths in the late seventeenth century were prolific, and there was money in mourning. That woollen lace was used in burials is clear from the monopoly in the making of woollen lace for burying the dead granted to Amy Potter, near St Paul's Church Yard, in November 1678. We do not know what this lace looked like.

In spite of the horror of society ladies at the thought of wool touching their skin, so lucidly expressed in Pope's well known lines c 1734 – 'Odious! in woollen! 'Twould a saint provoke! . . . No, let a charming chintz and Brussels lace Wrap my cold limbs and shade my lifeless face' – the Act continued to be enforced. However, the payment of only a £5 fine enabled people to be laid to rest in linen, and many chose this course. In 1730 there was a recommendation that the penalty should be increased and 'extended to the plantations in America and the islands', which would be much to the advantage of the wool trade.

Woollen laces known to have been made are:

(i) Yak. A torchon lace made in the East Midlands.

(ii) Pusher machine. Lama (mohair) lace, c 1850-70.

(iii) Stocking Frame. In 1804 plain worsted hosiery machines were adapted for the openwork patterning of woollen laces. Earlier, in 1750, mittens and gloves of wool were made on the Stocking Frame, ornamented with eyelet holes and rose leaves in openwork, some so elaborate that journeymen were paid 5s or 6s a pair for making them and might make two pairs in one day – a high reward for the period. In the mid nineteenth century Stocking Frames made shawls similar to those of the Shetlands. Leicester was traditionally associated with wool, Derby with silk, and Nottingham with cotton.

(iv) Warp Frames were adapted both for plain nets of gossamer silk and for patterned laces, some of wool.

Worker bobbins. See *Leader.*

Yak. A woollen bobbin lace, associated with the East Midlands. It appeared first in the 1870s and, though made mainly in creamy-white or black, it was occasionally dyed in bright colours. Early examples are said to have been made from the wool of the Tibetan yak, but since it was never more than a very utilitarian lace this seems unlikely. Later examples, of Yorkshire sheep's wool, were made in great quantities at High Wycombe up to the 1890s. One lace manufacturer of north Buckinghamshire used 300 pounds (136 kg) of wool per month. Designs were geometric, of a simple torchon, Cluny or Beds Maltese type. Yak was soon out of fashion, being prone to moth attack and to shrinkage.

Yardwork. The production of lengths of edging on the lacemaking machines.

Youghal. A needlepoint lace first made commercially at the Presentation Convent, County Cork, in 1852. Though ostensibly based on old Venetian raised points, it soon developed a pretty style of its own, quite different from any other, with picoted brides in the shape of rounded hexagons, with the sunlight and shade effect so characteristic of the late nineteenth-century revival laces, and with very natural flowers — wild roses in full bloom or springing as tight buds from trailing stems, pansies, fuchsias and garden anemones — all so accurately observed they seemed still to be growing. A Youghal fan was made for the wedding of Princess Maud, daughter of Edward VII, in 1896, but lack of adequate patronage shortened the life of the industry.

Ypres. A town in north-west Belgium, one of the main centres for the production of nineteenth-century Valenciennes after the monopoly of its manufacture had been acquired by Belgium. It also made good quality torchon lace, which was sold as souvenirs during the First World War.

Recommended reading

Abegg, Margaret. *Apropos Patterns for Embroidery, Lace and Woven Textiles.* Bern, 1978.

Aemilia Ars, Merletti e Ricami della. Milan and Rome, 1929.

Caplin, Jessie F. *The Lace Book.* Macmillan, New York, 1932.

Caulfield, S. F. A. and Saward, B. C. *Encyclopaedia of Victorian Needlework.* Dover Publications, New York, 1972 reprint.

Chapman, S. D. 'The Genesis of the British Hosiery Industry, 1600-1750'. *Textile History,* volume 3, December 1972.

Cole, A. S. *Ancient Needlepoint and Pillow Lace.* London, 1875.

Compton, Rose. *The Hamlyn Knitting Guide.* Hamlyn, 1980.

Coxhead, J. R. W. *The Romance of the Wool, Lace and Pottery Trade in Honiton.* 1952.

Cunnington, Phillis and Lucas, Catherine. *Costumes of Births, Marriages and Deaths.* Adam and Charles Black, 1972.

Delany, Mary. *Autobiography and Correspondence of Mary Granville, Mrs Delany.* Edited by Lady Llanover. London, 1861.

Despierres, G. *Histoire de point d'Alençon depuis ses origines jusqu'à nos jours.* Renousard, Paris, 1886.

Dillmont, Thérèse de. *Encyclopaedia of Needlework.* The Midlands Educational Company Ltd, Birmingham.

Downton Lace Industry. Salisbury Museum, Wiltshire, 1961.

Earnshaw, Pat. *The Identification of Lace.* Shire Publications, 1980.

— 'Lace Terms - a Multilingual Muddle'. *Antique Collecting,* 1980.

— 'The Dating of Lace: Pointers and Pitfalls'. *Antique Collecting,* June 1980.

— 'The Cost of Lace'. *Antique Collecting,* February 1981.

— 'Investment in Lace'. *Antique Collecting,* July/August 1981.

— 'Signs, Dates and Terms: Lace'. *Art and Antiques Weekly,* 27th June 1980.

— 'Lace - with Care'. *Art and Antiques Weekly,* 3rd October 1980.

— 'A Frivolity of Kings'. *Art and Antiques Weekly,* 28th November 1980.

— 'Lace for Collectors'. *Connoisseur,* August 1980.

— 'English Lace: Cottage, Commerce and Court'. *The Period Home,* June 1981.

Felkin, W. *History of Machine-wrought Hosiery and Lace.* David and Charles, 1967 reprint.

Fiennes, Celia. *Through England on a Side-saddle in the Time of William and Mary (1685-1703).* Simpkin Marshall, 1888.

— *The Journeys of Celia Fiennes.* Edited by Christopher Morris. Cresset

Press, 1947.

Freeman, Charles. *Pillow Lace of the East Midlands.* Luton Museum and Art Gallery, 1971.

Fuller, Thomas. *The History of the Worthies of England.* 1662.

Halls, Zillah. *Machine-made Lace in Nottingham.* The City of Nottingham Museum and Libraries Committee, 1973.

Hawkins, Daisy Waterhouse. *Old Point Lace.* Chatto and Windus, 1878.

Head, Mrs R. E. *The Lace and Embroidery Collector.* Herbert Jenkins, 1922. Reprinted, Gale, Detroit, 1974.

Henneberg, F. A. von. *The Art and Craft of Old Lace.* Batsford, 1931.

Hudson Moore, N. *The Lace Book.* Chapman and Hall, 1905.

Huetson, T. L. *Lace and Bobbins.* David and Charles, 1973.

Inder, P. M. *Honiton Lace.* Exeter Museum Publication, number 55, 1971.

Jackson, Mrs Nevill. *A History of Hand-made Lace.* Upcott Gill, 1900.

Johnstone, Margaret Taylor. *Ragusa, the Mystery Spot in Lace History.* Needle and Bobbin Club Bulletin, volume 10, number 1, 1926.

Jourdain, M. *Old Lace.* Batsford, 1908.

Kybulová, Herbenová and Lamarová. *The Pictorial Encyclopaedia of Fashion.* Hamlyn, 1968.

Lefebure, E. *Embroidery and Lace.* Grevel, 1888.

Lewis, Fulvia. *Lace.* Remos Sandron, Firenze, 1981.

Longfield, Ada. *Guide to the Collection of Lace.* National Museum of Ireland, Dublin, 1970.

Lowes, Mrs E. L. *Chats on Old Lace and Needlework.* London, 1919.

Maidment, M. *A Manual of Hand-made Bobbin Lace-work.* Minet, 1978 reprint.

May, F. L. *Hispanic Lace and Lace-making.* The Hispanic Society of America, 1939.

Meulen-Nulle, L. W. van der. *Lace.* Merlin Press, London, 1963.

Mincoff, E. and Marriage, M. S. *Pillow Lace.* Murray, 1907.

Palliser, Mrs Bury. *History of Lace.* Sampson Low, 1910.

Paulis, L. *Pour Connaître la Dentelle.* Antwerp, 1947.

— *Les Points à l'Aiguille Belges.* Brussels, 1947.

— *'Le Pompe'. A Study of the Technique of Sixteenth Century Bobbin Laces.* Needle and Bobbin Club Bulletin, volume 6, number 1, 1922.

Pollen, Mrs J. Hungerford. *Seven Centuries of Lace.* Heinemann, 1908.

Pond, Gabrielle. *An Introduction to Lace.* Scribners, New York, 1975.

Powys, M. *Lace and Lace-making.* Ch. T. Branford, Boston, 1953.

Ricci, Elisa. *Old Italian Lace.* Heinemann, 1913.

Risley, C. *Machine Embroidery.* Studio Vista, 1980.

Risselin-Steenebrugen, M. *Trois Siècles de Dentelles.* Musées Royaux d'Art et d'Histoire, Brussels, 1981.

Ruppert, J. *Le Costume*, II and III. Flammarion, 1931.

Séguin, J. *La Dentelle*. Paris, 1875.

Sharp, Mary (A.M.S.). *Point and Pillow Lace*. Murray, 1913.

Simeon, M. *A History of Lace*. Stainer and Bell, 1979.

Stoves, J. L. *Fibre Microscopy, its Technique and Appreciation*. National Trade Press Ltd, 1957.

Stubbes, Philip. *The Anatomie of Abuses*. 1583.

Thomas, Mary. *A Dictionary of Embroidery Stitches*. Hodder and Stoughton, 1968.

Treadwin, Mrs C. *Antique Point and Honiton Lace*. Ward, Lock and Tyler, c 1874.

Vinciolo, Frederico. *Renaissance Patterns for Lace, Embroidery and Needlepoint*. Dover Publications, New York, 1971.

Wardle, Patricia. *Victorian Lace*. Herbert Jenkins, 1968.

Westcote, T. *A View of Devonshire in MDCXXX*. Oliver and Jones, 1845.

Whiting, Gertrude (editor). *La Révolte des Passemens*. Paris, 1660-1 Reprinted 1935 from Needle and Bobbin Club Bulletin, volume 14, 1930.

Whiting, Gertrude. *A Lace Guide for Makers and Collectors*. Dutton, 1920.

Wright, Thomas. *The Romance of the Lace Pillow*. Armstrong, 1919. Minet, 1971 reprint.

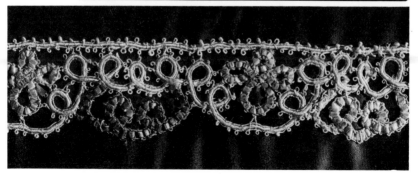

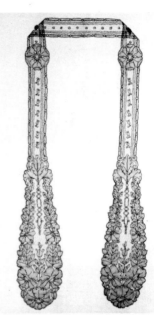

2. Bobbin laces from north and central France. **a** (above right). Black Chantilly, a narrow tie worked in half stitch c 1830. **b** (above left). Black Le Puy with rows of wheatears, cartouches of flowers, and a ground of brides. **c** (left). Blonde lace of similar design but different techniques: bobbin-made; needlerun on bobbinet; entirely machine-made.

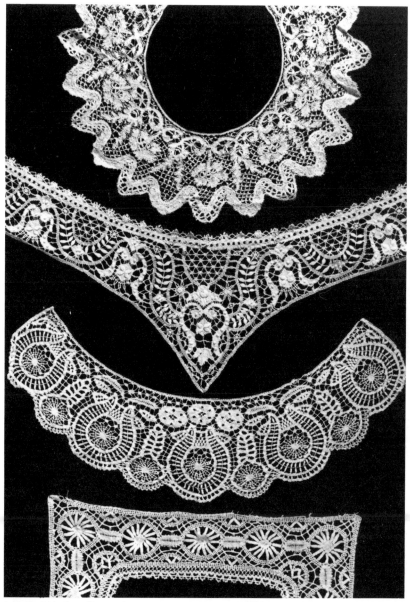

3. Bedfordshire laces (from top). **a.** With a plaited ground of tallies. **b.** With raised wheatears. **c.** Le Puy form with long lines of wheatears. **d.** Cluny form with divided trail.

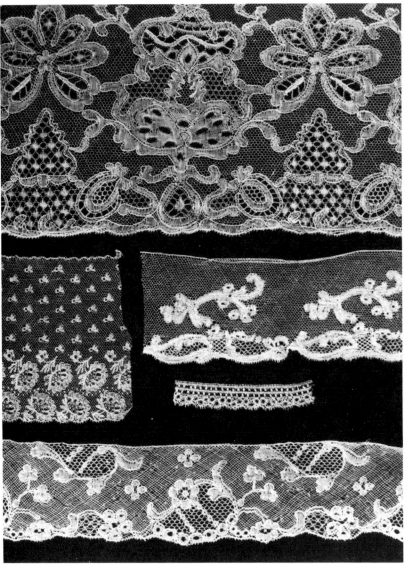

4. Buckinghamshire laces (from top, and left to right). **a.** The border of a veil attached at its heading to a matching net; Mayflower fillings are shown in the cones to left and right. **b.** A Bucks lace strikingly similar to an early nineteenth-century Mechlin design. **c.** A design called Regency, where the gimp thread passes not around the outline but through the centre of the toilé. **d.** Baby lace. **e.** An early form with a torchon ground, probably eighteenth century.

5a (above left). Brussels point de gaze, nineteenth century. The ornate design has raised rose petals and intricate fillings. **b** (above right). Brussels needlepoint, eighteenth century, part of a lappet extended by an edging. The exceptional fineness of the crystal-jewelled design is apparent in the x10 enlargement, **c** (below). Here the buttonhole stitches of the solid parts contrast with the bobbin-made droschel ground, the strands of which pass behind the toilé showing that it is a mixed lace and not an appliqué.

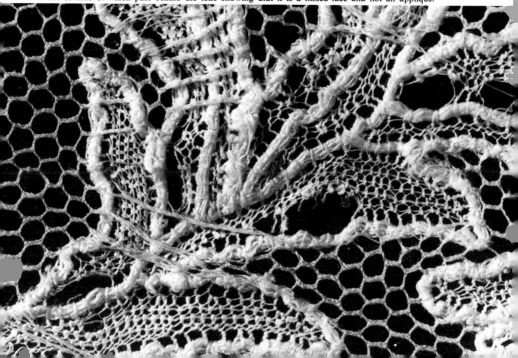

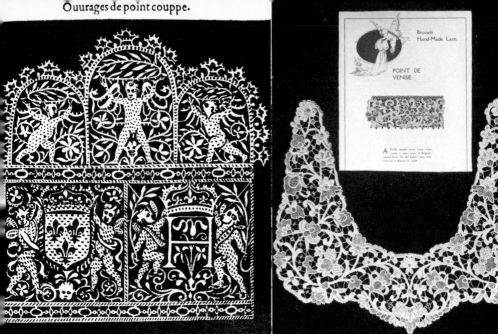

6 (above). Flemish/Belgian lace. **a** (left). An expensive form of cutwork. Though the Venetian Vinciolo designed this at the French court, his pattern book (1587) would have been available in Flanders, and his elaborate point couppes may have been among those ordered by Elizabeth I, at one time enamoured of Henri III's brother François, duc d'Alençon. **b** (right). Point de Venise, twentieth century, an exhibition collar similar to the design shown in the catalogue, 1912.

7 (below). Flemish bobbin laces, c 1700. **a** (left top). Mechlin. **b** (left centre). Valenciennes. **c** (left bottom). Binche. **d** (right). Twentieth-century point de fée.

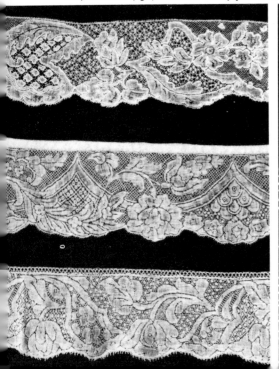

8 (above). Sixteenth-century bobbin laces: the first and third are probably Venetian, the second and fourth Genoese.

9 (below). Punto in aria. a (left). A copy of the lace worn by Lady Doddridge on her stone effigy in Exeter cathedral (1614). Mrs Treadwin's copy appears to be worked in a combination of cording and needle weaving, but the original lace which the stonemason copied could have been either bobbin (Genoese) or needlepoint (punto in aria). b (right). A bobbin-made copy of punto in aria, c 1600. The terminal carnation is flanked by young strawberries.

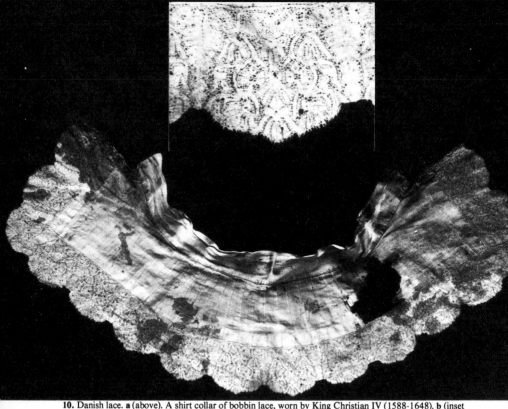

10. Danish lace. **a** (above). A shirt collar of bobbin lace, worn by King Christian IV (1588-1648). **b** (inset at top). A small portion of (a) enlarged, to show the design. **c** (below). Flemish collar laces, early seventeenth century, two designs.

11. *Portrait of a Lady* by Bartholomeus van der Helst (1613-70), possibly painted in Amsterdam, showing a cap, triple falling collar, cuffs and a shift beneath, all bordered with a Flemish bobbin lace very similar in design to fig. 10b, demonstrating the close relationship between Danish and Flemish at this time. Note the black lace.

12. Swedish lace. **a** (above). A collar of King Gustavus II Adolphus (1594-1632). The border, like a complex punto in aria, is in fact a bobbin lace; see enlargement of one of the insertions, **b** (below).

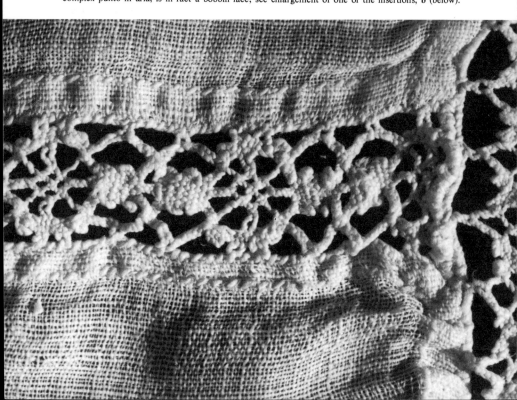

13a. Scandinavian lace: damask work around a panel of black embroidery dated 1768. The cloth is pierced with eyelet holes and darned to look like damask on the figures of cupids, peacocks and unicorns, separated by reticella squares. The 'damask' is enclosed by a double band of needle weaving.

13b. An ornamental towel end of drawnwork, the figures picked out in pale pink and blue. The edging is bobbin lace, Swedish, nineteenth century.

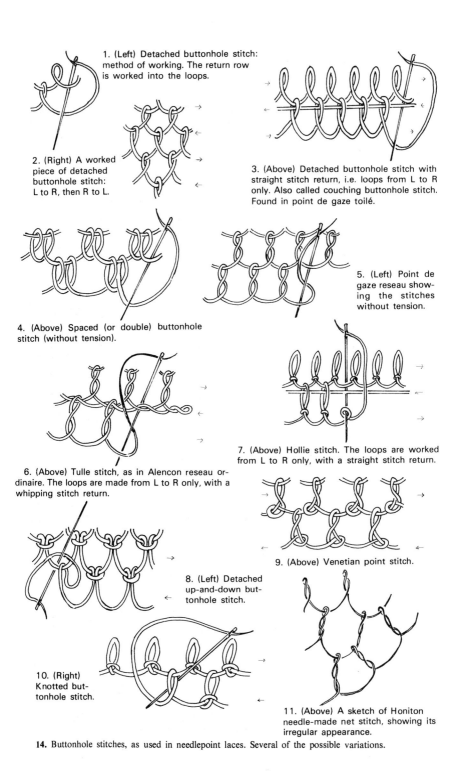

1. (Left) Detached buttonhole stitch: method of working. The return row is worked into the loops.

2. (Right) A worked piece of detached buttonhole stitch: L to R, then R to L.

3. (Above) Detached buttonhole stitch with straight stitch return, i.e. loops from L to R only. Also called couching buttonhole stitch. Found in point de gaze toilé.

4. (Above) Spaced (or double) buttonhole stitch (without tension).

5. (Left) Point de gaze reseau showing the stitches without tension.

6. (Above) Tulle stitch, as in Alencon reseau ordinaire. The loops are made from L to R only, with a whipping stitch return.

7. (Above) Hollie stitch. The loops are worked from L to R only, with a straight stitch return.

8. (Left) Detached up-and-down buttonhole stitch.

9. (Above) Venetian point stitch.

10. (Right) Knotted buttonhole stitch.

11. (Above) A sketch of Honiton needle-made net stitch, showing its irregular appearance.

14. Buttonhole stitches, as used in needlepoint laces. Several of the possible variations.

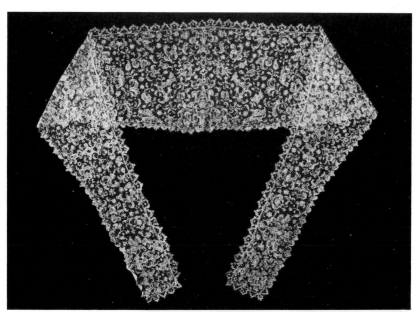

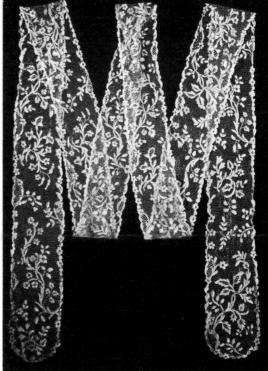

15. French needlepoints. **a** (above). A collar of point de France, c 1700. **b** (right). Argentan, a pair of 6 foot (1.8 m) long lappets, first half eighteenth century.

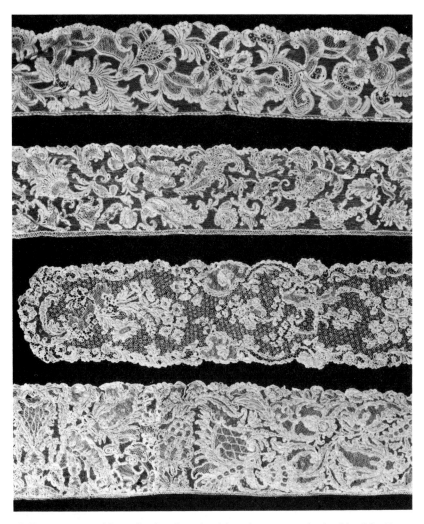

16. Four gossamer-weight needlepoints from the eighteenth century, variously claimed by France, Brussels and Venice (from top). **a.** The form most usually called reseau Venise. It is flat, with a bold exuberant design, and the reseau worked lengthwise. **b.** A very similar form, flat and with a similar reseau, but with the disseminated parts not unlike fragments of point de France. **c.** Argentella, with a slightly raised outlining thread closely oversewn with buttonhole stitch, and a characteristic reseau rosaceae. It is generally regarded as a form of Argentan. **d.** A conglomerated design, the cordonnet raised and oversewn as in (c), the fillings similar to point de Sedan, though finer. The scattered open parts are filled with reseau ordinaire, but running in different directions. (a-d) represent at least three distinct forms: the problem is to decide which name is most appropriate for them.

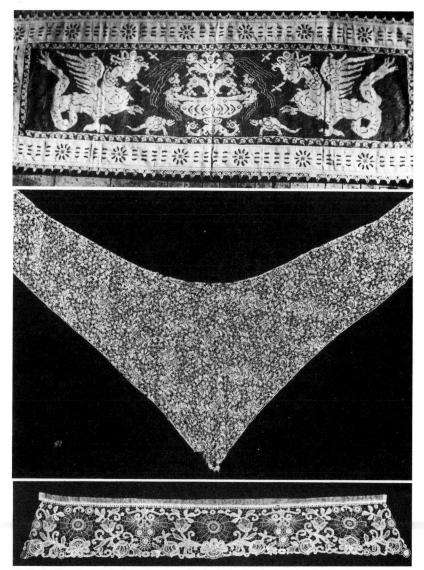

17. Design (from top). **a.** A sixteenth-century fantasy of fountain-gargoyles spraying water over mythical beasts and tailed turtles; filet. **b.** The crowded dizzying beauty of rococo swirls; Binche bobbin lace c 1700, with a snowflake ground. **c.** Art nouveau spider webs add a fairy-like quality to an unreal grotto of flowers; chemical lace, c 1900.

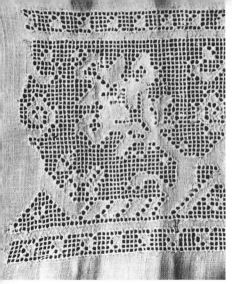
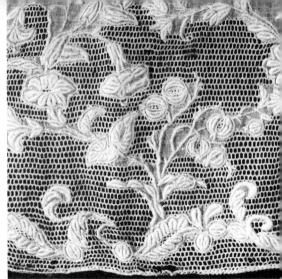

18. Drawnwork. **a** (above left). Sixteenth-century on linen. The basic closely textured cloth is shown on the left. On the right the meshes are formed by drawnwork, the designs by the untouched material. **b** (above right). A similar form, but of loosely textured muslin so that holes can be formed by drawing together rather than by drawing out the threads. Again the design is formed by the residual cloth, here strengthened by surface embroidery. Early nineteenth century, sometimes called Rhodes embroidery. **c** (below left). A lappet of Dresden work. The densely white parts are the original material made opaque by shadow stitch. The complex fillings, with every stitch evenly and perfectly formed, are characteristic of this mid eighteenth-century form. **d** (below right). Philippine drawnwork. The stiffness of this pina cloth conceals a loose weave which enables the threads to be pulled easily together. The work, as in (c), is beautifully executed, but the designs are naive rather than regal.

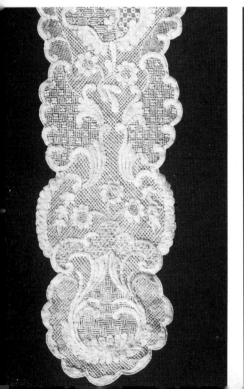

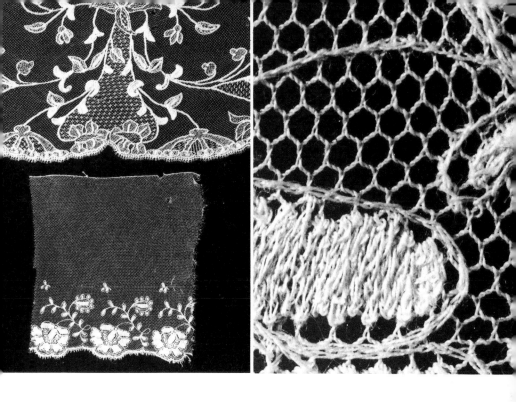

19. Embroidered nets. **a** (above left, top). The outline is hand-embroidered with a tambour hook, the fillings of needlerun variations, possibly Ghent c 1900. **b** (above left, lower). Machine embroidery, the short repeats regimented by Jacquard cards. **c** (above right). A x10 enlargement of (b) showing the lock stitches so densely crowded that they look confused. **d** (below left). An unusual hand-made torchon ground run in thick thread with punto a rammendo to form a striking design. Here handwork looks like machine work, but the enlargement **(e)** shows that it is not. Said to be Scottish.

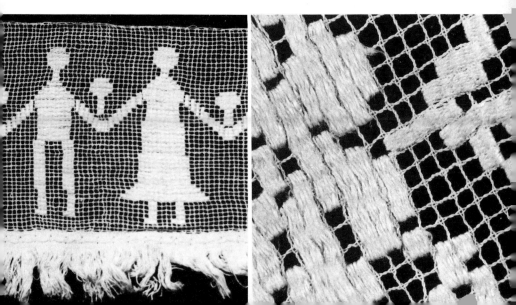

20. Fashion: court ladies wearing fontanges, lappets, engageants, tuckers and aprons, c 1690.

21. **a** (above left). Louis XIV c 1670, a drawing by Gagnières. **b** (above right). The lacemaker – a court lady stitches assiduously at her needlepoint lace on its parchment. Note her elaborate lace-bordered apron. **c** (right). Summer fashion, with point d'Angleterre very much in vogue. Both (b) and (c) late seventeenth century.

Habit d'Esté

Agraphe de Piereries.

gans de point d'Angleterre.

Manchettes doubles.

Manteau de gaze.

Iupe de point d'Angleterre Sur em fons de Couleur.

d'entelle d'Angleterre plissée.

Principal Lacemaking Centres
of Europe

SHETLAND

NORWAY

SWEDEN

New Pitsligo

Hamilton

Ayr

DENMARK

Carrickmacross

Limerick

Tonder

Youghal

Nottingham

HOLLAND

Bedford

Buckingham

SAXONY

Honiton

Bruges

Antwerp

Calais

Ghent

Mechlin

Dresden

Lille

Wuppertal

Brussels

Liege

Dieppe

Binche

Bayeux

Valenciennes

Caen

Sedan

BOHEMIA

Argentan

Chantilly

RUSSIA

Alençon

Luneville

BRITTANY

Augsburg

FRANCE

Vienna

SWITZERLAND

AUSTRIA

Le Puy

St. Gallen

HUNGARY

Aurillac

Lyon

Milan

Venice

Genoa

PORTUGAL

SPAIN

ITALY

Dubrovnik

SICILY

22. A map of Europe indicating the main areas associated with lacemaking.

23. Fibres. **a** (above left). Wool with scales x1500. **b** (above right). Cotton with a twist x750. **c** (below left). Coarse flax with nodes x1500. **d** (right). Silk x1500. **e** (below right). Nylon x1500. (a-c) staple, (d-c) filament fibres.

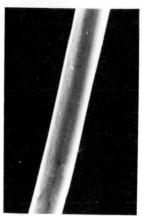

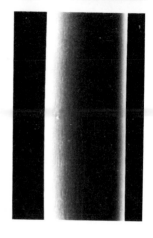

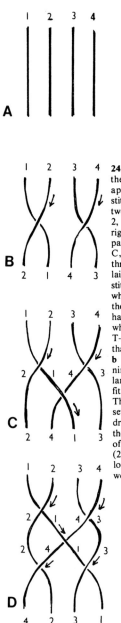

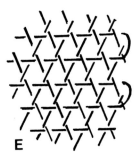

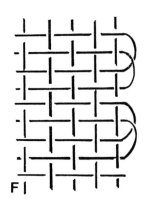

24a. Bobbin lace. A-F, the making and final appearance of whole stitch and half stitch. A, two pairs of threads (1 + 2, 3 + 4). B, the twist: the right-hand thread of each pair is laid over the left. C, the cross: the left thread of the inner pair is laid over the right. D, half stitch is formed of C-T; whole stitch of C-T-C. E, the grille formed by the half stitch repeats. F, the whole stitch formed by C-T-C repeats using more than two pairs of bobbins. **b** (bottom right). A nineteenth-century lace lamp made to hold a wick fitment. **c** (centre right). The technique of taking a sewing: the needle pin (A) draws thread (1) through the outer loops of the toilé of whole stitch (B); thread (2) is taken through the loop of thread (1) by a worker bobbin (C).

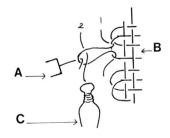

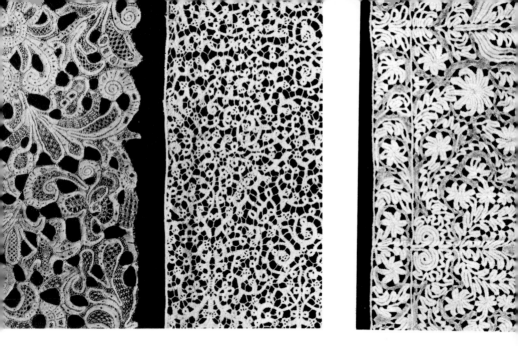

25. Italian bobbin laces. **a** (above left). Seventeenth-century Milanese with prodigal and diversified fillings, and almost no brides. **b** (above centre). Late eighteenth-century Milanese, the 'snail's head' pattern, small and nondescript, on the same scale as (a). **c** (above right). Eighteenth-century Palestrina, finely and evenly textured, but showing an East European (Austrian) influence in the continuous maze-like trails of the very formal design (see figs. 26 and 27). **d** (below). Abruzzi, a silk bobbin lace, early eighteenth century.

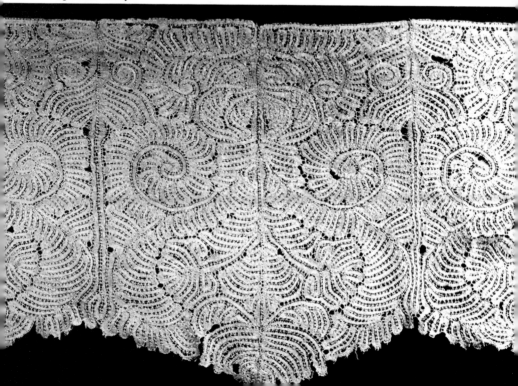

26 (above). East European bobbin laces. Russian lace trimming the dress of one of the young daughters of the last Tsar, killed in 1918. The traditional bobbin lace is made of thin red and blue trails curling their way through the deeply scalloped flouncings.

27 (opposite page). East European. a (top left). Bohemian, eighteenth century, part of a flounce 18 inches (460 mm) deep, showing the extremely complex, yet not muddled, intertwining of the contorted trail with its very short sewn-in brides. b (top right). Hungarian, eighteenth century. c (centre). Austrian, eighteenth century. d (bottom). Russian, twentieth century. This is loosely worked compared with (a-c); the ground occupies more space, and the trails are scarcely maze-like at all.

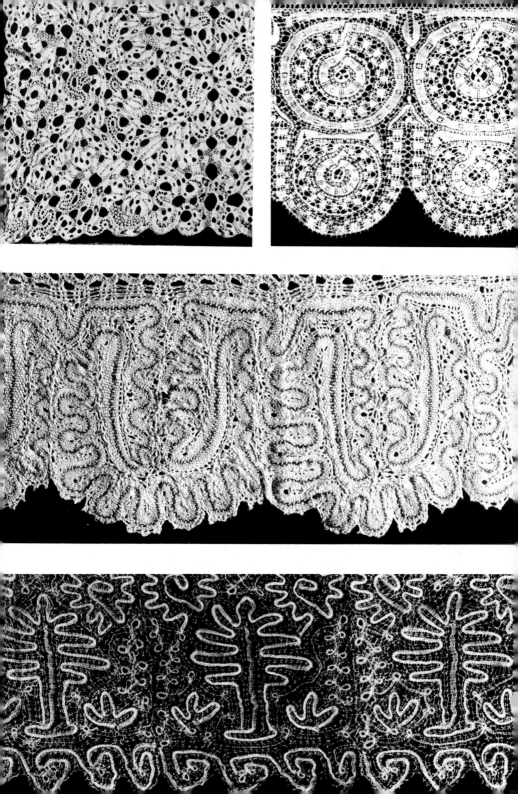

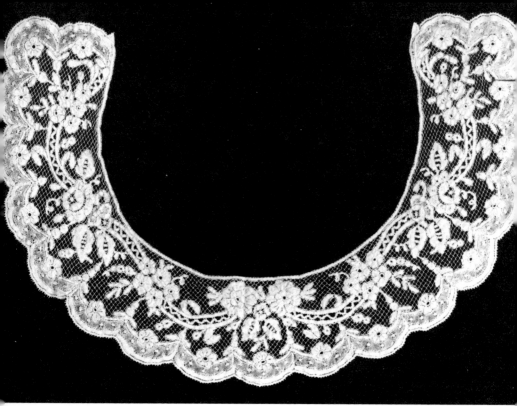

28. Valenciennes. **a** (above). A finely worked Peter Pan collar. **b** (below). A close-up of the reverse side of (a). Though Valenciennes is regarded as a continuous thread lace, the late nineteenth-century form made in Belgium and sometimes called 'Val de Ghent' has cut as well as attached threads, showing that the terms fil coupé and fil attaché do not form a satisfactory category in opposition to fil continu. Quite a number of cut ends can be clearly seen, and to the right the reseau continues behind the leafy tendrils of whole stitch.

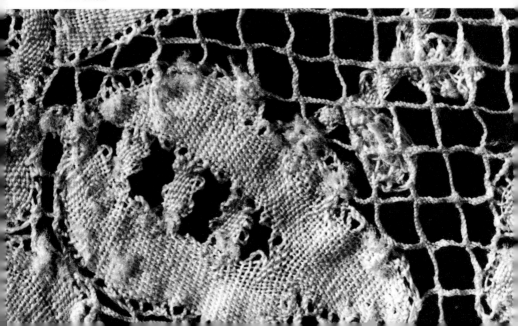

29. Chain stitch. **a** (above left). A hand-knitted baby cap said to have been worn by Lord Nelson. **b** (above right). Isle of Wight lace, a child's bonnet, in tambour work. **c** (below). A ×10 enlargement of eighteenth-century hand knitting — even with the complex patterning, the basically horizontal alignment of the loops can be seen.

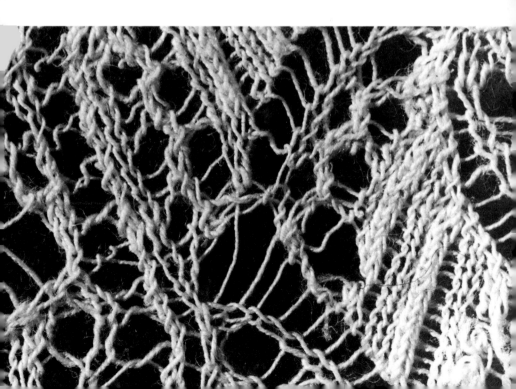

30. 'Knitting' machines. **a** (opposite page). An early Stocking Frame with a bench seat where the framework knitter could sit as he worked the foot treadle, c 1770. **b** (right). A stocking front with eyelet work, the sort of decoration which inspired the invention of 'point net' in 1769. **c** (below). Raschel machine, the knitting elements, showing the blunt-ended needles with the eye at the tip. Gauges vary from twenty-eight to forty-eight (i.e. fourteen to twenty-four needles per inch). Between 240 and 480 courses (rows) per minute can be worked, for widths varying from 75 to 130 inches (1.9 to 3.3 m), which is very fast indeed.

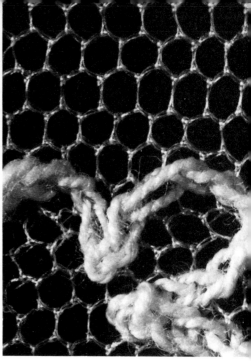

31. Looped nets. **a** (above left). Part of a silk square, decorated by hand with tambour work. **b** (above right). A x10 enlargement of (a) showing the 'point net' and the embroidering chain stitch. **c** (below left). A machine-patterned warp frame stole, c 1920. **d** (below right). A x10 enlargement of (c) showing the vertical (warp) alignment of the loops.

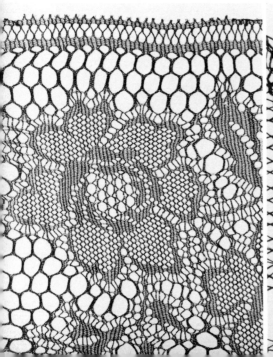

32. Machine lace. **a** (above). A Levers machine showing the vertical warp threads, the beams below holding the warps, spare bobbins (the working bobbins are not visible), and the dozens of widths of edgings being made side by side. **b** (right). A Jacquard apparatus, showing the large number of cards needed for a complex design. It is attached to one end of the machine and at the top can be seen the hooked steel bars which stretch outwards to manipulate the warps.

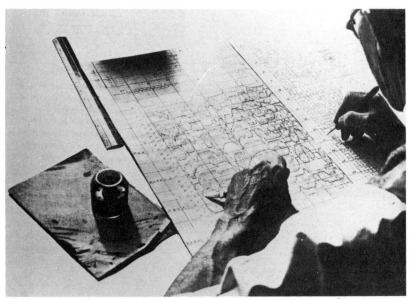

33. Machine lace. **a** (above). The draughtsman translates the artist's design (on the left) into a network of numbers (on the right) which plots every movement of every thread until the pattern is complete. **b** (below). The making of tulle illusion for royal wedding veils: (from the left) the strands of raw silk, one of the thousands of 'weft' bobbins in its carriage, and the very fine finished net.

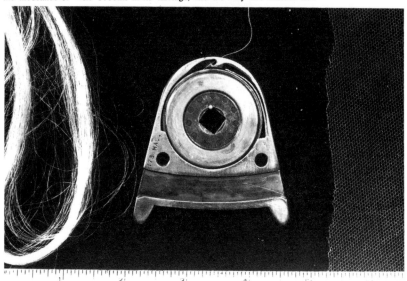

34. Poke bonnets. a (above). A contemporary cartoon of the absurdity of a fashion carried to extremes, c 1820. b (left). The 'curtain' which replaced the deep brim, a poke bonnet veil of needlerun embroidery on two-twist bobbinet, Nottingham c 1840.

35. Carrickmacross. **a** (top). Machine — the over-sewing stitch is made by the hand-embroidery machine, automated by the pantograph. The muslin shamrocks have their outline trimmed back by hand when the stitching is complete. Switzerland, second half nineteenth century. **b** (above right). Hand-made Irish Carrickmacross, with its characteristic open-looped border and needlerun fillings. **c** (above left). An appliqué of denser cloth outlined by chain stitch made either by hand with a tambour needle, or by the Bonnaz embroidery machine. Belgium, or possibly Ireland. **d** (below left). A close-up of (a). **e** (below right). A close-up of (b) showing that the outline is formed by a couched thread, which is absent in (a).

36. Swiss lace. **a** (above). Work done on the hand-embroidery machine. In spite of an unvarying rigidity of repeat, it is almost impossible to isolate features which indicate that this work was done by anything but human hand. **b** (below left). A close-up of work similar to the fillings of (a), and also machine-made. **c** (below right). An equivalent enlargement of Schiffli embroidery taken from the reverse side to show the general unsharp appearance and the central ridge in the solid parts, quite unlike embroidery by hand.

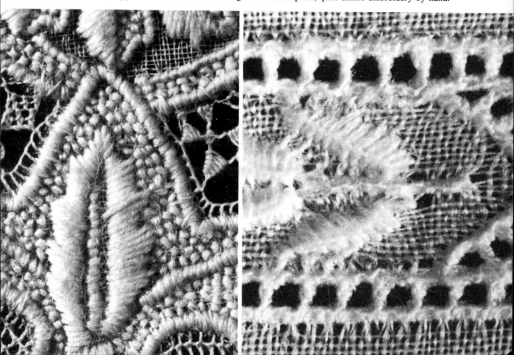

37. Imitation laces. a (above). Intagliatela, eighteenth century. The general form of the design gives a superficial impression of needlepoint, assisted by the odd petals of buttonhole stitch inserted in the linen flowers. **b** (below). Cording, a close-up of an imitation puncetto. Here there is no knotting, only binding around, darning and plaiting. Twentieth century, Italy. **c** (opposite, top). A clever imitation of needlepoint formed again by darning and cording. The tightly twisted thread which was used gives a crinkly appearance to the whole, making it look rather like chemical lace. **d** (opposite, bottom). A laborious imitation resembling point de gaze, in spite of having a ground of brides. The basic material is a gauze (leno weave), which can be seen within the petals of the central flower. Raised outlines have been made by heavy embroidery, and there are tiny fillings of buttonhole stitching. When the work was done, all the excess gauze behind the brides would have to be cut away.

38. The pierced look. **a** (above left). The trompe l'oeil appearance of lace made by pierced paperwork on a Japanese fan. **b** (above right). Hardanger work, Norway, early twentieth century. **c** (below). Ayrshire, detail of the bodice of a baby gown showing complex drawnwork fillings, c 1840.

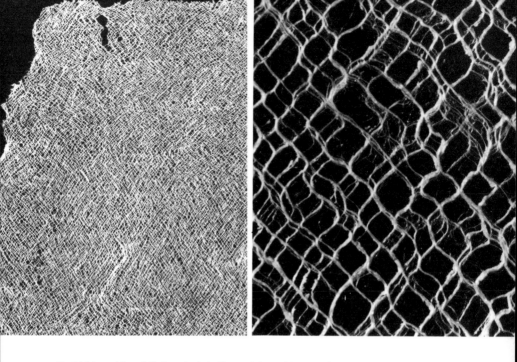

39. Oddities. **a** (above left). Lace bark, half natural size. **b** (above right). Lace bark enlarged, to show its mesh-like form. **c** (below left). E-lace-tic, india-rubber strands woven into a machine lace, c 1900. **d** (below right). Loom lace, eighteenth century. The irregular arrangement of the threads in the gauze-like weave gives this piece a strangely modern, abstract appearance.

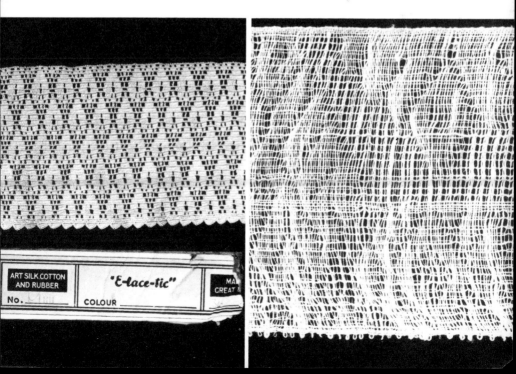

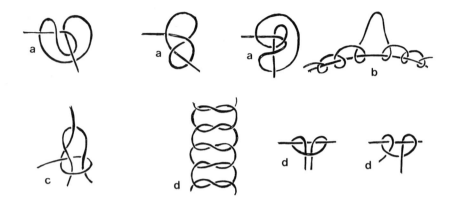

40. Knots. **a.** Knots used in Middle Eastern, Mediterranean and North African laces (from left: Smyrna, Armenian, bebilla). **b.** Tatting knot, showing a picot; a double reverse half hitch or double stitch or lark's head. **c.** Filet knot; a fisherman's knot or weaver's knot, sheet bend or mesh. **d.** Macramé knots: (from left) flat or square knot, double half hitch or cow hitch, reversed double half hitch or clove hitch. **e** (below left). Sixteenth- or seventeenth-century punto a groppo, part of a dentate border with wart-like excrescences. The knotting is clearer from the reverse side, but even there is so shrunk, hardened and crushed by washing, starching and ironing that the technique is not really distinguishable. Each 1½ inch (38 mm) tooth may have been built up by macramé work from threads of limited length, with the picots taking up the remains of the fringe. **f** (below right). Bebilla, part of a three-dimensional necklace or garland formed by delicate knotting. Nineteenth century.

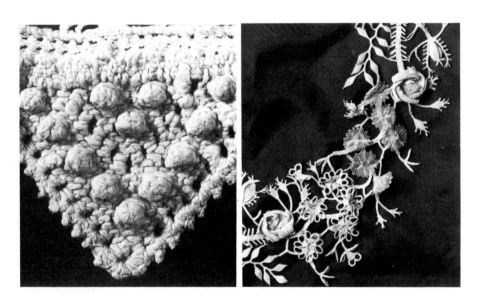

41. Knotting. a and b (above left). Middle Eastern knotted laces, twentieth century. c (above right). A close-up of (a) which shows the knotting very clearly. d (below left). Puncetto, Italian, twentieth century. e (below right). A close-up of (d); the knotting is very dense, but still distinguishable; compare fig. 37b.

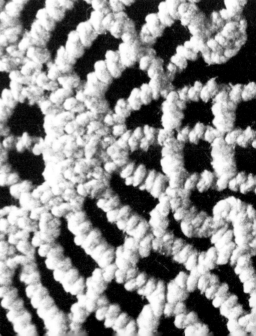

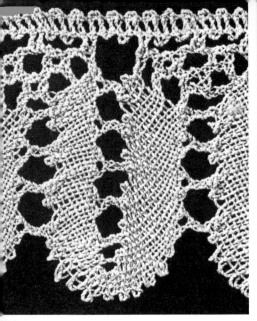

42. Spider lace. **a** (above left). Said to have been made from spider's silk, Madagascar, actual size. **b** (above right). Tenerife lace — the radiating fibres crossed by concentric circles bear some resemblance to a spider's web. **c** (below). Torchon lace, showing the scalloped fan (or shell) border, the torchon ground with point d'esprit, and the many-legged spiders hanging within the half-stitch diamonds, the sides of which are at a 45 degree angle to the footing.

43. Representations in lace. **a** (right). Hollie point, from a baby's cap, with a post-fall representation of Adam and Eve, clutching their fig leaves, and observed by the serpent twined around a pomegranate tree (Latin *pomum granatum*, apple with many seeds). **b** (below). A fragment of hair lace enlarged to show the technique, a combination of buttonhole stitch and needle weaving. The entire piece bears the sentimental message 'Though far apart yet neere in heart'.

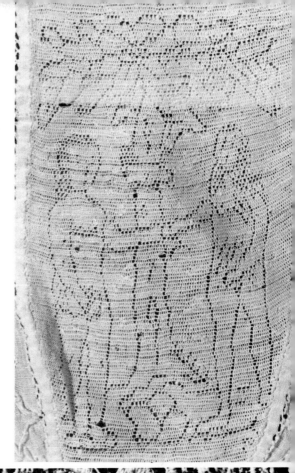

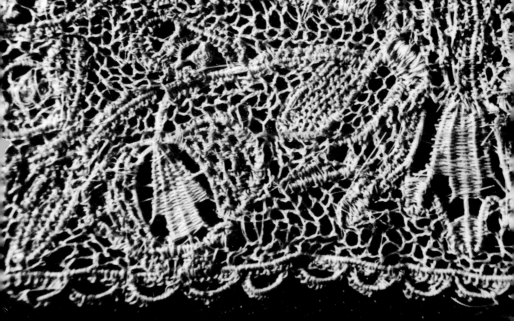

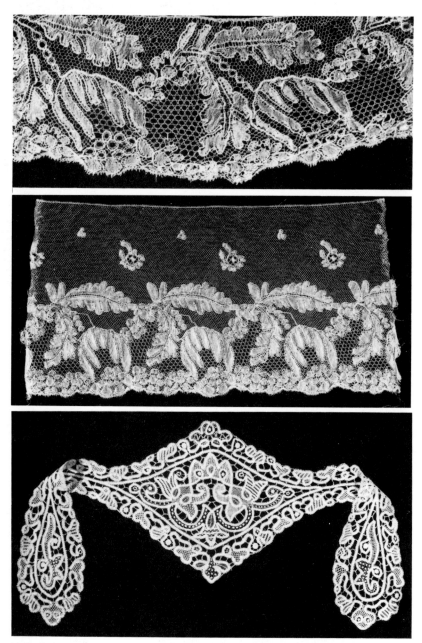

44. Trolly lace. **a** (top). Reputedly made in Devon. **b** (centre). Reputedly made in Buckinghamshire. **c** (bottom). A fall cap of Branscombe lace, c 1880.

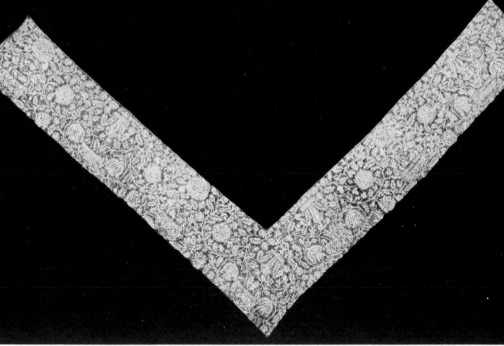

45. English bobbin lace(?). **a** (above). A rare and beautiful length attributed by Frances Morris to seventeenth-century Devon because of the design of acorns and oak leaves, Tudor roses and Prince of Wales feathers. The inscription *Carolus Rex* is taken to refer to Charles II of Great Britain, and the initials *CB* to be those of Catherine of Braganza, to whom Charles became betrothed in 1661. *Vive le Roy* then makes sense, though *CB Baronet* remains enigmatic. **b** (below). In this enlargement of (a) there is a suggestion of a two-headed eagle, though Portugal had escaped from the rulership of Spain in 1640 and was independent. In other respects it most closely resembles the 'Dutch' laces of contemporary portraits and was probably commissioned from Flanders. There is a slight nuance of German-Milanese influence in the form of the eagle. The lace is non-continuous and has a round Valenciennes ground. Although now in the form of a V-shaped collar, it shows a clear join to one side of the angle.

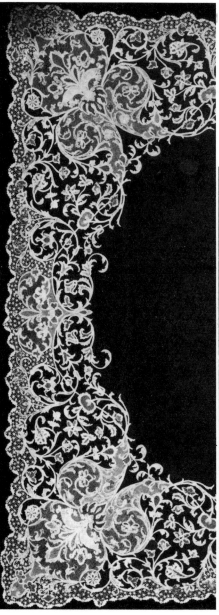

46. Queen Victoria. **a** (below). Her Coronation gown trimmed with Honiton, 28th June 1838. **b** (left). Part of her wedding veil, about 54 inches (1300 mm) square. Honiton appliqué on three-twist bobbinet.

47. English lace revivals. **a** (right). The Bucks Lacemaking Industry, 1931 (founded 1906). **b** (below). Ruskin lace: a drawstring purse, c 1890.

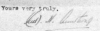

Mrs. Armstrong, Olney

Lace Maker

BUCKS. ENGLAND.

(THE BUCKS. LACE-MAKING INDUSTRY.)

Miss E. .Scott,
Thames Ditton.

15th April, 1931.

Dear Madam,

Thanks for the practical help you have given our Industry.

I wonder if you would help further by giving the name of the Matron or Secretary of any institution, also names and addresses of some wealthy and kind hearted people either in England or overseas to whom I could send our price list.

Perhaps this will result in a few much needed orders for the Workers, many of whom are idle owing to the distress in this district. Of course, your name would not be mentioned in the matter

The Workers have just completed a good selection of Lady's Silk Bags and Cushion covers in various colours. Also there are several articles of Lingerie for disposal cheap. These are perfect in every way except for being somewhat soiled with handing round as samples. I shall be glad to send them on approval.

Yours very truly,

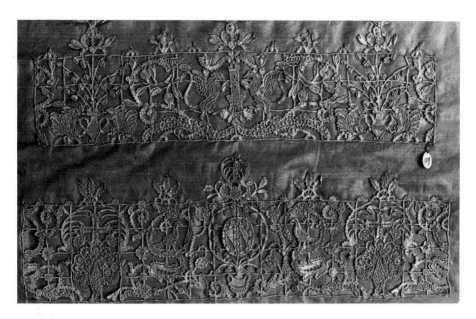

48. Continental lace revivals. **a** (above). Aemilia Ars, first quarter of the twentieth century, based on designs by Passarotti, 1591. The heraldic symbols represent the marriages of noble families: above, Roina — Angellini; below, Gozadini — Gozadini. **b** (below). Vienna: a raised needlepoint collar made at the Vienna Lace Centre by J. Stramnitzer. The original collar of which it is said to be a copy is shaped like a rabat, and this would date it at around 1660, a good deal later than the postulated attribution. However, the magnificent proficiency of the late nineteenth-century Austrian work has indisputable provenance.

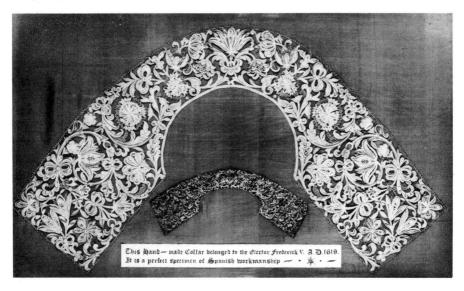

Acknowledgements for illustrations

The cover photograph and Fig. 46b are reproduced by gracious permission of Her Majesty Queen Elizabeth II. The map (Fig. 22) was drawn by Richard G. Holmes. Other illustrations are acknowledged as follows: Art Institute of Chicago, 45a, b; Jocelyn Baker, 18a; Le Bibliothèque Nationale, Paris, 20, 21a, b, c, 34a; Birkin and Company, Nottingham, 32a, b; British Lace Federation, 33a; Buckinghamshire County Museum, Aylesbury, 44b; Lynda Clayden, 47a; Cooper-Hewitt Museum, the Smithsonian Institution's National Museum of Design, 1a; lent to the Science Museum, London, by N. Corah and Sons Ltd, Leicester, 30a; Elizabeth Czabafy, 39d; Dover Publications Inc, 6a; Graves, Son and Pilcher, Hove, 29a; John Heathcoat Ltd, Tiverton, 33b; Karl Mayer Textilmaschinenfabrik GmbH, Obertshausen, 30c; Audrey Kerrison, 47b; Livrustkammaren, Stockholm, 12a, b; National Gallery, London, 11; Phillips, Fine Art Auctioneers, 24b; Gabrielle Pond, 40f; Dr Joyce Rigby, Queen Elizabeth College, London, 23a, b, c, d, e; Royal Albert Memorial Museum, Exeter, 9a; Samling pa Rosenborg, Kobenhavn, 10a; Sotheby's Belgravia, 48b.

Also by Pat Earnshaw

The Identification of Lace

The aim of this book is to guide the reader through the intricacies of identification, listing and illustrating the points to look for in each lace. It covers the whole range of lace from all parts of the world, selecting for examination those major types which the collector or dealer is most likely to come across or hear about. There are over 150 photographs, arranged to assist comparison of diagnostic features.   *ISBN 0 85263 484 6*

'Pat Earnshaw's book will prove invaluable. The information she provides is clearly, concisely and logically presented. She explains how to distinguish between laces made by the same technique in different areas and at different times. She also defines lacemaking terms and clarifies various problems and anomalies in lace terminology. What is more, and the most remarkable thing in a book of this price, is that the photographs are superb...'   *Textile History*

'The immensely readable historical section, the concise description of all hand-made and machine laces, together with very fine photographs, make a comprehensive reference book which should be a "must" for beginners and seasoned lace enthusiasts alike and, incidentally, extremely good value at the price...'   *Lace Guild*

'This is a very impressive book which belies its slim appearance ... something of a godsend. Especially useful are the excellent photographs which home in on the salient features, enlarging the minute admirably... A valuable work, extraordinarily cheap...'   *Antique Collector*

'It seems to have all the answers...'   *International Old Lacers*

The Identification of Lace is available from booksellers or in case of difficulty from Shire Publications Ltd, Cromwell House, Church Street, Princes Risborough, Aylesbury, Bucks, HP17 9AJ, UK.